Schoolboy, Cowboy, Mexican Spy

BOOKS BY JAY MONAGHAN

Lincoln Bibliography, 1839–1939 (2 volumes)

Diplomat in Carpet Slippers:
Abraham Lincoln Deals with Foreign Affairs

Last of the Bad Men: The Legend of Tom Horn

The Overland Trail

This Is Illinois: A Pictorial History

The Great Rascal:
The Life and Adventures of Ned Buntline

Civil War on the Western Border, 1854–1865

The Man Who Elected Lincoln

Swamp Fox of the Confederacy:
The Life and Military Services of M. Jeff Thompson

Custer: The Life of General George Armstrong Custer

Australians and the Gold Rush:
California and Down Under, 1849–1854

Chile, Peru, and the California Gold Rush of 1849

Schoolboy, Cowboy, Mexican Spy

BOOKS EDITED BY JAY MONAGHAN

John Hope Franklin, *Civil War Diary of James T. Ayres*
Robert L. Kincaid, *The Wilderness Road*
Philip D. Jordan, *The National Road*
John Drury, *Old Illinois Houses*
Theodore Calvin Pease, *Story of Illinois*
Francis Philbrick, *Laws of Illinois Territory, 1809–1818*
Mary Waters, *Illinois in the Second World War*
The Book of the American West
R.B. Townshend, *A Tenderfoot in Colorado*
The Private Journal of Louis McLane, U.S.N., 1844–1848
Charles A. Storke, *After the Bugles—The West*

Schoolboy, Cowboy, Mexican Spy

Jay Monaghan

With a Foreword by
Ray Allen Billington

University of California Press
Berkeley • Los Angeles • London

University of California Press
Berkeley and Los Angeles, California
University of California Press, Ltd.
London, England

TO MILDRED
A fellow adventurer in all my books
who knows that some names in this narrative
have been changed to protect descendants
while preserving the truth of real events

Contents

Foreword

During the past decade, a spate of autobiographies by historians have not only glorified the vertical "I" but have told us a great deal about the lives and thoughts of some of our leading interpreters of the American past. These reminiscences, most would agree, have been only mildly interesting. The historian is usually content to record the past rather than live an adventuresome present, confining his worldly experiences to an occasional dabbling in politics, and showing a marked preference for intellectual speculation rather than hair-raising adventures. The results seldom provide exciting reading.

James Jay Monaghan IV is a first-rate historian, but any reader who expects to find in this book a bland rehash of historical theories or a day-by-day chronicle of how this or that monograph evolved is doomed to a very happy surprise. Jay Monaghan could, if he so willed, write such somniferous reminiscences as have some of his colleagues, for his later years were as packed with intellectual adventuring as were his early years with physical excitement. Born in 1891 of Quaker parents, educated at Vevey in Switzerland and the Friends Central School of Philadelphia, a graduate of Swarthmore College in 1913 and with a graduate degree from the University of Pennsylvania, he was fully equipped by training and competence to follow a normal academic career, and to write a normally dull autobiography.

He entered the world of historical scholarship when he was in his middle forties, in 1935, as an interviewer of Indians for the Colorado Historical Society—a pioneering version of what we would today call "oral history." There followed a brief period as a professional researcher in Kansas and Nebraska, then a stint as supervisor of a depression-created federal project to analyze and index Illinois newspapers. This baptism into the world of historical record-keeping started Jay Monaghan on his way; between 1939 and 1945 he served as historical research editor for the Illinois State Historical Society, then as historian in charge of the library and secretary-editor of the historical society between 1946 and 1950. After a period of teaching abroad, he "retired" in 1953 to become special consultant for the Wyles Collection of Lincolniana at the library of the University of California at Santa Barbara.

During these years of administrative bustle, Jay Monaghan somehow found time to write a whole shelf-full of books, all of them highly respected by his peers. They emphasized two aspects of the past. One stressed the Civil War; here he contributed such standard works as *Diplomat in Carpet Slippers: Lincoln Deals with Foreign Affairs* (1945); *The Civil War on the Western Border* (1955); *The Man Who Elected Lincoln* (1956); and *Swamp Fox of the Confederacy* (1956). The other dealt with the West; in this field he was responsible for such universally acclaimed volumes as *The Legend of Tom Horn* (1947); *The Overland Trail* (1947); *The Great Rascal: The Life and Adventures of Ned Buntline* (1953); *Custer: The Life of General George Armstrong Custer* (1959); and two useful books on the Forty-Niners from overseas: *Australia and the Gold Rush: California and Down Under* (1966), and *Chili, Peru, and the California Gold Rush of 1849* (1973). As if these were not enough, he has found time to edit the *American Trails Series*, and to produce a whole galaxy of essays and articles for journals scholarly and not-so-scholarly. Jay Monaghan, then, is a superior professional historian, writing voluminously and scattering seeds of knowledge everywhere.

But for a good many years—before he decided in 1935 to stop making history and start writing history—Jay Monaghan lived an adventure-packed life that would turn any wild-west enthusiast green with envy. It began in 1908 when he fled the placidity of Philadelphia's Friend's School seeking excitement during a summer in western Colorado. There he joined a wagon freight train that gave him his first taste of western life, then turned to cattle punching on neighboring ranches. The next summer this slim youth was back again, an experienced cowboy now, with a fine mare of his own, "Queenie," who that fall carried him across the Rockies to Denver and was his companion in a boxcar ride back to Pennsylvania.

Jay Monaghan is at his best when describing life on those Colorado ranches. His memory, aided by letters written home at the time, is vivid; his prose sparkling. We share with him the quiet beauty of the desert, the thrill of ordering his first "cigar" in a saloon, the dangers and hardships of the cattle trails, the agonies of taming wild horses, the satisfaction of winning the respect—and friendship—of westerners with such appealing names as Hawkshaw, Tricky Bisquits, Skull Crick Jones, Moon Eyes, Spike-you-son-of-a-bitch (whose last name was never revealed), and End-gate Edna. Here is the West, accurately depicted, and made as appealing to us as it was to young Jay.

The climax of these early days—and of the book—came in the spring of 1911 when news of stirring events along the borderlands—the Madero Revolution in Mexico—lured him from his Swarthmore classes. His adventures at El Paso and Juárez during the next weeks provide as much excitement as any modern thriller. Even to hint at what he did would rob the reader of the greater excitement of reading Jay Monaghan's own description of his role in that rebellion. Sufficient to say that he finally escaped unharmed, and in time to drive an army mule team to the Sacramento Mountins of New Mexico, then take off on a grizzly bear hunt in Sonora, before returning that fall to his junior year at Swarthmore.

This volume ends on that note, but with a hint of things to come when (after being rejected as a recruit for Donald B. MacMillan's expedition to the North Polar region) he returned to the West to begin a new career. Jay Monaghan does not detail his further experiences in this book, but those of us fortunate enough to be counted among his friends have heard something of the next years: operating cattle and sheep ranches in western Colorado and Utah, opening the northwestern ranges of Colorado to sheep-growing, teaching school at the Uintah Indian Reservation, serving as president of the Rio Blanco Wool Growers Association, helping operate the Colorado State Wool Growers Association, and occasionally taking part in some of the wars between cattle and sheep ranchers that rang down the curtain on the wildest days of the Wild West. All this before 1935 when Jay Monaghan forsook the six-gun for the typewriter and the hurricane deck of a bronc for an administrator's chair.

This, then, is a bang-up adventure tale, skillfully told by a master storyteller. But it is something far more. To read is to understand why this stripling of a lad left behind hearth and traditions to endure the hardships and discomforts of life on a still primitive frontier. Jay Monaghan's love of the West radiates from his pages; we can sense with him the irresistible attraction of that land of distant horizons. To read his pages is to enjoy the experiences that thrilled him, but it is also to understand what the West of those days meant to Easterners questing for adventure or opportunity. There is much to explain the lure of the West to would-be emigrants. We can now hope that this is only the first of a series of reminiscenses that will continue his adventures and preserve an authentic image of a frontier rapidly fading from the nation's memory.

The Huntington Library   Ray Allen Billington

1

A Freight Wagon Trip with Specimen Jones

*Still, still do they whisper, those aspens
Of voices, tall stories and play;
Over all there will linger a shimmer,
So full was the joy of that day.*
—W. H. Furness

Dee Wilkins took a deep drag on his cigarette. Exhaling the
smoke he said, "We ken do'er. We're two good men and a boy
what ain't no slump." The boy enjoyed these flattering words
because he probably was something of a slump. A tenderfoot
schoolboy from Philadelphia, he had never done any physical
work during the seventeen years he had been alive. He stood
only five feet, six inches above the wagon-wheel ruts in the dirt
road in front of McLearn's country store in the railroad town of
Rifle, Colorado. Weighing a little over a hundred pounds, he
looked like a midget beside the two six-foot, spider-legged men
with him, but his light weight would make him popular later as
a jockey racing with Indians. This morning, however, brute
strength was needed to load five tons of groceries into two
freight wagons for delivery in Meeker, across the divide.

In 1908 the prevailing contract of a dollar for hauling a
hundred pounds of freight fifty miles to Meeker did not include
loading and unloading, and if a freighter had to wait an extra
day to get help he lost money. No wonder Dee Wilkins said,
with another puff on his cigarette, "We've got to get going
today. I can't afford settin' here with six big horses eating their
heads off in the livery barn."

The boy looked at Dee's lean frame and haggard cheeks. His
mustache, a mere black line, hooked down at the corners of his

mouth. This face reminded the boy of the Specimen Jones drawn by Frederic Remington in Owen Wister's *Red Men and White*. Dee's helper, named Charlie, appeared much younger and fuller-bodied, more like one of the western characters W. H. D. Koerner painted. The boy admired the drawings of both artists, and he set to work with a will helping these two models of men he knew very well in books. Forty-eight-pound sacks of flour were easy to lift. Wooden cases containing pasteboard boxes of Arm & Hammer Soda (called "sody") were heavy; so were cases of canned tomatoes. Crates of Union Leader tobacco in tin boxes made awkward but light loads. Coffee beans (called "java") packed in burlap bags weighing eighty pounds each proved too heavy for the boy to lift. Kegs of whiskey taxed the combined strength of all three of them but, as Dee had said, he and his helper were good men and the boy was "no slump." Setting the kegs upright so they would not roll seemed sensible, but the boy wondered why Dee put them at the end gate of the trail wagon. He learned the reason before the trip ended. By noon both wagons were loaded.

The boy had been hired at four bits a day to tend a brake on the trail wagon. He knew four bits was a sum of money but, coming from the East where this term was not used, he wasn't sure how much. He knew nothing about wagon brakes or the possible danger ahead of him, but when he looked at the loaded trail wagon he realized that on a steep downgrade, if not checked, it would hit the lead wagon a crushing blow. This might wreck both wagons and send horses, men, baking soda, and kegs of whiskey hurtling over a precipice.

The only West the boy knew was in books. He could repeat whole paragraphs of Owen Wister's *Virginian*, had read Francis Parkman's *Oregon Trail*, Mark Twain's *Roughing It*, and Stewart Edward White's *Camp and Trail*. He knew that the then president of the United States, Theodore Roosevelt, had been a mighty hunter. The boy had lost himself for hours in Teddy's *Hunting Trips of a Ranchman*, *Ranch Life and the Hunting Trail*, *The Wilderness Hunter*, and *Hunting the Grizzly*. The boy also knew that Meeker had been built as a fort after an Indian massacre in 1879 and that Roosevelt had shot mountain lions in that country, but it never occurred to him that he would later own one of the ranches where Teddy stayed while hunting, and sit in Teddy's favorite armchair—a chipping sparrow in the eagle's nest.

I was that seventeen-year-old boy. I wanted to be a part of the West I had read about and I did not want to be a tenderfoot with a family back east, although my parents expected me to come home to Philadelphia in the fall when classes started at Friends Central School. My mother had sewed a return ticket in the hip pocket of my trousers but I was determined to make my own living this summer even if I pulled a wheel off—a good western expression.

When the two wagons were loaded I followed Dee Wilkins and Charlie to the livery barn for the horses. Dee paid his bill and Charlie asked for his gun. In those days the town marshal ordered every incoming horseman to leave his gun at the barn. The stableman unlocked the desk in his office and handed Charlie a Colt .45. Charlie wore no holster so he stuck the six-shooter in the waistband of his Levis. With his thumb he clicked out the gun's little reloading gate, which, when hooked over his belt, left the big black handle in plain sight and prevented the barrel from slipping down inside the leg of his pants. This casual accessory gave Charlie a reckless appearance he no doubt enjoyed. I had been reared a Quaker, and I thought, Charlie is like young William Penn who hesitated to join the Society of Friends if he could no longer wear his sword.

We harnessed the teams in their stalls, led them to a water trough, and then past the Winchester Hotel to the wagons. I had owned a horse back east as long as I could remember. While still a toddler I rode on the flat saddle in front of my father, who was a lawyer, so this part of the new job was easy for me. However, I knew nothing about neck yokes and lead bars for hitching six horses to a wagon and trailer.

Dee skillfully backed his wheel team to positions on each side of the lead-wagon tongue, and stood beside the near front wheel, where he watched us as he shook tobacco from a Bull Durham sack into a cigarette paper for rolling. Charlie swung his team in place ahead of the wheelers and waited on the off side, cutting a chew from the plug of Horseshoe tobacco he carried in his hip pocket. I had no trouble placing my lead team in front, but then I showed my ignorance. Charlie, on the off side, worked quickly—snapping reins to bits, passing lines through rings on bridle headstalls, slipping neck yokes through pole straps. I watched from the near side of the line of teams and tried to do everything he had done, but he worked fast and was soon down the line of horses past the wheelers where I could not see. To catch up I made my first mistake. I started hooking the traces for each horse to its singletree.

"Hook them tugs last!" the boss shouted. "Always." His cigarette was rolled now and I saw him seal the paper with his tongue. A dexterous twist with his right hand crimped the end so the tobacco flakes would not fall out the open end. His command to "hook them tugs last" made me feel stupid. Certainly if a horse's traces were hitched to a wagon before the harness for controlling him was in order he might pull everything to pieces. I never made this mistake again.

Finally Charlie and I held out the six lines for the three teams to Dee. He lighted his cigarette, inhaled the smoke, grabbed the lines, and climbed to the wagon seat. Charlie spat copiously at the front wheel, scrambled up beside Dee, grasped the rope to the long iron brake handle, and held it without pulling. I climbed up the near front wheel of the trail wagon, slid across to the off side of the seat, and grasped the rope to the brake handle as Charlie had done. Looking ahead I could see, above the load on the lead wagon, Charlie's raised arm holding the brake rope, and both men's flat-brimmed hats. (The curled brim on cowboy hats became fashionable when movie cameras needed more light on the wearer's face.) Dee's head turned, facing me. The straight brim of his hat, straight black mustache, and grim mouth formed three parallel black lines. He gave me a half nod and turned to his horses. Charlie released his brake. I pulled my brake handle out of the brake comb and let it swing free, releasing my brake. The six horses recognized the sound of the two chugs loosening the brakes and leaned forward in their collars. With a slight jerk the wagons moved forward out of Rifle, Colorado, into the West I had read about, the West of ropes and saddles, spurs, bed rolls, coffee pots, guns, and hobbles.

A half mile out of town we came to a dry wash—an arroyo just like a Remington picture. The road ahead went squarely over the edge. Here was the first hazard of the trip. I saw the lead horses disappear down the steep bank. A moment later the lead wagon's front wheels followed them. I saw Charlie jam the brake on his hind wheels, and they skidded over the rim. My front wheels followed. This was the critical moment. With "forty hundred" of freight on my wagon it might hit the lead wagon a crushing blow unless checked. I pulled on the brake rope with all my might, locked the brake handle in the comb, and felt my rear wheels stop and skid to the bottom of the gulch, where I released the brake. Already the lead horses were arching their necks for the pull up the far side of the wash. It was heavy going because the wheels of both wagons sank in the loose sand, but six stout horses dragged us across and up onto the sagebrush flat beyond. The road ahead seemed level so I dared look back toward Rifle. The village was already shrinking in the distance, and I thought that must have been the way Medicine Bow appeared "throught the great still air" to Owen Wister on his first drive across Wyoming with the Virginian. My father knew Wister in Philadelphia, so his book always had a personal appeal to me.

The wagons lumbered northward through the sagebrush along what was known as the "government road," although the government had certainly forgotten it after abandoning the Meeker fort. From my perch on the rear wagon I could not see the wheel horses, but the heads of the swing team were visible, as were the backs, heads, and pointed ears of the leaders. While we traveled at a walk, I had time to enjoy the scenery. We were rumbling up a long valley bounded on the east by a barren, gullied ridge dotted with a few scattered cedars. West of the road a line of green treetops indicated a sunken creek. Beyond them a bare concave slope skirted the flat-topped Book Cliffs, rising two thousand feet into a cloudless sky that Frederic Remington might have painted. We belonged in this picturesque landscape. Our horses and wagons were a part of it.

After two hours we came to a long, level-roofed building beside the road. Here was the station where Thad Harp's stagecoach from Rifle to Meeker stopped to change horses for the steep climb out of the valley. The wide door into the building stood open and a man, followed by his helper, came out. Our wagons stopped.

"Seen a sorrel down the road?" the man asked. "E got away yestiddy. I need a extry hand to hunt fer him. The stage for Rifle'll be here in half an hour. The three fresh hosses I've got is plenty to pull her on to Rifle, 'cause its a downgrade, but the stage driver'll have to trot along in the missing wheeler's place to hold up that end of the neck yoke." The man paused to smile at his little joke and gave us time to smile, too. Then he continued, "He won't do that and I'll ketch hell."

A job hunting horses out on the open range for a dollar a day instead of my job on the trail wagon appealed to me. Changing horses at an overland stage station was part of the West I wanted to know and be a part of, but I wasn't going to quit on my first day's work and leave the boss shorthanded. I might come back, though, after reaching Meeker.

We drove on and in due time met the Concord stagecoach coming down the road at a brisk trot. The driver gave Dee the grim half nod I had learned was typical of range men. I saw his eyes glance sideways at me, but there was no greeting, and the stage flashed by. I looked back through the flying dust and watched the "rear boot" and spinning wheels disappear. There went the overland stagecoach Mark Twain described in *Roughing It*—a sight I have never forgotten.

That afternoon when the sun set behind the Book Cliffs it still shone on the bare eastern ridge. Darkness would not come for another two hours but the boss ordered a halt. There was no water in the stream above this spot so we camped here. Charlie and I pulled the brake ropes tight and jumped down to unhitch the teams. Dee, still on the front seat holding the lines in his hands, shouted, "Unhook them tugs first," but I had not forgotten my mistake.

We tied the horses along the wagons on the side away from camp and dragged off their heavy harness. Then Dee told me to lead them to water, two at a time; he and Charlie would "build the biscuits" (a range expression for "get dinner"). When I came back with the last team I gave each horse a flake of baled hay. Then I walked around the wagons to the campfire and stopped in my tracks. Dinner was being prepared in a manner totally new to me. The fire crackled under any empty Dutch oven and its upturned lid. Beside them an iron frying pan held bubbling hot water. Dee was mixing dough for biscuits in the open top of a sack of flour he held between his knees. Charlie was cutting slices from a hard chunk of yellow "saltside" and flipping each slice into the bubbling frying pan to "try out" the salt so we could fry the meat. The boss, with hands whitened by the flour, told me to put a big handful of coffee beans in the empty salt sack I'd find in the mess box, then get a hammer from the lead wagon's jockey box. With this I was to crush the coffee beans using, for an anvil, the wide flat tire of the nearest wagon. I liked the job. Pounded coffee smelled good—rich and spicy. Dee, still mixing bread dough, pointed with his lips (a Ute Indian gesture I learned later) to a big coffee pot. He asked me to fill it half full with cold water and put the pulverized coffee on top. It floated, and Dee said, "Now, put the pot on the fire and when she boils the java will turn over. Take her off then, add a cup of cold water to settle the grounds, and she's ready."

After that first meal the pipe I was learning to smoke tasted good. Darkness had fallen and the firelight on the wagons would have made a Remington picture. The time had now come to unroll our beds. I noticed that Charlie wrapped his Levis around his beloved six-shooter for a pillow. We lay down. The sky was black above the wagons and a brilliant planet appeared large, white, and without a twinkle in the dry, western air.

Next morning, after watering and feeding the horses and eating breakfast, we started on the long pull out of the valley. Dee watched the horses and stopped every hundred yards or so to let them rest while we brake tenders locked the hind wheels of our wagons. The horses, I soon learned, understood this procedure as well as we did, and something was evidently on their minds—probably mischief. In those days I had no appreciation of a western horse's constructive imagination, but I soon enjoyed a never-forgotten demonstration. I knew, of course, that they were animals lacking Victorian modesty and inhibitions. Direct expressions could be expected from them and halfway up the slope, between two of the regular stops, one of the wheelers, named Togo for an admiral in the recent Russo-Japanese War, "wanted to powder his nose." He had probably been waiting all morning for this opportunity. Charlie jammed on his brake and waved me to follow. I did so, and from my seat on the stalled trail wagon I could hear the splashing as Ol' Togo drained his radiator. I kept my hand on the brake handle, ready to release it and continue the climb. Little did I know draft-horse psychology. When that horse finished, another started. The third waited his turn, then the fourth, fifth, and sixth. For twenty minutes the wagons could not move. I wondered if Togo, after such a long rest, might be able to repeat. Charlie told me that mules were smarter than horses, and with an opportunity like this a draft mule would do his best, even if it burst a blood vessel. However, Ol' Togo didn't, and we moved on up the slope with twenty-four draft-horse hooves pounding out what sounded to me like chuckling laughter.

Finally, we reached the top. The road for the next few miles rose and dipped over rolling sagebrush country before we came to Alley's ranch. Here Thad Harp had established a stagecoach dinner station in a two-story mid-Victorian residence more appropriate for Camden, New Jersey, I thought, than for Colorado's frontier. Several freight wagons were parked nearby and we stopped among them. Charlie and I watered and fed the horses and started cooking dinner while the boss attended to some business in the house.

A small boy, probably one of Alley's sons, popped out the door and ran toward us. He had bright, eager eyes and words babbled excitedly from his mouth, which lacked two upper front teeth. "I seed a railroad train," he shouted. "You bet! Pa he taken Mom and me to see it in Rifle. Pa tolded me to watch out and not get skeert if the train turned around. I tolded Pa to not job me with no dry sell. Trains didn't turn 'round and I didn't skeer. Cowboys doan skeer and I'm a-gonna be a cowboy. The horse don't live I kaint ride."

Charlie stopped him by waving toward me and retorting, "I'll bet you can't even ride this man if he gets down on all fours like a horse."

"Betcha I can," the kid replied, with a toothless grin.

Being called a man pleased me but I was not prepared for this proposition. However, it seemed to be fun so I got down on hands and knees. The child mounted and I bucked him off. He got up, remounted, and I bucked him off again. He was crying mad now. His face swelled with anger and turned red.

"Lemme go get my spurs," he shouted. "I'll ride you, or while I'm quittin' you I'll peel your hide off from your tailbone both ways."

Fortunately, the boss returned in time to stop more rodeo events. He rolled a fresh cigarette, climbed up to the driver's seat, lighted it, and we lumbered away from Alley's big white house along a dirt road through dusty gray-green sagebrush. Within a mile I saw another large frame residence standing in a dazzling, emerald-green alfalfa meadow. A second big house was in plain sight about a mile beyond it. These residences, both elaborately mid-Victorian in architecture, had been built in the 1880s by newly rich miners from Leadville who invested in cattle. Some lost their fortunes here as quickly as they had made them and moved on. Their fine homes, built immediately after the Indians had been driven off, seemed to contradict the so-called Turner thesis taught me by school teachers who had not read Turner carefully. Certainly the frontier here, instead of beginning with the primitive and developing to the more advanced, had done the reverse. Turner, of course, had carefully guarded himself against his interpretation.

I was told that the present owner of one of these fine houses, a Mr. Longstrang, had married a "catalog woman." He answered her advertisement in a "Lonely Heart" magazine, and people said that on their wedding night, before crawling into bed with her, Mr. Longstrang had pointed to the clock and said, "Mamie, this is a working ranch, not a playhouse! When you hear that alarm go off in the morning, I want to hear your feet flap on the floor."

True or not, she kept the big house clean, dutifully prepared his meals, and entertained herself by making a Longfellow Corner in one room. She placed a bust of the poet there and bought new books of poetry by mail. Her husband had no interest in Longfellow but was not jealous of him. His interests were out in the barn where he spent his spare time except for meals, which he ate hurriedly.

Mr. Longstrang evidently liked to believe himself a gay deceiver. On Sundays he would tell his wife, "I've built a blind in the lower forty, so I'm goin' down there and shoot a duck or rabbit for supper." Then he would shoulder his gun, but instead of going down in the meadow he took a short cut to

Alley's for a game of poker, being careful to shoot once or twice during the afternoon to fool his wife into believing that he was hunting. Maybe he wasn't fooling her as much as she fooled him by always believing his story. In any event, while he was happy playing cards she was also happy reading and rereading without a single interruption *The Courtship of Miles Standish* and *Evangeline.* Book in hand, she peopled her solitary life with Hiawatha, Nakomis, daughter of the moon, and the mighty Mudgekeewis. I was never well acquainted with Mamie Longstrang but I did know her sufficiently well later to believe that she was happy with her books—a contented woman very sure that she had not let the good life pass her by.

Beyond these big frame residences we came to a large log house built of straight and true lodge-pole pine more suitable, it seemed to me, for the Rocky Mountain landscape. Certainly architect Frank Lloyd Wright was correct when he said a residence should be built with the natural material surrounding it. The man who lived here was a great talker. His tongue wagged constantly. He was nicknamed "Wagon-Tongue Jones" to distinguish him from "Skull-Crick Jones" and "Red-Wash Jones." Wagon-Tongue Jones had a daughter the boys called "End-Gate Edna." Charlie had evidently been jilted by her, and in camp that night he cut his usual chew from the plug of Horseshoe and gave it an extra after-dinner dip in the round can of Copenhagen snuff he always carried. Thrusting this into his mouth, he said, "Somebody lied to Edna when they told her she was pretty."

"You're a sorehead," Dee retorted, "Have you ett some loco weed? Just because she and you licked salt together out on the ranch that don't mean she'll go to the dance with you in town. Can't you think? Have you got a head on your shoulders, or just a neckbone that's haired over?"

Charlie's mouth was too full of tobacco juice to reply, and I wondered whether Specimen Jones ever talked like Dee Wilkins. Whether he did or not, Dee was certainly his "spittin' image."

Beyond Wagon-Tongue's ranch there was no house for almost twenty miles, except Harp's last stage station for changing horses. On the right side of the road a ridge five or six hundred feet high had been formed by uptilted strata. Called the Hogback, with its concave slope and sharp rocky crest it resembled a gigantic ocean wave starting to break over. On the left side of the road there was a massive mountain called, with western understatement, the Little Hill. Between these promontories our road traversed a mile-wide flat, carpeted with sagebrush. Here the road became very bad. Wagon wheels had cut ruts so deep in some places that the axles dragged, stalling the wagon. To avoid these spots teamsters made new roads by driving beside the old ruts, but these also soon wore down, becoming impassable. In some places a driver had to choose between a dozen ruts, and he might drive half a mile before he discovered that his selection became deeper ahead and he would soon stick fast.

There was no way he could go back, and getting out of deep ruts was often difficult. If the high center ahead was short and the road better beyond, a teamster might haul rocks on a "stone boat" from the Hogback to fill the ruts, but this took time—maybe half a day. Another way to get out of deep ruts was to break down the sides with crowbar and pick and pull the wagons out on a bias. This gave the horses uncertain footing across other deep ruts, and if a horse fell he might break a leg. Also, when a rear wheel was suddenly pulled higher than the other wheels the wagon might upset. Then a full day would be required to get both wagons right side up and reloaded. Considering these hazards, the standard charge of a dollar a hundred for freighting across the divide was not high, but skilled men made a living at it.

At one stretch of road where the ruts were shallow we met a southbound freighter with empty wagons. The boss stopped our teams for a chat. The strange driver had a face spreckled with black dots like a guinea. His nose was long and sharp over a receding chin that gave him the look of a snipe or shore bird. The boss asked him which ruts ahead were best to take.

"Them furdest to the east is best," the man replied, pushing his hat back on that birdlike head; I noticed that his ears were oddly crumpled.

The boss thanked him. We parted, each driving away under the big sky, but I noticed that our boss took the ruts farthest west, instead of east. We camped that night on the flat above a deep gulch where there was water. I asked why we hadn't taken the more easterly ruts recommended by the freighter. Dee gave me a Specimen Jones look and, taking a deep draught on his cigarette, replied, "That man is Skull-Crick Jones. Even his name will lie, and steal too, when it gets a chanct." Dee paused for the smoke to come out through his nose and mouth. Then he continued, "If we got stuck it wouldn't earn Skully a thin dime, but it wouldn't cost him nothin's neither. You gotta watch them freighters. Did ya see his ears? I dun know f'r sartain but I hear tell the K Ranch riders ketched Skully alterin' brands. They throwed and ear-marked him like a calf; crop and split on the right, a swaller-fork on the left. Skully could-a had the law on 'em f'r that, but he dassent. If he did, they'd a-jailed him f'r rustling."

Dee took a second drag on his cigarette and said, "Skully's a card. He's his own worst enemy, alus cheatin' so' he'll make a million dollars. Rube Ball called him onct and said to him, sez he, "Skully, you wouldn't know what to do with a million dollars.'"

Dee exhaled, and with smoke and words coming out together he continued, "Skully sez to Rube, sez he, 'The hell I wouldn't. I'd put new clappers on my lead team's bells, I'd get brass studded housing for my wheelers' hames, and I'd have the best goddamned freight outfit on the Meeker-Rifle road. Don't tell me I wouldn't know what to do with a million dollars!'"

That night we greased the wagon wheels. I supposed we'd jack up each axle and slip off the wheel, but this is not the way it is done. Each wagon wheel is held on the axle's iron spindle or "skeen" by a square nut threaded to screw so the wagon wheel, moving forward, constantly tightens it. In hot, dry western weather, wagon spokes and felloes ("felleys" in freighter lingo) shrink, loosening the iron tires. To correct this a freighter invariably left his wagon standing overnight in a river ford where the dry wood swelled to its original size. To drive a wagon into a stream, unhook a team, and lead or drive the horses back to shore through waist-deep water was not easy. A tenderfoot who prided himself on being a constructive thinker might save his horses from the deep water by backing his wagon into the stream. A fine idea, indeed! This would unscrew his axle nuts and he'd lose his wheels.

Fortunately, our wheels had not yet dried out sufficiently to rattle, but Dee's method of greasing them seemed dangerous to me. He unscrewed each nut, took hold of the top of the wheel where he had a good leverage, and with a jerk pulled it off until the spindle was exposed. Then he told me to take the small wooden paddle in the grease can, lubricate the inside of the hub thimble, and fill the little groove on top of the "skeen" with grease. When I finished, Dee pushed the wheel back in place with another jerk and screwed on the nut, while I wondered—and still wonder—what might have happened if Dee had, by mistake, pulled the wheel out an inch or two farther, permitting the axle to fall to the ground and the tons of freight to crash down on us.

At this camp there was no firewood except dead sagebrush, but every roundup cook knows that no kindling makes a hotter blaze. Dee said we'd be in Meeker tomorrow, so tonight was our last chance to celebrate. He had saved the wire from our baled hay and put several wire ends in the fire. I soon learned why the whiskey kegs for Rube Ball's saloon had been stored at the trail wagon's end gate. Dee took the hammer I had used to pound the coffee and drove down one of the metal hoops on a whiskey keg. Then with red-hot wires he started burning a hole between the keg staves. Before long a little stream of whiskey spurted out into the Mason jar Dee held. He filled it and a big tin cup. Then he stopped the hole with a wooden peg and drove the hoop back in place, covering it. Dee said he hated a thief, but did we realize that it was good businessmen—really keen businessmen—who had made America great! And a good businessman, he said, must outsmart a competitor just as he had outsmarted Rube Ball, who would never know that his whiskey had been tapped.

Dee set the big tin cup of liquor on the mess box and, taking the full Mason jar, said, "I'll cache this down in the wash. It'll shorten our return trip."

He was not gone long but when he came back and looked at the liquor in the cup he had left he must have realized that Charlie and I were also pretty good businessmen. Without a word, however, he divided what we had left into three drinks. Giving one to each of us, he said with magnanimous solemnity, "Here's to Rube Ball's good health!"

Charlie rocked his cup gently and with appreciative eyes replied, "Bread's the staff of life; whiskey is life itself."

Dee held up his cup and, looking at each of us in turn with the grim smile I had learned to know, said, "Drink hearty." Then he turned to me and added, "A man your age in a saloon can't drink. There's a law agin it. When treats is set up f'r the house, and your turn comes to order, you must say, 'I'll take a ci-gar.' Remember that." (I thought, yes, just like always remembering to "hook them tugs last.")

Next morning our wagons coasted down the last few miles toward White River. From my seat I could see far to the north "through the great still air" a magnificent broad unfenced valley, pearl gray with distant sagebrush. Within an hour we crossed White River, turned upstream, and drove three miles to the abandoned fort, which had become the town of Meeker. The officers' quarters were residences now. Built of hewn logs and steep-roofed to shed snow in winter, they stood along the north side of the old parade ground which had become an open field with a church on one end, a saloon and hardware store on the other. South of the field stood a bank, a restaurant, Rube Ball's two-story brick hotel, his saloon, and Oldland's big general store. This store was our destination. Here each loaded wagon was weighed on ground scales, then unloaded and weighed again. Mr. Oldland figured the weight of the goods received and paid Dee in greenbacks and big round silver dollars. A man wearing a marshal's badge followed us to the livery barn, where we watered and unharnessed the horses. The strange man told Charlie to leave his gun in the office and waited until Charlie did so. I looked carefully at his badge. It was marked 'U.S. Marshal," and I have often wondered if it was genuine. An effort was being made at that time to prevent men from carrying guns in small western towns, but surely as exalted an officer as a United States Marshal was not being assigned to every little community. When the man left, Dee counted out the money he owed Charlie. Then he handed me two silver "cartwheels"—the first money I had ever earned—and said, "Now the drinks is on me."

What could please a seventeen-year-old boy more than going into a real western saloon with Specimen Jones and a genuine

W. H. D. Koerner cowboy! Dee led the way through the
Meeker Hotel lobby, which was filled with the mounted heads
of deer, antelope, and bighorn sheep. Under them I noticed
gigantic elk-horn chairs made in the exact pattern used for the
chairs fashioned from red-deer antlers I had seen in Blair
Castle when traveling with my family in Scotland. I wondered
whether this style had originated in the Highlands or here in
the West. In the lobby there was also a large framed photograph of the heads and massive shoulders of two polled
Herefords. While we looked at them with wonder the famous
Rube Ball himself came out from behind the hotel desk. He
was a handsome, well-dressed, pleasant-speaking man, even if
he lacked Dee Wilkens's business ability. He told us with a
smile that one of the oldest cowhands in the county had admired that picture, saying, "Them's splendid bulls, be'ent
they?"

Mr. Ball said the hotel guests who heard him had slapped
the fellow on the back and laughed, because the animals in the
photographs were not bulls but prize-winning cows back east
somewhere. A few registered bulls were being shipped west to
improve the range stock, but no one out here had ever seen
cows like those.

Dee Wilkins thought this anecdote called for the drink he'd
been talking about and led us through a hotel side door into
Rube Ball's saloon. The room was crowded. We walked along
the bar past coatless men wearing broad-brim hats. At the back
of the room, where card players sat at round tables, we found
an open place at the bar. A white-aproned barkeeper asked
what we'd like. I had already become accustomed to the sun-
burned faces of outdoor men and I remember being shocked at
the barman's pale pink, indoor face.

"I'll take whiskey," Dee said with a half-nod invitation to
Charlie and me.

"I'll take a beer," said Charlie.

I can still hear my boyish voice in that frontier saloon say
with proud, youthful assurance, "I'll take a ci-gar."

This was a great moment. I had said the right thing, and I
knew now that I liked life Out West. With two round silver
dollars in my pocket, and no job, the future held no fears for

me. I was determined to go places and see the Wild West, but it never occurred to me that before school started in the fall I would camp with the West's last band of renegade Indians, disgruntled Utes being brought back to their reservation by the United States Army. They had bolted the new reservation assigned them after the Meeker Massacre, hoping to join the Sioux up at Wounded Knee.

2

A Frightening Experience

O, beware of Mudjekeewis,
Of the West Wind, Mudjekeewis;
Listen not to what he tells you.
—The Song of Hiawatha

A man destined to be nationally known as author and literary critic listened, like many young men of his day, to what the West Wind told him. Seeking adventure, he traveled in a Meeker-Rifle stagecoach the same month and year I tended brake on the freight wagon. Hermann Hagedorn took his bride on their wedding trip to a ranch in the Meeker country. His graphic account of their journey along the "government road," published by Macmillan in *The Hyphenated Family*, correlates excellently with my experience. Here is what he wrote:

The second lap of our journey was brief, taking us . . . by train from Glenwood to Rifle, where we were to spend the night and take the stagecoach, the following morning, for Meeker, the scene of a famous massacre by the Indians, some thirty years before. . . .

The four-horse stagecoach we climbed into next morning was of the Concord type, subsequently made familiar by Western horse operas; with the inside seats facing each other, the driver's seat level with the coach roof, and the baggage strapped on behind. There were only two passengers in the stagecoach besides Dorothy and myself: a wide-bosomed Negro woman on the way to some ranch, "up-country," as cook, and a rough, burly, heavily moustached character who appeared to be some sort of judge. . . . The judge made himself less agreeable, regaling us with tales of manslaughter and hangings which to us cotton-wool babes-in-the-woods lost none of their grisly quality by the casual manner of his narration. I must have been more tough-fibered than Dorothy, for when, at a stage station where we changed horses, the judge to her relief, joined the driver up front, I followed, hoping—not vainly—for more.

We stepped straight into the West of romantic fiction that day. The road could be called such only by courtesy. It was actually a series of parallel ruts cut deep in the gumbo-mud and only recently dried out. The coach was carrying U.S. mail and had a schedule that had no mercy on passengers. We lurched in and out of the ruts, pitching from side to side in our seats, never certain that, at the next lurch, the coach might topple over. Now Dorothy was in the colored cook's lap and now the cook in Dorothy's. I don't know how I clung to my perch at the far left of the driver's seat.

Hagedorn's account stirs up vivid memories: my first job after being paid off in Meeker was back at Thad Harp's White River stage station. Half a century later my wife and I were next door neighbors of the Hagedorn family in Santa Barbara, and all of us have wondered whether Hermann and Dorothy might have been in one of the coaches that I met every day with a fresh relay of horses. The job lasted only until the missing wheeler at the Rifle station was replaced. At that time a man driving north to Bear River gave me a lift in his buckboard. These vehicles were very popular. There was room under the seat for a grub box, and a bed or two could be lashed on the slats behind it.

I never asked the man his name. That was impolite in those days. A stranger might be escaping from something. In a crowd each man was soon given a name like Slim, Shorty, Curly, or Red. My new friend was probably in his upper twenties and certainly Slim. I noticed that he always watched the road ahead, never looking at me. His profile was sharp, his cheeks suntanned, his jaws square, resolute, determined. In camp, when he pushed his hat back on his hand, his forehead appeared very white above brown cheeks. He was an attentive listener, not a talker. For an hour at a time no word passed between us, but when he spoke I listened.

After a long silence he said, "An Indian told me once that Sináwa [Ute for God] gave man two ears and one mouth, so I reckon it must be better for man to listen twice as much as he talks."

We camped that first night at the mouth of a foothill canyon known as Nine Mile. A ranch house stood here, evidently built by one of those men with eastern ideas who had made money in the Leadville mines. Below the big two-story house forty acres of irrigated alfalfa made an emerald blotch on the pearl gray sagebrush. Zane Grey had not yet written *Riders of the Purple Sage,* so sagebrush was still gray. I noticed a white pillar of deer antlers in front of the fine house on the neglected lawn. Evidently when the ranchman killed a buck he put the head on this pile, and the sun soon bleached the skull and antlers white. I learned later that in the Meeker country, where every man shot his meat regularly, these antler pillars were fashionable front-yard decorations. They reminded me of the much higher elk-horn pillars built by Indians in the 1830s. I had seen one of these painted by Karl Bodmer in a copy of *Graham's Magazine* that I found among rare publications in a Philadelphia library on Chestnut Street.

We never saw the ranchman in the big house at Nine Mile. Campers unloaded along the creek below his barbed-wire fence. We joined a wagon man who had already unhitched there. A big lobo, or gray wolf, was tied to one of his wagon wheels. I petted the animal's head. He submitted but did not wag his tail. In that country coyotes were plentiful and after dark their staccato howls surrounded us. Yipping like lunatic laughter, they seemed to be daring us to come and catch them if we could. For a tenderfoot this chorus was exciting, but it disturbed the wolf tied to the wagon wheel. I saw his tail curl up defiantly. He pointed his nose up at the stars and his deep bass howl boomed across the sagebrush.

There was authority, defiance, even majesty, I thought, in that long-drawn howl, and also powerful notes of savage melancholy. No coyote replied. The plains, the rimrocks, the mountainsides were silent. In the dark I heard the wagon man's voice: "Them little bastards knows who's boss," he said. "We'll hear no more from them this night." He was right.

In the morning we left the wagon man and drove up Nine Mile Canyon. The road was not steep and the horses trotted much of the way. Topping the Divide, I noticed a clump of small trees with little round leaves sparkling in the sunshine. The tree trunks looked white, not the paper white of birch trees, but alive like human bodies.

"Them's quaking aspens," the driver said. "They grow at high altitudes where the air is cold. The leaves shiver even in July and August."

Driving down the Divide's north slope I saw more vegetation

new to me. The bare, grassy slopes were dotted with clumps of serviceberry bushes—pronounced "sarviceberry" Out West. Many western words were derived from Spanish, but I soon learned that others were from cockney English. The British who had participated in the boom days for cattlemen following the Civil War were skilled livestock breeders and many of them, or their "sarvents," must have talked cockney English. Certainly the cockney idiom persisted in several western words. A cow with a mottled white face was called a "brockoface." The name must have originated as "brock-face"; in England a badger is called a brock. A stream I crossed later also had an oddly Anglicized name. French fur traders had named it the St. Vrain but it was now called the Savory, an English appetizer (spelled Savery on maps). In like manner the river named Purgatoire by the French became Picketwire in cowboy lingo.

Our road led us out of the foothills into what was called Axial Basin, a gigantic saucer six or eight miles across. The plain looked very flat but the road ahead disappeared down a slight depression, came up smaller in the distance, went down again and up once more until it vanished on the vast basin floor. After the foothills, this sudden expanse did something to us: Slim began to talk. We hadn't driven a hundred yards before a "jackass rabbit" leaped out from behind a bush and raced away at marvelous speed, his long ears laid flat on his body. Spurts of dust indicated that his feet hit the ground only every twelve or fifteen feet. When twenty yards away he made a sky hop, five feet straight up, and, with jackass ears erect, he looked back to see if he was being chased. Evidently satisfied, he galloped away at a slower pace.

On the treeless plain, with nothing to compare it with, the jackrabbit seemed very large. Slim, breaking his usual silence, said that in some lights, morning or evening, a jackrabbit at one hundred yards might be mistaken for an antelope at twice that distance. Men who risked a distant shot were apt to set their rifle sights too high, and the bullet would plow up the ground harmlessly a good hundred yards beyond the mark.

Slim, having begun to talk, continued. "The big vegetable in these parts," he said, "is Tom Isles. He's quite a blower, a real windjammer from who laid the chunk. Tom alus talks big, about takin' part in things that never happened. He ken kill a deer furder away and a bear closer than any other man, but he makes up fer them lies by never bein' downhearted even when he's tuckered out. Alus, he's ready to help a fella buildin' fence, or at a barbecue, a sick spell, or a buryin'."

For the next two hours we exchanged remarks as we drove across the basin. Dots on the plain far ahead of us were either cattle or horses—it was not easy to tell the difference until the dots moved. Slim, talking frequently now, explained that dots moving in long lines were cattle while horses usually, but not always, traveled in a more compact group. When grazing, both kinds of animals spread out, but occasionally one of them would make some movement that identified it as a horse or cow.

That afternoon we forded Bear River—really a large creek— and Slim remarked in his sudden way that we would camp tonight at Dummy and Craney's roadhouse. Dummy, he said, was a "deef" mute, and Craney, with a thin neck and long, pointed nose, looked something like a sandhill crane. Slim said we could get a good meal there and sleep under the buckboard as we had at Nine Mile.

"Them fellas beat any you ever see," Slim concluded. "They're moneymakers. Sure as shootin' you better watch out fur them. They charge a fella two bits fur unrollin' his bed on the stone floor in their barn, and to spite any man who saves money by sleepin' outside, Dummy'll disturb him two or three times durin' the night. Even when it is clear, he'll point to the sky like a storm is comin'. Being unable to talk, Dummy makes gestures that keep a sleeper awake most of the night."

I missed meeting Dummy and Craney on that trip because we crossed a road that Slim said led to the Two Bar horse camp, only four miles away. That was exactly the kind of camp I wanted to see, so I got off the buckboard, thanked Slim for the two-day ride, and walked away carrying my sleeping bag. Slim drove on and in no time became a tiny figure crawling toward the horizon; then I realized how big the world is when a lone man finds himself on foot in the center of a vast plain. Never before had the line where the sky meets the earth seemed quite so far away, but a buzz at one side of the road made me jump and brought me back to practical life.

Thank God for rattlesnakes! This one was coiled under a sagebrush. I could find no stick or stone with which to kill it.

Finally I saw a splintered stalk of dead sagebrush, broke it
loose, came back to the snake, and beat it until I dared put my
foot on the squirming head and crush it to death. Then, with
my penknife, I cut off the rattles, put them proudly in my
hatband, and during the rest of the afternoon every time I
turned my head suddenly the rattles scared me.

At the horse camp I found only one man. He was about my
age but much tougher. He seemed glad I had stopped.

"I hain't saw nary a man f'r three days." The youth smiled as
he pushed back his broad-brimmed hat. "But I shore as hell
jobbed my last boss. Over to Craig, I see that son-of-a-bitch
hitch his team in front of Ledford's saloon. The bastard went
inside and when nobody was lookin' I untied the horses and
whipped 'em down the road. I'll bet they wrecked that buggy
and diden stop 'til they reached the home ranch. I heered tell
folks done that to Ora Haley, his own-self onct, an' it made him
mad as God was that time when he drownded the world."

This was the first time I heard the name Ora Haley, but it
meant much to be in the days ahead. The young cowboy at this
horse camp did not dislike Haley. His only objection to the
present job was the grub. With thousands of cattle around him
his only meat was "salt-side," or what he called, with a suppressed smile, "sow-bosom." Then, he repeated an old range
cliché: "Out here they's more cattle and less milk, more sage
chickens and less eggs, an' you can look furder and see less
than anywheres else on earth."

In front of the cabin at a marsh water hole I noticed a
multitude of redwing blackbirds and suggested that we shoot a
few for dinner. It had never occurred to this cowboy that they
were edible, and I was pleased to suggest anything practical to
an "old hand." We shot six. I ate the first to prove they were
not poison, then both of us found their dark meat delicious.

Next morning a buckboard driven by two men stopped at our
camp. They were headed for Craig, and I went with them
across the wide sagebrush plain. Three on the seat was not
crowded and they talked all the way about Queen Ann, a
notorious cattle rustler in Brown's Park.

"She can ride and swear with the best of the cowboys," the
driver said, "but when in town she's so delicate butter won't
melt in her mouth."

This expression, common then in the rural West, was new to the Philadelphia schoolboy and I never forgot it.

"I saw Queen Ann once," the other man replied. "I knew she must be old but her face was painted up so good she looked young."

She was just thirty years old at that time. Her greatest notoriety was yet to come in trials for cattle stealing in 1911 and 1913, but her early nickname, "Queen of the Rustlers," stuck in my mind. Later I had the good fortune to know her quite well. She filed on a homestead near a claim of mine. When called "Queen Ann" she always smiled, but when scoffing neighbors voiced her other nickname, "Queen Zenoby," she pouted. Zenobia Peak was a gigantic nearby mountain.

That summer day when we drove into Craig the town I had heard so much about seemed quite small. We came first to the big red livery barn where my new friends stopped to stable their horses. The livery man, sitting in a rickety chair tipped back against the barn, was too busy to get up. He was diligently picking his teeth with a yellow straw and, although we were only a few feet away, he shouted, "Hi, strangers! What'll a man see when he ain't got his gun?"

Without another word we unhooked the horses, watered, fed, and stalled them. Then we walked downtown together.

"Don't worry about that man," one of my companions said, "He can't talk without shoutin'. Known as 'Whispering Bob Green,' he used to be Justice of the Peace. When he married folks, people all over town, from the 'coat house' to the livery barn, could hear him say: 'Jine hands.'"

In Craig, "downtown" was the corner where the road we came in on crossed the road leading north to Wyoming. Houses occupied three of the corners. The fourth was an open field evidently used as a race track and ball park. On the corner we came to, Ledford & Kittell operated a one-story false-front saloon. The double doors stood wide open. It was dark inside and my friends asked me to join them for a drink. Not caring for a *ci-gar*, I thanked them and asked to be excused. They seemed relieved and walked in without me.

Standing on the wooden sidewalk between the saloon and the hitching rack for horses, I noticed a slat-backed bench against the wall, shaded by a tall, many-branched box elder.

Here in the heart of a genuine cow town I could leisurely observe true western life. I sat down. Across the road, on the opposite corner, I saw a false-front building that displayed a sign, J. W. HUGUS & CO. A shabbily dressed loafer stood under the canvas awning at the front door. Large letters on the awning above his head said GENERAL MERCHANDISE. Something about the loafer convinced me that he was a tricky character. He wore his hat too low over his eyes, which gave him a stealthy appearance, as though he were hiding from something.

On the other corner, across the sixty-foot-wide street leading north to Wyoming, I saw "a parcel" of men. Some wore coats, some unbuttoned vests. They stood on the board sidewalk in front of a square two-story building. A swinging shingle over their heads was marked BANK. Other buildings that I could see along the street beyond the bank had the false fronts I had seen in western movies back east, movies in which the sentimental cowboy actor William S. Hart shot it out with bad guys.

Craig boasted two hotels. The men in front of the bank had evidently eaten dinner at Ma Webb's, where a good meal was served for two bits. The more aristocratic Baker House, a few doors up the street from Ledford's saloon, charged an extra dime for most of its similar services. The men on the bank corner were waiting for three wagons and a buckboard to pass before they could cross to my side of the wide dirt street.

Sitting at ease on the bench, I wondered why Craig, which seemed smaller than Meeker, had so many more strangers. The town was fifty miles farther from any railroad than Meeker, but I knew that a wagon road from the Colorado plains to Utah passed through Craig. Absentmindedly pondering this geography, I felt my sleeve being twitched. Turning my head, I looked into the slinking eyes of the sinister man I had seen in front of the Hugus store.

"What'll ya take fer that?" The main pointed to my black silk cowboy neckerchief, and I noticed that his fingers all curled in the way they do on a hand that always takes.

"It's not for sale," I replied curtly, but he sat down beside me.

The buckboard and wagons had passed now and the men from the bank corner were walking around the hitching rack and stepping up on the board sidewalk in front of the saloon.

Most of them stopped to talk where they could spit into the street, a western custom even for men who did not chew. Two of them sat down beside me on the bench, crowding me closer to the inquisitive stranger. They were evidently travelers because I heard one say to the other, "From here on, water will be scarce all the way to Utah. There's a couple o' towns, named Lay and Maybell, but they's only a couple o' houses in each of them, and then seventy miles to Green River with no fence ner cabin in that lower country."

The furtive seatmate on my other side glanced with apparent disapproval at the men who had just arrived, then whispered, "What kiney watch hev ye got?"

To get away from this pest I joined the standing men. They did not notice me, and I heard one say to another, "That ain't much money, but if I had it I wouldn't buy no land up here. I'd buy me a camp outfit and a dozen cow critters and pull out fer the lower country. A man ken live cheap down thar and the mavericks is plenty. Soon yu'd hev a bunch o' yer own."

"But with Queen Ann and the rustlers," the first man replied, "wouldn't they rub a feller out?"

"No. She only works the big outfits, and since Tom Horn's been hung its easy pickins for her an' the rest of us. I knowed one fella with nothin' but two steers. He was so handy with a rope an' iron, both them steers had calves, reglar. A man willin' to work ken make a stake fast, down in the lower country."

Everybody referred to the "lower country" as a place apart. That man Tom Horn also intrigued me. I determined to learn more about both, and during the summer ahead I learned plenty.

More men joined our little group on the sidewalk. One was evidently a politician, because I heard him tell the man beside him in a loud voice—evidently pitched for the rest of us to hear—"Them fellers in the legislater told me I must vote their way or they'd hang my hide on the fence." He paused to see if he had an audience, then with a smile of self-appreciation continued, "I tol 'em go ahead, hang it on the fence, but be sure the brand shows plain."

I was drinking in every word of the western talk so new to me. One of the newcomers asked a better-dressed young man,

"Reverend, tell me about this Chirography. I'm fur eddication but agin 'solidation o' county schools. Is the Chirography like that?"

"You mean the Chautauqua," the minister replied. "That is like a traveling circus under a big tent. Instead of clowns and acrobats, lecturers on a stage discuss current events. It is good and educational but they charge admission and take out of town some of the little money we have."

My obnoxious seatmate had followed me into the crowd and nudged me again. The minister may have noticed him, or perhaps the scamp was a town character. In any event, the minister reached out his hand to me and said, "Are you new in town?"

I owe Preacher Ellis a debt of gratitude. He helped me get permanently away from the too-friendly pest who showed so much interest in my scarf and watch. The minister also proved to be a good companion. He did not bore me talking about morals and how to save my soul. Instead, his wife cooked us an excellent supper. The letter I wrote home about him shows that I was still very young. My father kept it and showed it to me with a laugh when I returned home. I had written: "There is a minister in this town, *but* he is a very nice man."

Next morning at the red barn I exchanged with Whispering Green the usual formalities concerning conditions on the range and the chance of a job. He told me, with his usual shout, that help was needed on a ranch behind Cedar Mountain, a thousand-foot mesa west of town. The ranch was five or six miles away. I liked hiking and trudged off on one of the most dangerous walks of my life. The country around Cedar Mountain was unfenced. There was no other ranch all the way. On one side of the road the mesa sloped in a concave arc up to cedars near the flat crest. On the other side sagebrush flats stretched out endlessly into a sealike pearl-gray desert. Finally, I came to the big house. At the front door tall, unkempt weeds told me that this entrance was not used. At the back door, on the barn side of the house, I saw a bench and two washbasins under a mussed towel on a roller. This indicated the main entrance, so I knocked.

"Landy sakes! How'd you get here? Where's your horse? Ye must be half starved!" The buxom female cook who opened the door was dressed in a fresh calico frock that displayed ample curves. She spoke with short, sharp sentences, and I learned that the boss was not shorthanded. Two men were "let go" yesterday.

She offered me a chair and said nothing about the possible danger of walking back to town alone. Instead, she handed me a chunk of fried beef sandwiched between slices of sourdough bread. I ate this with relish while studying an elaborate calendar on the wall. It showed, in color, heroic Texas cowboys driving a herd of longhorns. The commission firm of Clay, Robinson & Co. sent these big calendars with a new picture each year to ranchmen whose cattle they had sold. A man who displayed a Clay, Robinson calendar in public view on the wall of his house ranked with the cattle-owning aristocracy, superior to the humble homesteader who only hoped to be a rancher some day.

After eating, I thanked the woman for my lunch, and as I went out the door I noticed on the corral a fresh beef hide hanging with the brand in full view. This was good social conduct Out West. It assured visitors that the ranchman was eating his own and not his neighbors' beef.

I had experienced no trouble on the trip out from town and expected none going back. After walking for perhaps an hour along the west side of Cedar Mountain I heard a rumble of hoofs behind me. I turned around and saw a herd of some twenty-five or thirty cattle running down the mountainside toward me. No rider was driving them and I saw another bunch about the same size also running toward me. The two herds joined and when a hundred yards away they stopped. I watched them a few minutes, then continued walking down the road. Soon I heard the trample of hoofs again—louder now. I turned once more and this time, when they were fifty yards from me, the cattle stopped.

I shall never forget that row of cattle, standing company front, with their brown faces, black eyes, and high horns and their ears cupped forward. If they ran again they would be on me. Certainly the worst thing I could do would be to run. There was no tree on that vast sagebrush flat for me to climb. I stood there looking at that menacing line of horns. What was best for me to do?

3

Boots That Saved My Job

I love to watch the rooster crow,
He's like so many men I know
Who brag and bluster, rant and shout
And beat their manly breasts, without
The first damn thing to crow about.
—John Kendrick Bangs

Range cattle in those days had never seen a man on foot and they were apt to run toward him with curiosity, especially in the early summer when they were gaining flesh and feeling frisky. The cattle that ran after me probably had no intention of attacking, although they might do so. Certainly when a herd stampedes, the leaders, pushed by those behind, are unable to stop suddenly and anyone in front of them will be trampled to death. Cattle, like sheep, run in tight herds that make it possible for a few riders to round up a thousand head. If cattle start running down hill, others will often join them. Of course I did not know any of their habits when I stood in the center of the vast sagebrush flat confronted by a line of horned cattle.

At one side of the road I saw a dry gulley, three feet wide and three or four feet deep. I would feel helpless lying down in there but getting out of sight of those menacing cattle seemed wise. That there might be rattlesnakes in that wash never occurred to me. I jumped in, and lying down felt helplessly unsafe. The cattle might stampede over the gulch, fall into it, and crush the life out of me. To escape this possibility I crawled on hands and knees down the wash as fast as I could go. It soon became sufficiently deep for me to stand up and walk.

I shall never know what the cattle did when I disappeared, because I saw something in the gulch that took all my attention from them. It was not rattlesnakes I might have met but a white object half buried in the side of the wash about three feet below the rim. It appeared to be a part of a buffalo skull. With my pocket knife I began to chip away the adobe mud holding it, and I soon discovered that it was indeed a cranium just like those Charlie Russell drew beside his signature of his western paintings. I wondered, and still wonder, whether that skull belonged to the gigantic ancestor of our modern bison. Certainly many centuries must have elapsed to deposit three feet of hard clay over the flat where the beast had died and been buried until rain cut this deep wash, exposing the skull.

I did not dig it out. It was much too large to carry away, and if uncovered I feared it might fall to the bottom of the wash and be destroyed by the flood that would follow the next hard rain. I decided to come back some day, however, and take this rare specimen—but I never did. Later, when I collected buffalo skulls for J. D. Figgins, patron of the Colorado Museum of Natural History in Denver, who was classifying varieties and species of bison, I planned to get that skull, but it was a long distance from my ranch and I did not make the trip. On the day I found it I examined the white cranium for an hour, I'm sure, before I remembered the cattle that had chased me into the gulch. Then I peeked up over the top of the wash. All the cows were gone!

Animals have short attention spans, and when I disappeared they probably forgot their curiosity and grazed away. East of the road I could see no cow on the concave slope of Cedar Mountain. Some may have been hidden in the distant trees up near the crest but I saw none. West of the road the sweeping sagebrush flats stretched out endlessly to the horizon—to the distant lower country I had heard so much about. Far-off dots might be cattle, or they might be horses. Certainly they were too distant to be dangerous.

I climbed out of the wash and stood for a moment in plain view, wondering if the curious cattle would reappear. None showed up anywhere, so I walked down the road toward Craig, but I was nervous, alert, watching constantly. After a hundred yards I stopped and looked back across the vast open plain. No animal was visible. Reassured now, I strode away but still watched for hiding places ahead. After an hour, I felt as safe

and happy as I had that morning on my walk out to the ranch
alone in the sharp, motionless western air. In due time I
rounded Cedar Mountain and saw the green line of cottonwood
trees along Bear River. Soon Craig and the big red livery barn
came in view. I suspected that I would spend another night in
that horseman's hotel, make new friends, perhaps, and enjoy
more pioneer gossip.

When I reached the barn I heard what sounded like two
pistol shots, and they seemed to come from the street in front
of Ledford's saloon. Here was the real Wild West at last, and
two more shots convinced me that I had better go no closer,
although I did want to see what was happening. In front of the
barn, Whispering Green's rickety chair was overturned and
deserted. For safety I stepped into the barn. Whispering
Green's office was empty. Seeking him, I walked back between
the ammonia-scented stalls to the corral. No man was there but
I heard more shots up by the saloon. Where had everybody
gone? I didn't want to be hit by a stray bullet and I didn't feel
safe standing there alone. I walked back through the barn stalls
and looked out again through the big front door. There was still
not a man in sight and the shots continued at the street corner
in front of the saloon. For the second time that day I wondered
what to do next.

The shooting lasted so long that I decided it was not a fight.
No man could still be alive after such a bombardment. Perhaps
they were making some tenderfoot dance the two-step to a
tune of carefully aimed shots. It seemed foolish to investigate
but I wanted to see without being seen, so I walked quickly up
the street, ready to dart behind the nearest house at any
moment. Looking in the alley to the back of the saloon, I saw
nobody. The absence of people was disconcerting—really
ominous, threatening, foreboding.

I hurried along the side of the saloon but was not prepared
for what I saw before I reached the box elder tree at the
corner. Across the street from Ledford's saloon, on the bank
corner, the wooden sidewalk was packed with women, a solid
wall of them in sunbonnets and long dresses that hung to the
board sidewalk. They were watching something in the street. I
looked eagerly around the saloon corner and saw a man in

checked cotton shirt, overalls, and broad-brim hat standing in the dirt road with a long whip in his hand. The slim whipstock was three feet long and the lash at least ten. The man held it coiled like a lariat in his left hand. He set up an empty Sego milk can, walked ten feet away from it, turned around, and with his whip made the lash snap like a pistol shot when it hit the can. His marksmanship with that whip was deadly, and with rapid fire he chased the can up and down the street like something alive. The apparent fusillade must have attracted the audience of women. The man's skill was really remarkable.

An observer sitting on the bench under the box elder told me the performing whip-master freighted supplies to Craig from Rawlins, Wyoming. I wanted to see Wyoming but a crowd of admirers surrounded the performer after his exhibition, so I waited until feeding and watering time at the barn before asking him for a job. Whispering Green told me the outfit had twelve horses pulling two wagons and each had a trailer. Six men was the usual number for this outfit and I may have kept some man from a job by offering to tend a trail brake for the trip and my meals. Certainly I had found no work in Craig.

We started early the next morning. Rawlins was almost a hundred miles north of Craig, and there were very few houses along the way. From my seat on the boss's trail wagon I could not see all his teams, but I pitied any of his horses that failed to obey his commands. With that whip he could make the hair fly and cut a horse's hide as with a knife, drawing blood. We camped the first night on the wide open flats of upper Fortification Creek. Drinking java around the fire, the men talked about the only village we would pass on the trip. Baggs, Wyoming, the men said, was a haven for drinking, shouting, shooting cowboys. A man who was wanted by an officer in either Colorado or Wyoming could enjoy life in Baggs because the state line was so close to town he could always dodge the law. Such men were usually free spenders.

"Considerin' the town's size," one of the wagon men said as he held up his mustache with his left hand so he could drink his coffee, "merchants, hotel and saloon men get rich quick in Baggs."

"Yeah!" the man sitting beside him replied. "An' I heerd say that the stage driver's wife from Rawlins said she liked the Bagg end of her husband's route the best."

"They'll even blagguard women in that town," the man with the big mustache retorted.

Baggs, when our wagons trundled through it, had little more than a dozen dreary one-story buildings strung along a single street. There was a three-story hip-roofed hotel with a front porch. Although it was the most pretentious building in town, I had completely forgotten it when I learned, four years later, that a well-liked cowboy, Chick Bowen, was shot by the marshal, Bob Meldrum, in front of that hotel. Chick's only crime, according to the outraged popular account, was to stand on that hotel porch and yell. This seemed an innocent act but cowboy yells in town at that time—shrill and provocative—were a challenge to law and order. They put a chill in a peaceful person's spine that cannot be forgotten. The yells I remember were usually accompanied by pistol shots, and very often similar yells and shots down the street responded to them. The town marshals, I knew, always hurried, grim-faced, toward such disturbances, but Chick Bowen is the only cowboy I can recall who was shot for yelling.

Local gossips gave personal reasons to explain why Bob Meldrum killed Chick Bowen. Bob was having trouble with his wife, who was accused of being unfaithful, and some said Bob may have been jealous of Chick. A much more probable reason for Bob's hostility was Chick's sympathy with the small ranchers who rustled from the big outfits. The apparently peaceful and picturesque village I drove through that day was seething with secret fears and hatreds. Cattle and horse stealing had almost become an acknowledged occupation on the surrounding range. It was difficult to get a conviction in court when a majority on a jury were fellow rustlers. Only five years earlier Tom Horn had been hanged as an assassin paid by the big outfits to kill rustlers who could not be convicted in court. Since Horn's hanging, rustling had become more open, more daring. At Queen Ann's trial in 1911 for butchering a Haley heifer, Chick Bowen testified that Haley's foreman told him the big outfits planned to "get rid of Queen Ann." Those were ominous words in Baggs, Wyoming. Tom Horn had been hanged for "getting rid" of rustlers marked by the big outfits. Chick Bowen's testimony at Ann's trial was said to have prevented the jury from convicting her. The disgruntled big outfits marked Chick and hired Bob Meldrum to do the job.

This, of course, is only speculation. Bob Meldrum was a surly fellow, but men like Bob did help bring law and order to the frontier. A few years later, when I was in the cattle business myself, I employed a surveyor named Harry Ratliff who had lived for years in the Baggs community. I found him to be an energetic, dependable, and fearless man. He told me that the cattlemen, when I passed through Baggs, had organized a Snake River Stock Growers Association, which planned to continue Tom Horn's method of controlling cattle stealing. Their written constitution provided that the directors appoint a committee of three who, to prevent detection, would secretly draw straws to determine which one should employ a stock detective to assassinate suspected rustlers. This provision may have been written to frighten rustlers. It was stricken from the final record but Bob Meldrum was employed as a stock detective. He distrusted small ranchers, terrified horse and cattle thieves, and was feared and hated as much as Tom Horn had ever been.

Three months after the day I drove through Baggs, Bob Meldrum became the town's first marshal. The merchants who welcomed a lawless stranger with money to spend needed a man to protect their property. Bob Meldrum had the qualities for that ugly job.

Across the street from the hotel where Chick was shot stood the only building in Baggs that impressed me. It had a broad false front that was freshly painted white. In black letters, over the wide-open doors, I read FOUR ACE BEER HALL. The entrance was sufficiently high for a horseman to ride in and drink from his saddle at the bar.

Driving north from Baggs we crossed Snake River, pulled the wagons out on the Wyoming plains, and camped that night on "the Muddy." Here I heard for the first time about the renegade Ute Indians I was destined to camp with that fall. I do not know what brought up the subject or where the teamsters got their information, but it seemed to be common knowledge that a band of Utes who were moved to Utah after

the Meeker Massacre had been unhappy on their new reservation. Hoping to resume their wild life on the plains, some three
hundred of them rode north with their families in 1906 seeking
the Big Horn Mountains—the legendary country where the
Sioux had celebrated after killing Custer. The Army overtook
them on the wide plains between the Black Hills and the Big
Horns. The Utes, outnumbered by the soldiers, refused to
return to their reservation but consented to go with the Army
to the Sioux reservation at Wounded Knee in South Dakota.

The Sioux did not welcome the Utes. Instead, they charged
them pasturage for their hundreds of ponies, and after an
unhappy summer the Utes agreed to be escorted by the Army
back to Utah in 1908. They were now ahead of us somewhere,
in an ugly mood, on their return trip. Two of the teamsters
who told me this, feared that the Indians might slip away from
the soldiers and take revenge on settlers. Others said the Utes
had better stay with the soldiers lest the settlers take revenge
on them. This started an argument and we went to bed without
settling it.

Next morning we continued our slow voyage north across the
sea of sagebrush. I knew that the Indians must be many miles
away, and from my seat at the brake on the trail wagon I
amused myself by imagining them on the skyline racing toward
us as Frederic Remington pictured them. I did not realize that
we were slowly driving uphill until we came to a country where
there was no sagebrush. We traveled across this rough, grassy
land for some ten or fifteen miles. The sod was deep, and grass
grew even in the sides of deep gulches and on rocky peaks the
men called "pee-nuckles." This, I learned later, was the Continental Divide.

Crossing to the lower sagebrush country beyond, we came
suddenly to the edge of an escarpment and looked down on the
long line of the Union Pacific Railroad, with Rawlins only a
mile away below us. The stockyards, the stables, and what we
learned later was a house of prostitution were south of the
tracks. We had barely watered and unharnessed our teams
before we learned that a man named Rhoden was shipping in a
big herd of Texas longhorns, cattle that were expected to be
"sniffy" and hard to handle. He was hiring any man who could
ride to help hold them the first day or two after being uncar-

red. The job would be temporary; as soon as the cattle recovered from the fright of the trip and filled their paunches with
grass, the outfit's regular cowboys could trail them to the
summer range on the Little Snake.

I was told that the rich man hiring the cowboys was across
the tracks in Hugus's store. Hugus seemed to have a store in
every town. I found the man to be quiet and short-spoken,
with a determined face deeply lined by hardships, perhaps by
hunger, too. He wore a frock coat, celluloid collar buttoned on
a white cotton shirt, no necktie, and conspicuously shabby
"catalog shoes"—a cheap pattern with the "gunboat toes" worn
in Philadelphia by dressed-up menials. Certainly he was not
my idea of a rich man but he had calm strength, character and,
in spite of his odd clothes, real unaffected dignity. I was told
later that this was not Mr. Rhoden but his straw boss, who
ramrodded the outfit on the range—an odd character, yes!
Later I was told that he went to Washington once with a
delegation of cattlemen to see the President concerning grazing
rights on the newly created national forests. His wife told him
to be sure to buy a necktie. He objected, saying he would be in
Wasington only two days and only half an hour with the President. He could not wear out a necktie in that length of time.

I asked this odd fellow for a job. He asked me no questions
about my experience working with cattle, so I did not have to
stretch the blanket—very much. He said I could start work at a
dollar a day the next morning: "Put your bed and saddle in the
company cart down at the livery barn and be there at six
tonight when the cook drives out to the wagon." I learned later
that "the wagon," short for chuck wagon in cowboy lingo,
meant the camp.

Everything was coming my way now, except I did not have a
saddle and I lacked the money to buy one. While "figgering"
what to do about this, a young man about my age came in the
store, also seeking a job. He was a talker—a bragger, I
thought—and he said he'd been riding for the "Figger Fours."
In a loud voice, obviously keyed for everybody to hear, he
announced that the "Fours" was a cheap outfit.

"They give me a string of six hosses," the cowboy said, "all
no good! I spurred the first one across some rocks so's he'd
break a leg. My second hoss had sprung knees. I seed that right

off, so I whipped him down a steep grade to make him fall. A good hand like me knows how to jump clear, and that fall finished that hoss. The third one in my string was bad to toss his head, hit me onct in the nose. I hit him back with the butt of my quirt, knocked out his eye. I told the boss I was quittin' fer the outfit's good. I wanted to learn 'em how to get shut o' them no good broncs. Now they'd hev to buy good mounts and with them they ken keep good men, like the Two Bar done."

This loud-mouthed abuser of horseflesh, this bantam rooster crowing when he had nothing to crow about, disgusted me. To my surprise, the frock-coated boss hired him without a question and I wondered how long I would last with such a man on this cowpunching job. The young fellow slapped the six-shooter in his belt and swaggered out of the store in his high-heeled boots.

Years later, when I began to study history seriously, I met that boy in many books, first as one of the powder monkeys on John Paul Jones's *Bon Homme Richard* (the story of a naval battle my father first read to me). I met him again in Captain Marryat's stories, and when I studied the career of Ned Buntline I found dozens of terrible young midshipmen who "strutted the deck, slapped the hilts of their dirks, and sputtered oaths at seamen older, wiser, and larger than themselves."

Thoroughly detesting this kind of overgrown boy and not being sufficiently old myself to be amused, I walked to the back of the store where three elderly men were sitting in armchairs around a stove. This was evidently an established place for gossip, summer or winter, because the weather was warm now and the stove was cold. The men must have heard that young braggart's loud talk and I hoped to hear them criticize him. I was disappointed. One of them said, "Who is that fella?"

"For a kid he's a top hand," another replied. "They call him Hawkshaw for some reason. I don't know what. He ken outride any two men. Wilse Rankin told me that when Hawkshaw starts to turn a steer every other man in the outfit remembers something that needs fixin' on his saddle and gets off to 'tend it."

"Yes," another said. "Hi Bernard told me that on the shove-down last fall when they changed horses at dinner time

Hawkshaw beat every man in the race to the wagon, saddled his fresh horse, and instead of settin' down f'r coffee he put a slice of beef between two biscuits and loped back to the herd eatin' it. Some man, him!"

I still did not like Hawkshaw, the name of a character, I learned later, in Tom Taylor's English play, *The Ticket-of-Leave Man*. British stockmen probably brought the name west with other idioms. To me the Hawkshaw in Hugus's store was an unpleasant individual of bright, ugly colors. I dreaded working with him, but a good-looking cowboy followed him into the store to buy a shirt and I heard him say, "My name's Robinson, Jim Robinson. Charge it to Al Rhoden."

That was the name of my employer. Another cowboy came in, bought some socks, underwear, Levi Straus overalls, and said, "Charge it to Al Rhoden."

This put an idea in my head. I knew that a cowboy should wear boots. In case of a stampede at night he must dress quickly and there was no time for lacing shoes. I asked the clerk in the store to show me a pair. The cowboy boots of that day had sharp heels that made walking difficult but were excellent for digging into the ground when the man wearing them wanted to stop a bolting horse he had just roped. The high tops on old-fashioned boots that reached up almost to a rider's knees were good, too. In later days when leather became expensive, low embroidered boot tops became fashionable. They looked nice in town but were bad for rough riding. Gravel from a horse's flying hooves always fell in the low, open tops and a man had to dismount to shake it out.

The high-topped boots in Hugus's store fit my feet, felt smooth and comfortable. I told the clerk, "My name's Monaghan, Jim Monaghan. Charge it to Al Rhoden."

These were the exact words the two cowboys ahead of me had used. They were easy to remember but I saw the clerk hesitate and look at the straw boss for confirmation. This was a tense moment in my young life. Had I done the wrong thing? Was I or was I not accepted in this brave new western world? With great relief I saw the straw boss nod. The charge would be honored. Rhoden was really hard up for help! Wearing brand-new high-heeled boots, I followed the two cowboys out the door into the clear Wyoming air.

An odd incident a few days later made those boots an important purchase in my life. At the time, however, I was worried. I wondered how in the world I was ever going to get a saddle by six o'clock that evening in order to join the cowboys down at the wagon. A saddle was a big investment, not one I could *charge to Al Rhoden.*

4

"Keep Jesus Out of This Game!"

The feller was a cowboy that come from Swenson's ranch;
They called him Windy Billy from Little Deadman's Branch.
His rig was kinder keerler—big spurs and high-heeled boots;
He had the reputation that comes when fellers shoots.
  —The Cowboy's Christmas Ball"

June on the high plains of Wyoming can be magnificent. A lung full of free, sagebrush air, iced by wind from the snowy Medicine Bow Mountains, makes a young man wearing new cowboy boots forget that he may lose his job for lack of funds to buy a saddle, but he is sure to remember and understand the refrain:

> Where seldom is heard a discouraging word
> And the deer and the rattlesnakes play.

Breathing that couplet, I walked down a Rawlins side street, and in the modest display window of a humble saddle shop I saw a quantity of hand-crafted leather goods. There were leather cuffs and leather spud belts six inches wide with brass studs depicting stars, circles, even well-known brands. There were chaps—both bat-wing and shotgun—some with silver conchos down the sides. There were even leather turndown collars for the collarless cotton shirts of that day, and leather neckties, both bow and four-in-hand, that clamped on those leather collars. With curiosity, and more time than money, I climbed the three steps to the entrance and walked in.

That year a new fashion in saddles had come to Wyoming. The old square skirts were being replaced by lighter, round skirts to be used over a thick corona pad instead of the usual folded saddle blankets. The craftsman who operated the shop greeted me with a Yorkshire accent. He had evidently come west with some of the early British stockmen. An affable man, but a close trader, I heard later that he was honest and economical, that he had come to Rawlins ten years earlier with a ten-dollar bill and a clean shirt and had not yet changed either one. He looked at my boots and, evidently assuming me to be at least a would-be cowboy, explained that these new corona pads were better than blankets. They could not wrinkle and make a horse's back sore. On a long, fast trot they never worked back out from under the saddle "gaulding a horse's weathers." In addition, when saddling up, a pad lay flat on a horse's back even in a Wyoming wind, and all cowboys knew that the usual morning breeze made it very difficult to keep blankets flat until the saddle was swung on top of them.

The shopkeeper rubbed his calloused hands together, saying that every cowboy who could afford it was buying these new round-skirted saddles. He said he had taken a pretty good old model as down payment for a new one and could afford to sell it for fifteen dollars. That took every cent I had but it was a Thompson Saddle, a name as well known in the Rocky Mountains as Colt and Winchester. During the years ahead that Thompson carried me many miles in Mexico as well as in the United States. The shopkeeper even gave me a burlap bag, the kind cowboys of that day used for checking saddles when traveling by train.

Down at the livery barn the crew of riders I found waiting to be hauled to "the wagon" did not resemble Frederic Remington cowboys. Hawkshaw was there. He spied my boots and, in a tone of contempt that I disliked, he asked, "Whatja pay for them clodhoppers?"

This was none of his business and I made no reply.

"Them round-toed boots is no good," he asserted. "A genuine cowhand wears sharp-pointed toes that help find the off stirrup when a man swings aboard. Real professionals never wear store boots, alus has 'em tailor-made. Alligator skin is the most expensive. They're waterproof."

I would hear all these flimsy excuses for cowboy finery repeated many times later by youthful riders trying to hide their vanity by pleading utility.

A rough Scandinavian at the wagon attracted my attention. Coarse and heavy, he had fists as big as hams and feet so flat the boys said his insteps punched holes in the ground. I pitied the horse that had to carry such a giant. He was red-headed, red-faced, good-natured, noisy, quick to say whatever came into his mind and quick to laugh, especially at his own jokes. Dry, scorching western winds had chapped his lips until they were swollen and bleeding. He licked them constantly for relief, making his face under his red hair very red indeed. Somebody told him he could cure those sore lips by chewing tobacco. He said no. He was a Mormon, and the church objected to tobacco. Henceforth, the men called this red-faced beauty the Pink Angel.

Another new man had only one leg. He wore a cowboy boot on it and evidently was no stranger to range life. He was well over six feet tall, and the crutch under his right arm made him look like a head under a big hat with two legs each five feet long. When he walked, each stride covered at least six feet. A normal man had to run to keep up with him. The boys called him High-Pockets. That crutch, he said, was as good as a leg for clamping him on a horse but, with his right hand holding it, he could not throw a lasso. In wet weather he carried a little snowshoe for the end of his crutch to prevent it from sinking in the mud. He was a grim young man of few words. His lifelong suffering had cut deep lines of pain in his face. I never saw him smile, but he never complained the way Hawkshaw was always doing.

My first meal at the chuck wagon up on the ridge that night was a treat to remember. Perhaps it was the picturesque setting, the slim men in high-heeled boots and broad Stetson hats, the kettles on the pot-rack, the covered wagon and, far below, like a checkerboard on the plain, Rawlins, Wyoming. The chuck wagon food tasted good—beef fried in a Dutch oven, sliced potatoes browned to a spicy crisp, boiled dried peaches, sourdough biscuits, and molasses dip.

"Sorghum, ugh!" Hawkshaw snorted in his impudent manner. "The Two Circle Bar riders 'ud get Log Cabin Maple Syrup. Ol' Noey [Noah] Rhoden alus thinks cowboys want to eat like he done when a boy."

Hawkshaw was interrupted by a middle-aged cowboy who had been helping the cook. "Al Rhoden feeds us pretty well,"

the man said. "At shippen time last fall he tol' the boys who
took his stock to Chicago, that he'd pay f'r their meals out thar.
Yas, an' he'd pay f'r their whiskey but he'd be goddamned if
he'd pay f'r their women. What more'n that c'n a man ask?"

Hawkshaw made no reply. When authority spoke he seldom
answered. I looked at the speaker's solemn face, his squint
eyes, crow-footed at the corners. Those eyes had a hard, level
look from constantly watching for objects a long distance away.
Frederic Remington would have understood his face. I learned
that he was the outfit's nighthawk, always called Boston, which
may have been his real name, although nicknames were more
popular. Boston's job was to night herd the horses, or "cavy," a
bad pronunciation of *caballo*, Spanish for "horse." Texas hands
called a cavy the *remuda*. A night herder's job was important.
To fill it a man must know the range, know horses, and ride
alone hour after hour in the stillness of the night. A hundred or
more geldings soon divide into social groups with independent
grazing habits, and a good nighthawk must know each group
and keep track of it in the dark—even in pouring rain when
bolts of lightning crack the heavens and explode in a rider's
face. To lose the horses would leave the entire outfit helplessly
afoot.

I learned to know Boston well in the years ahead, and to
respect him greatly. He was hawk-featured, seldom talked, was
never sociable, but he found satisfaction, even grim joy, in his
success at this lonely work. He belonged to an endangered
species, as extinct now as the horse Indian. Both are gone and
the western world they lived in has gone with them.

A few of the regular cowboys who had spent the day in
Rawlins rode into camp and unsaddled. A shrill yell in the
distance told us that the wrangler was bringing in the cavy. To
corral the horses we stretched ropes from the wheels of the
chuck and bed wagons. Holding the rope ends, we made a
U-shaped pen for the horses until Boston, with a skillful ground
throw, lassoed the night horse he wanted. Saddling up, he
drove the cavy back south out of sight for his lonely vigil. The
day wrangler helped himself to supper from the pot-rack and
Hawkshaw, free of Boston, tried once more for an audience.

"They's three ways to brace a Jane," he commenced, "an'

two of 'em is wrong. Never let a girl think yer stingy, but never let her pull yer leg neither. Here's what I done onct. I had on a new silk shirt. Cost me twelve dollars. She said, 'I'd love to have that shirt.' I yanked it offen my back right now, tore it in half and handed her the pieces. That let her know I diden care a goddamn about the twelve dollars but she coulden impose on me neither. That's the way to get along with woming. Let 'em know you're smart as they be."

No one, other than Boston, had questioned Hawkshaw's philosopical commentary. Instead, we began to unroll our beds at places that looked level, or nearly so. I heard one man say, "A rattlesnake just went down this hole, but with my bed over it he can't come up."

I personally was more afraid of Hawkshaw than the rattlesnake and carried my bed as far from his as posible, but I did not go sufficiently far. He had a pack of cards and wanted to start a game.

"Either stud or twenty-one," he announced in a loud voice.

Two or three booted men stamped across to Hawkshaw's bed to test their luck. "Let's take the little bastard's dough," one of them said, "and earn back what we lost in town."

I soon heard the peculiar western habit of snapping each card as it was played.

"The boss don't allow no card games in camp," our cook shouted.

"The boss ain't here," Hawkshaw retorted.

Darkness came. Most of us crawled into our beds but the gamblers fixed a "bitch lamp"—a burning rag for a wick in a can of melted grease—to continue playing. The game must have been stud poker because I heard a deep-chest voice say, "One card fer me," and the card snapped.

"Three cards fer me," another voice said, and one at a time three cards snapped.

"I'll take two," and two snapped.

A pause, and we sleepers buried our heads in what we used for pillows until disturbed by, "I'll raise you two."

"I'll stay in."

"I'll raise you five."

"I'll raise yu *ten*."

"Don't chip-rack me," an angry voice challenged.

A much angrier voice—this time the cook's—shouted, "Fer Chrisake shut up. Let a fella sleep."

"Keep Jesus out o' this game," Hawkshaw replied, and I heard muffled laughter in the beds around me—even from the Pink Angel's.

Nobody was getting much rest, but the gamblers did begin to talk more quietly and most of us soon fell asleep. At midnight a hand shook me awake. In the dark I could not be sure who had disturbed me.

"Jim," a man's voice said, "did you buy a pair of boots at Hugus's store?"

Something in the man's voice made me suspect that Al Rhoden himself, not his straw boss, had awakened me.

"Yes," I replied, barely raising my head from the rolled Levis I used for a pillow. Hawkshaw had taught me that Out West I should never say "Yes, sir." Hawkshaw explained that all men were created equal, and for a man with pride "sir" was "a son-of-a-bitch what ain't yet bornded"—a common saying of that day that I soon learned to repeat myself.

"Ugh," the man replied, exactly the way Hawkshaw had when he saw the molasses. Saying no other word, he disappeared in the dark. I expected to "ketch it" come morning, but I had worn the boots and could not now take them back. The gamblers had evidently stopped playing when the boss arrived. The camp was quiet and I decided to enjoy sleeping until dawn.

I shall never forget the next morning and my fear of "ketching it" from the boss for buying those boots. The cook awakened us before dawn shouting: "Come and get it, before I throw it out!"

Men stirred in all the beds. Throwing back the tarpaulin covers, they stood up, pulled on pants and boots, tucked in their shirt tails. Then they rolled their beds and tied them with ropes.

In the darkness, the cook's fire under the kettles on the pot-rack attracted everybody. Deference for the boss and the awkwardness of the four green hands caused some confusion, but men were already helping themselves to the victuals. Two men were still washing their faces in the outfit's two washbowls. A third man held a cup between his knees, splashed the water in it onto his hands, and rubbed his face—resourceful, certainly. I tried this myself and wiped on the black silk scarf around my neck. My toilet completed, I picked up the plate and the "reloading tools" the cook had laid out for us on his cupboard shelf. Then I joined the line filing past the pot-rack. We sat on the ground, tailor-fashion, to eat with our plates on our folded legs. Hot coffee and meat tasted good in the half light. The foreman, in work clothes this morning, looked better dressed, I thought, than he had in yesterday's silly city clothes. He sat on the ground eating with an older man who was evidently Al Rhoden. The two men talked quietly together, occasionally glancing at me. I expected them to call me over and say something about those boots. They did not, however, and I thought perhaps they did not want to embarrass me in front of all hands and have me quit.

Before we finished eating, Boston drove in the cavy. The cook shouted to all of us, "Put your plates and reloading tools here in the roundup pan!"

We did so and then ran to man the ropes used for the cavy-corral. A single strand with a man serving as fence post would hold these horses but he must be watchful. When he saw a horse lower its head to slip under the rope and escape, he had to swing the rope quickly so that it threatened to slap the animal's face. Horses soon learned this danger and stayed away from the rope barrier. At the corral's open panel I stood with Hawkshaw, the Pink Angel, and High-Pockets, whose swinging crutch warned any horse that hoped to bolt past us.

The job of catching the horses each rider selected for the day's work was given to Nate Jackson. Nate was Hawkshaw's age but as different from him as two men can be. A top rider and roper, Nate was quiet in a crowd and never bragged or slapped his six-shooter. Everybody liked Nate Jackson. The foreman told him what horses to rope for us new riders and he, without swinging the lasso over his head to frighten the horses, threw what was called a "hooleyann." This was a vertical loop that sailed over a half dozen horses' backs and tossing manes before it flipped horizontally and snared the head of the desired animal. The wisest horse, one that has learned to dodge a horizontal loop, can never tell which way a "hooleyann" will turn and thus cannot evade being caught.

The mount assigned me this morning was a chunky little bay

named Buttons. I looked carefully at the small AH branded on his shoulder because from now on I must remember this horse even when he ran with a half a hundred others in the remuda. More horses would be assigned to me in the days ahead and I must know "my string" by name and description. From now on I, not the foreman, would call for the horse I wanted each morning and it was part of my job to select the best horse for the day's work. I would also be responsible for each horse's condition, and I wondered if Hawkshaw would abuse "his string" the way he had done when riding for the Figure Fours.

The old hands named the mounts they wanted. Nate roped them all and we riders led our horses to the saddles which lay on the ground near our beds. The wrangler drove the cavy out of camp while we saddled up. Now, I thought, Al might speak to me alone concerning those boots, but a new and serious incident distracted all of us. High-Pockets was in trouble. His horse feared the strange big hat on long legs that took six-foot strides. In terror he snorted and shied away. High-Pockets held him with one hand but with the crutch in the other he could not pet the horse's neck and reassure him. One of the cowboys had to hold the bronc until High-Pockets threw on his saddle, cinched it and mounted. His long crutch swinging across the horse's rump must have resembled a whip because the animal flinched and when turned loose tried to buck, but High-Pockets was a good rider. He kept the horse's head up and we all mounted, ready for the day's work.

I would like to go back some time to Rawlins, climb the ridge south of town, and locate the spot where we assembled that morning around the chuck wagon. Sitting on our horses, we looked down on Rawlins and could see the railroad stretching like a thread to the eastern horizon. The sun peeped up exactly where the railroad disappeared and a slow-moving freight train chugged along the track, seemingly pulling the sun up into the Wyoming sky. Nate Jackson was the first to notice it and we all watched until the sun rose above the plains. Then one of the older cowhands said, "That train must be bringin' our caddle."

A happy exclamation rippled across the group of horsemen, and if Al Rhoden planned saying anything to me about those boots he was diverted for the fourth time. After all, I had done exactly what his other hands were doing in the store and his straw boss had acquiesced, so there was little he could say except to call me extravagant. Perhaps I felt guilty and imagined it all.

Hawkshaw's voice rang out: "Let's go!" And without waiting for the foreman to speak, he galloped down the hill, his shirt ballooning in back, his elbows flapping like a bird in flight. I had been taught in the East to hold my elbows at my sides when riding at a gallop, but I kept my criticism of his horsemanship to myself. The cook evidently felt no such restraint and shouted after him, "Any bed that ain't loaded in the wagon will be left behind when I drives off today."

I suspected that the cook was beginning to dislike Hawkshaw very much. We all dismounted to load our rolled-up beds in the wagon. Then we remounted and raced down the hill. The horses felt good, wanted to run, and we didn't like to disappoint them. High-Pockets kept up with the best of us. Older men and the owner, with his foreman, brought up the rear. We beat the train to Rawlins by only a few minutes.

The engineer backed his train into the siding for the stockyards and spotted two cars loaded with cattle at the two unloading chutes. Then he left the other cars that were also full of cattle on the track for us to unload as best we could. Without saying "hello, good-bye, or go to hell"—an expresion of that time—the engineer chuffed away with the remainder of his train while we watched helplessly as it shrank in the distance until it disappeared, leaving only a skein of smoke in the big sky.

All the stock-car doors were sealed. The railroad agent, a leisurely man, finally came down from the station with a crowbar and some papers for Al Rhoden to sign. He broke the seals on all the car doors and we shoved open those on the two cars spotted at the chutes. The steers hesitated to come out. Cowboys with prod poles began to poke the animals at the car ends. Finally, one venturesome "critter's" long horns appeared at the open doorway. The animal made an uncertain step out of the car, then rushed down the chute with the whole carload rumbling after him into the pen below. They were lean, colorless cattle, all three years old or older. They appeared alert and frightened. When they crowded together their horns hit and clattered. These animals in open country were sure to require different handling than our native cattle. No wonder the foreman had hired all the extra help he could find.

Our first real problem came after unloading the two cars at the chutes. With no locomotive to move the empty cars and spot the loaded cars we seemed to be in a predicament, but not for the station agent and the older cowboys. First the two empty cars were uncoupled. Then with one man at the brake wheel on top and others with crowbars under the wheels, the cars were inched, one by one, down the track. The same tedious method was used to bring the loaded cars to the chutes. At last all the cattle were unloaded and the time had come for me to see how hungry Texas longhorns would perform when turned loose in open country.

I noticed that both Al and his foreman appeared to be a trifle apprehensive. They tried not to show it but they mounted their horses before there was any reason to do so, and the foreman idly wrapped his reins around the saddle horn—a strange action. Al, beside him, squeezed and wrung his gloves as though they were wet.

A lot of money was at stake in these cattle, but more important to the cowmen were their reputations. Their older cowboys had come to this country with trail herds from Texas, but that was years ago when they were in their teens. Some of the middle-aged cowboys had chased wild cattle in the renowned "lower country." They had roped, hobbled, or neck yoked them to "gentle oxen" until they were tame, but that was very different from handling a big herd of longhorns in open country. For me to watch the way expert horsemen handled half-wild cattle, and to work with them, was one of the great events I had come west to experience. As soon as that stockyard gate opened I was going to witness a closing scene of the real Old West.

5

"Have You Seed Gompers?

In my wild erratic fancy visions come to me of Clancy
  Gone a-droving "down the Cooper" where the western drovers go;
As the stock are slowly stringing, Clancy rides behind them singing,
  For the drover's life has pleasures that the townsfolk never know.
    —Banjo Paterson

I was surprised that the people in Rawlins showed so little interest in the release of those cattle. Cowboys, of course, were not new or even interesting to them. Rawlins was a railroad town with fine shops and banks. Cowboys might be socially acceptable back East where Owen Wister's novel, *The Virginian*, was being read and discussed, but out here cowboys were laborers who ranked with the Union Pacific section hands. The big merchants and bankers in Rawlins were concerned about a cattleman's credit, not his ability to throw a rope or control half-wild steers. Even the girls in the bawdy house south of the tracks showed no interest in us at the cattle pens. Two of them rode by on horseback, but they did not look our way—unusual for prostitutes. We looked at them and Hawkshaw even shouted an obscene remark that shocked me, as I was shocked later by the way men talked in front of Indian squaws. I learned that such words were proper conversation with Indians.

The prostitutes were smartly dressed. I noticed their neatly cut breeches and English boots. In those days breeches on a woman were considered improper. A true lady rode sidesaddle in a skirt so long she could not walk on the ground without pinning it up. When she mounted, her escort or a groom cupped his hands like a stirrup, and with her left foot in them he lifted her up onto the saddle.

Sitting on our horses beside the cattle pens, we waited for

orders. The boss explained that when the cattle streamed out we must be careful not to frighten them, to stay well back, permit them to settle down and graze. If they ran, we must head them up the steep ridge south of town. Cattle like to run down hill, but not up. That slope would tire them, make them quit running and stay together. The boss said he intended to release only one pen of longhorns and see how they acted. Then he would open other pens and let all the cattle out to join them.

"Station your riders about fifty yards apart in a big circle,' the boss told his foreman, and added in a low voice, "Put good men on both sides of them two idjits."

I pretended not to hear that last remark and hoped that I was not one of the two idiots. Nate Jackson and another of the old hands rode off to distant positions. The foreman pointed to places for the rest of us. Everyone seemed to become more nervous the longer we waited. I saw Al squeeze and wring his gloves again, but he nodded to the foreman, who dismounted, unhooked the gate to one of the pens, and stepped quickly back to his horse, being careful, I noticed, not to run. That would make his horse shy away and leave him afoot.

The gate swung open and the hinge made a strange sound—a squeak and jolt. The steers inside heard this and the first one to run out held his head low, watching that hinge. Two followed him, both shying away from that suspicious hinge. Behind them three crowded out together, rubbing the gatepost opposite the hinge. All the cattle in the pen followed, horns rattling as they jostled one another to get away.

Surrounded by the distant circle of riders, these cattle threw up their heads to look around, stopped running, and soon began nipping anything they might eat. So far so good! The foreman opened the other yard gates one at a time. Each bunch ran, as Al had hoped, to the grazing animals outside and stopped. Before long the entire shipment was unloaded—a nice herd of longhorns, and they had not made the expected trouble, at least not yet! Instead, all of them seemed willing to be driven at a walk up the side of the ridge south of Rawlins. We cowboys rode along both sides of the line of cattle, keeping them headed in the same direction. We passed the wagons on the crest and a mile or two beyond came to good grass. Here the lead riders stopped the herd and all the cattle spread out to graze. Al and his foreman watched them a few minutes and then separated. Al rode back toward the wagons.

That evening, as the sun slipped slowly below the sagebrush desert horizon, we bunched the cattle a little but not into a tight herd. They seemed accustomed to horsemen. Some of them began to lie down and chew their cuds. The foreman assigned four of the old hands to stay on guard, and the rest of us followed him at a fast trot to the wagon for supper. This was the first time since our morning race to the train that we had ridden faster than a walk. When we dismounted at the wagon the Pink Angel was a sight to behold. The steady trotting had worked his pants up his legs above his knees. His shanks were bare except for the cheap cotton socks that had rolled down over the tops of his shoes, but nothing—not even his chapped and bleeding lips—squelched his spirits.

We ate a good supper and, before we finished, the wrangler brought in the cavy. Each of us saddled a night horse for the work ahead. It was dark now and the foreman told me to go to bed if I wanted to, but he would rout me out at ten o'clock for my night-herding trick. Tired and eager to lie down, I took off my hat, pulled off those precious boots, put my glasses in them for safety, rolled up my Levis for a pillow, and crawled into the sleeping bag. The next minute, so it seemed to me, the fore-man began to shake the blankets. Crawling out, I joined High-Pockets and two of the regular hands at the wagon, where they were drinking coffee in the dark. The night was pitch black and I wondered how we would find the herd. There was no road or trail out to the bed ground, but the two old hands started without hesitation. High-Pockets and I followed them. First one and then the other of our leaders lighted cigarettes. The smoke and the men's quiet voices came back to us. Sud-denly, after riding less than a mile, one of our leaders, in a surprisingly loud voice, said:

> "We are the jolly cowboys
>   Who ride the western plains.
> Our trade is cinching saddles
>   And pulling bridle reins."

I looked at High-Pockets with a questioning smile. That grim and usually silent man replied, "The herd must be close. Never

ride up to bedded cattle without singin', talkin', lettin' 'em
know that men, not varmints, is a-comin'. A sudden noise in
the dark, a horse crushin' a sagebrush or stumblin', can start a
stampede."

The rider ahead of us continued his recitation:

> "We chase the long-horned cattle
> And tie them down with ease
> Or rope the fork-ed lightning
> And ride it where we please."

High-Pockets was right. The bedded cattle were close and
we stopped a short distance from them. Many were still chewing their cuds. Chanting cowboys circled the herd, riding at a
fast walk in opposite directions.

"Peculiar, be-ent it," High-Pockets said, readjusting the
crutch under his right arm. "I never a-fore see half the riders
a-goin' that-a-way, but it do keep a critter from slipping out
behind a rider's back, an' I reckon, too, the boss is shore
a-feared we'd get to talkin' and bunch up if we all rode in the
same direction."

In the dark I heard a rider approaching us. His words were
plain:

> "Beware all ye ladies who live on the flat.
> Beware of the rider who wears a white hat.
> He'll . . ."

Before he finished the line this cowboy rode up to us. With
the half nod typical of the Old West, he reined his horse away
from the herd and without saying a word trotted off toward the
wagon to get his night's rest. One of the hands who had led us
out to the herd took this man's place, circling around the cattle.
As he rode off he recited in a plain voice:

> "My father was hanged as a horse thief.
> My mother was burned as a witch.
> My sisters ain't fit f'r a flop house,
> I'm a cow-punching son-of-a-bitch."

The next of the circling cowboys came in from the opposite
direction. He chanted:

> "I fogged them caddle, an' I fogged 'em hard,
>   An' I eat sowbelly 'til I shit pure lard,
> Singin' 'Tie, yie, yippy, yappy, yay!'"

This refrain was popular with the cowboys, and High-Pockets
relayed this man, chanting:

> "Oh, the caddle's on the range, the pony's on the grass,
>   Man without his woman is little but an ass,
> Singin' 'Tie, yie, yippy, yappy, yay—yappy, yay!'
>   Singin' 'Tie, yie, yippy, yappy, yay!'"

The cowboy High-Pockets had relieved trotted off in the
darkness toward the wagon. My turn came now to relay the
next rider from the other direction, and when he came I rode
away, around the herd. It was good to feel a willing horse
between my knees and all I had to do was keep separated from
the other riders and not disturb the cattle. I must stay back
from them fifteen or twenty steps, and I soon learned that my
horse, if given his head, judged this distance more accurately
than I did.

On each circle I recited the poetry I could remember, then
began counting in French. My parents had sent me to school
one winter in Switzerland so this was easy, and the cattle did
not seem to mind. Each time I rounded the herd I met and
passed High-Pockets and the other riders going their way.
Each of us gave the customary solemn sideways western
glance. This was fun, like play-acting, and overhead the stars
twinkled brightly. I located Cassiopeia, and watched for that
constellation every time I circled the herd. I knew that it
rotated slowly around the North Star and wondered if it would
change position very much during the two hours of my watch.
Only one thing worried me. How would I ever find the wagon
when my watch ended? I could never ride off into the darkness
alone the way each man we relieved had done. This was a real
danger, because a horseman who missed the wagon and continued riding would be hopelessly lost come morning—not only

lost in the wilderness, but laughed at by all hands if he ever found camp again.

With this apprehension troubling me, the two-hour watch passed quickly. Perhaps I worried too much about getting lost while riding back to the wagon alone, but I remember that on my last lap around the herd I breathed more easily when I saw that High-Pockets and other members of our watch were waiting, instead of riding away singly to bed. The foreman had joined them. He had come to relieve us and take the graveyard watch, the most important guard. At midnight, cattle have finished chewing their cuds and most of them stand up, stretch, curl their tails over their backs, and, if not held back, graze away to refill their paunches.

These unpredictable longhorns might make trouble at this time and the foreman himself had come out. He kept all of us with him until he was sure the cattle would not try to break away. Then my entire watch rode back to the wagon together. This ended the danger of my getting lost, but something else disturbed me. We extra riders were sure to "get our time" since the longhorns were behaving so well. If so my career as a cowboy would come to an end, but come what would, I slept soundly the remainder of that night.

Before dawn the cook's "Come and get it" aroused me. I pulled on my pants and boots and hurried to the pot-rack, fearing that this would be my last meal at the chuck wagon. The meat and coffee tasted as good as usual, and before we finished breakfast a sharp yell told us Boston was bringing in the cavy. I saw the foreman speak quietly to the Pink Angel and to High-Pockets. The rest of us ran out to man the rope corral. Nate Jackson began to catch our horses while the two men the boss spoke to carried their beds to the empty bed wagon. The Angel seemed happy. Smiling and licking his chapped lips, he seemed glad to be let go. He belonged behind a plow, not on the hurricane deck of a cow horse. Having joined the outfit to accommodate a short-handed boss, he wanted to quit. High-Pockets appeared grim, but he had experienced too much misfortune in life to be much chagrined. A good cowboy when mounted, he often needed help to swing aboard a skittish horse, and once in the saddle he was apt to be short-tempered and abuse his mount. I suspected that these faults ended his job ahead of mine, but I felt sure the tin can would be tied to my tail next.

Boston drove the two men back to Rawlins in the bed wagon. I wondered when he ever slept. He caught up with us at our noon camp, bringing a load of red rock salt in the wagon.

The next day we crossed the Continental Divide. The cattle seemed well broken to trailing now, and they walked in a long column with two riders up front pointing the leaders. The rest of us—the swing and drag men—rode at each side and behind. We came to a rough, rocky place and I heard a rattle of horns up ahead. This noise always meant that the cattle had bunched. The wild scenery with a nearby granite outcrop towering in the sky reminded me of a picture I had seen of cowboys roping a grizzly bear. I hoped we had met one here and spurred ahead to see, but was disappointed. The lead cowboys had only cut off a small bunch of cattle to drive them through a defile that had stopped the big herd. With these as leaders, the herd followed and before long all the cattle streamed down the western slope of the Rockies onto the vast plains—a magnificent panorama spiced by the smell of sagebrush freshly crushed by hundreds of hooves.

In the open country Hawkshaw found an opportunity to display his horsemanship. We swing men rode fifteen to twenty yards out from each side of the marching column. Sage chickens were plentiful, and coveys of them often roared up at our horses' feet. Because many of the birds were young, they could fly only about a hundred yards and then came down exhausted. Hawkshaw knew this, and with whip and spur he raced after every covey. Arriving at the birds' landing spot before they had recovered, he would leap off his horse and pick up one or two of the young birds. With them he remounted and holding them up for us all to see, he exultantly wrung their necks.

I hoped that we'd have sage chicken for dinner but Hawkshaw said, "No! The son-of-a-bitching anti-Christ cook won't fry 'em."

Hawkshaw's senseless profanity was interesting but I disliked his senseless killing of wild life. Both were common in those days.

Driving the cattle had become routine now. Many of them took the same place in the column every day. They became

personalities, not just longhorn steers. Although they mixed
together on the bed ground every night, in the morning certain
ones always took the lead. Others were content to plod along in
the center, and the weakest dropped to the rear where they
were abused and whipped to keep them in the society of their
fellows. I soon learned that there were one or two radicals that
watched for every opportunity to escape. Whenever we crossed
a deep wash where nobody could notice, or skirted a dense
clump of mahogany bushes, these rascals, with two or three
followers, would try to slip away. My horse, Buttons, proved
to be more watchful than I was, and several times I felt him
start to head off a would-be escapee. We riders soon learned to
know these liberals by sight and gave them names. The foreman enjoyed his little jokes and would ask, as he rode around
the herd watching our progress, "Have you seed Gompers
lately? If he's a-missin', we is shore out some caddle."

"I shore haven't saw him this mo'ning," I might reply, proud
of my mastery of cow-camp grammar.

Sometimes the boss called the offender Debs, sometimes
Ballinger, a man blamed, along with Gifford Pinchot, for creat-
ing national forests and limiting grazing thereon. Never did I
hear him refer to Karl Marx, a hero of the big cities who was
apparently unknown out where the wind blew free across unfenced ranges.

The cattle were so easy to handle now I was sure I would be
paid off, but to my surprise Hawkshaw was first to "get his
time." He did not like that and I remember how his hard eyes
met mine. "They's keepin' you," he growled, "to pay fer them
six-bit boots."

Hawkshaw was no doubt right. He was smart, intelligent, a
good worker, but nobody seemed to like him. Camp that night
was strangely quiet without his know-it-all voice. For the first
time, I listened to the conversation of the old hands while we
ate on the ground at the end of the chuck wagon. They discussed the bucking horses scheduled for Frontier Days over at
Cheyenne. The worst broncos, they said, were Carrie Nation,
Calamity Jane, and Powder River. The "favor-ite" still seemed
to be Old Steamboat, but a new "champe-en" named Young
Steamboat had "throwed" every rider who had forked him this
year.

"The hoss don't live what kain't be rode," a voice drawled, "when the right man comes along."

"You bet," the cowboy beside him replied, looking up from the plate in his lap. "An' the woman don't live what kain't be made, when the right man comes along."

"On this ride we ain't lost no men to the women," a third voice said. "Last year we lost a good hand, name o' Ralph Murphy, over to Rock Springs. One day he quit. Said he was marryin' a skirt in town—knowd her since infantry. Next day he come back to the wagon all upset. Said she'd turned him down, flattern a pancake. He'd never hev nuthin' more to do wid no woman again s'long as he lived. No married life fer him, not on yer tintype. 'With me,' sez 'e, 'the name of Murphy will die.' Curious idee o' hisen warn't it? We joshed him so bad about bein' the last of the Murphys it stuck in his craw, an' made him pretty hot. He got on the peck and quit fer good. Said he was goin' to Arrowzony, real cow outfits down thar."

Now for the first time I learned more details about the Indians, gossip the cowboys had picked up in Rawlins and kept repeating, over and over. They blamed all the agitation on the stupid government in Washington. One of them said, "That fool senator, Henry Dawes, knows Massachusetts but he don't know Utes."

The famous Dawes Act of 1887 had granted United States citizenship to Indians who would renounce their tribal holdings in exchange for deeded farms. That sounded fine, but caused all the present trouble. The three hundred Utes now wandering across Wyoming had accepted this exchange and immediately sold their land. With the money they traveled north across Wyoming killing all the game while their thousand horses ate the grass necessary to winter the ranchman's cattle. Settlers were frightened. They appealed to the government and were told that these Utes were United States citizens— free men, no longer under the Indian Department's jurisdiction.

The cowboy who told me much of this concluded: "Dawes meant well, but hell's full o' them kiney folks."

From another rider I learned that the "sit-u-ation" had become so critical in 1906 that the War Department had sent soldiers to investigate. They found the Utes on the Montana

border and reported them to be in small groups, all well
supplied with meat, flour, and ammunition. A few had wagons
but most were moving their tepees with travois as their ances-
tors had always done. These Utes knew their rights as United
States citizens and refused to return to the Utah reservation
where they had sold their farms. Finally they agreed to go to
the Sioux reservation in South Dakota, but that was a mistake.
They learned what Indians have always learned: alien tribes
treat one another worse than white men do. After one year
with the Sioux, these Utes were eager to return to Utah. The
Army purchased draft horses and wagons for the trip, and now
in 1908 the Utes were up in Wyoming somewhere, going
home. Angry and demoralized, they might take revenge on
some lonely cowboy, sheepherder, or homesteader. This
bloody prospect, according to the cowboys, was all the fault of
"them idjits in Washington."

The cowboys' dispositions improved noticeably when we
came to quaking-aspen country. Lush meadows separated the
groves of dancing leaves. Having traveled across the hard
sagebrush flats, we felt a touch of magic in the green wall-to-
wall shag carpet of fresh sod between the trees. The smell of
grass, freshly grazed by hungry longhorns, drifted back from
the herd. This was a smell to remember, always associated with
looming mountains and air fresh from timberline. The horses
felt good and showed new vigor, as did the cattle. Every
morning we cut back the drags, leaving thirty or so with a big
chunk of red rock salt.

"I see plenty larkspur up heah," the foreman said to Boston,
who drove the salt wagon to each new camp. "It's pizen, so
don' salt the caddle near them weeds, if you ken help it."

The blue flower with its spurred calyxes was easy to recognize. I dismounted to pick one and discovered another plant
altogether new to me, a little inconspicuous rose-purple blos-
som that grew deep in the long grass. A man on horseback
might overlook it, but having dismounted, I examined it closely
and saw a tiny elephant's head with big protruding ears and a
trunk curved up. Picking the flower, I handed it to the foreman
who rode up beside me. I expected him to tell me its name and
throw it down contemptuously, because these flowers were
abundant in the semi-alpine meadow and he must have ridden

over them countless times, but he pushed his hat to the back of his head and looked down at the flower with real curiosity. I shall never forget his rugged, sun-scorched face, as I saw it, framed in the circle of his hat brim with Colorado's brilliant blue sky for a background. He examined "the posy" in his calloused hand, studied the elephant head, and drawled, "I never see it afore. Ain't that suthink? Wall, I swan!" I had heard that expression on a Victor Talking Machine record, but never before in real life.

The work had really ended now. All the cattle were turned loose until shipping time. Two men started to build a summer camp. With sharp axes they cut quaking-aspen trunks quickly and built a cabin of sorts in a single day. Two other men, each driving his string of horses, jogged off to distant camps. I rode down out of the mountains on the chuck wagon to a town named Hayden. The cook wore a clean shirt for this occasion, and the foreman dressed up in his frock coat, but omitted the celluloid collar and those ridiculous shoes. At the livery barn we found loafers talking earnestly about a "shooting scrape." Eph Donaldson had killed a man named Tiption, and at the funeral something had happened which many people did not believe. I hoped to hear the whole story here in town but had little time to listen. My check, after paying for those boots, left me only enough for two meals, so I had to get a job quick or take my time being hungry—but I did prize those boots. Wearing them, I felt at last like a real "boy what ain't no slump." Very soon I was to learn how genuinely important those boots were to me.

6

A Chip Off the Old Chuck Wagon

The lark is up to greet the sun,
The bee is on the wing;
The ant its duty has begun,
The woods with music ring,
    —Jane Taylor

Hayden had been built on a gentle slope south of Bear River. The town's single street boasted a big livery barn at the lower end and, at the upper, a hotel run by two good-looking young women known as the Bowman girls. The street crossed an irrigation canal on a bridge built of boards that were said to have caused a runaway at Tipton's funeral. The boards had rattled like thunder when the new and elaborate hearse—the town's pride—was driven over them. This frightened the horses and, with a downhill pull, the runaway became spectacular. Two cowboys with ready ropes may have anticipated this accident; certainly they enjoyed displaying their skill on the town's main street. Lassoing the leaders, they stopped the horses before they reached the barn.

The usual bench in front of a western saloon attracted me. I sat down, wondering where I might find a job. The men walking past me were discussing the runaway. Some blamed the driver for being unprepared. Others were certain that cowboys had planned the event as a practical joke. Still others said there had been no runaway—just stories about one. I was not much concerned. I wanted a job.

Two men stopped on the board sidewalk with their backs toward me, and one of them said, "My caddle's ready to ship. Really fat this year. Got rolls of fat, even over the roots of their tails. I'd like to get 'em on the market afore the rush begins this fall, but I can't find the help I need to gather 'em. The cowboys that's any good have all good steady jobs at summer camps."

"Rhoden's wagon come in for supplies las' night," the other man said. "An extry hand come with it. He's only a boy but he must be good. Of all the extry help they hired at Rawlins, he's the only one they kep' to the end. Musta handled caddle to suit them, and they's partic'lar. He's here in town some'eres. You'll reco-nize him. He's wearin' new brown boots."

I liked everything I had heard except that last sentence about the boots. Hoping not to be noticed, I tucked my feet under the bench and like Br'er Rabbit I lay low until the men walked away. Then I strolled down the wooden sidewalk to E. Wagner's saddle shop. While looking in the display window one of the men I had heard talking stopped and hired me to help round up and trail his beef to the railroad. He said his name was Norvell, Jim Norvell.

I was disappointed when I met the two cowboys he hired to work with me. Neither ranked with the men I had met at the Rhoden wagon. One, younger than I was, had come to town with his father, a homesteader north of Hayden. We professional cowboys—I liked to consider myself one—called such people nesters, mossbacks, or scissorbills. This nester evidently owed money for groceries at Norvell's store, and his son's pay would renew the family credit.

"Cowboys is all no good," the nester told me with the forceful assurance of an evangelistic fundamentalist. "None of 'em will work, just ride a horse. Haf to saddle up to shut the front gate. I hope this job makes my boy sick o' cowboying. If it don't, he's ruined fer life. Once a cowpunch, alus a cowpunch. They'll never do nuthin' else. The hull lot o' them ain't worth the dirt it ud take to bury 'em."

This complainer's son had a shabby outfit. His saddle was what local people called a kak or cactus. The stirrups were very long, and to reach them the boy, with his short legs, might punch the crown out of his hat—to use another western expression. He wore no spurs and his only "persuader" was thirty inches of hard-twist rope he carried for a quirt.

The other cowboy Norvell had hired for the job matched, at first glance, the scissorbill's definition of worthless, but I found

him to be one of the most likable "worthless men" I have ever
known. On foot, Biscuits—the name we gave him—seemed too
heavy and short for a cowboy. He wobbled in his high-heeled
boots. His face was round and a cigarette usually dangled from
his smiling lips. There was no hint of the grim, set features that
come so often from hard years on the open range, but there
was something about Biscuits that proclaimed him to be
genuine, a true product of the cattle frontier:

> Born in the tules, suckled by a boar,
> Two rows of jaw-teeth and holes punched for more!

Biscuits's cowboy clothes were picturesque but not theatrical. They belonged on horseback out on the open range. He
carried a six-shooter inconspicuously in a chap pocket. His
father had been a Wyoming cowman back in the 1880s, and
when Owen Wister's *Virginian* became popular he had written
and published at his own expense a book about cowboy life on a
railroad stock train. His son, Biscuits, hired now to ride with
me, was a teller of funny anecdotes, as his father had been. A
true chip off the old chuck wagon, Biscuits would build up a
character in his stories, make him big in every way, and then
with one word annihilate him. He would say, "I knew Jeff well.
He had a heart in him big as a watermelon—seed."

He told me, with a glint of mischief in his eyes, that he had
been born in Nevada, California, and all around, that he had
ridden for Ora Haley's Two Bar and the Swan Cattle Company
on Chugwater but preferred living by his wits—using his brains
trading horses. He admitted he could not ride a bucking horse
but on the Fourth of July he usually appeared in some town's
rodeo. For twenty-five dollars he would mount the worst horse
they had and be bucked off in front of the grandstand. "I can
make as much money that way in thirty seconds," he told me,
"as they'll pay me fer thirty days' hard work on the ranch.
That's quicker, and much safer, than stealing."

Biscuits had ridden into Hayden on a handsome black mare
named Queenie, leading behind him a swaybacked gelding he
called Pegasus. The striking difference in the two animals
helped Biscuits make a living. Queenie's coat shone like
polished ebony and she had bright, eager eyes, an arched neck,
and pointed ears. Pegasus always needed currying. His long

tail, matted with cockleburs, made his legs look shorter than they really were. His ears hung out sideways and he had long hair on his feet like a draft horse. One look at him, standing beside Queenie, would convince any man who knew horses that a burro could beat Pegasus in a race. Biscuits had not become rich matching him against better-built horses, but he usually made expenses and had plenty of fun. It was important, however, to move from village to village faster than the gossip concerning the unusual speed of his dilapidated horse. He made money in Craig, but Hayden was only seventeen miles farther up Bear River and the news reached there before Biscuits could arrange for a profitable race. He already owed a bill at the livery barn, and to avoid having his horses attached to pay it he negotiated with Jim Norvell.

I never learned the details of Biscuits's deal, but I know Jim paid his livery-barn bill and hired him and his two horses to help with the roundup. I did not know for sure, but suspected that Biscuits feared a good horseman might change Pegasus's appearance. Clipping the fluff out of his ears would improve his head. Cutting off the long hair on his fetlocks would make him look less like a draft horse. Shortening his tail by pulling out the long hairs would make his legs look longer and more like a race horse's. These alterations, however, would deprive Biscuits of his livelihood. For this reason, I surmised that he insisted, in his agreement with Jim Norvell, that he and he alone ride and handle Pegasus. When the deal was closed, Biscuits and Jim shook hands, which in those days was as good as a signature.

Later that afternoon I learned that I was to ride Queenie under Biscuits's supervision. This pleased me very much because Queenie was what a later generation would call a quarter horse. Quick to start and very fast for a short distance, she could stop and turn on a ten-cent piece. Her natural gait was a single-foot, smooth to ride and faster than the jog trot of most cow ponies. I was in high spirits that evening when the pretty Bowman girls at the Oxford Hotel served an excellent supper to me, Biscuits, and Chip—the name we had given the scissor-bill boy. When night came the three of us unrolled our beds and slept—of all places—on Hayden's main street in front of the Norvell store.

The roundup was on Elkhead Creek, a stream that runs into

Bear River from the north. The valley had steep, bare sides covered with good grass. After driving the cattle down on our first circle we often looked back and saw that one or two had escaped our "gather." Then somebody had to make the long, slow climb back to the top and drive down those renegades. This task revealed Queenie's greatest weakness—if you could call it a weakness. She always wanted to run up that steep slope, and the hotter she got the faster she wanted to run. If let go she probably would have killed herself, and I earned Biscuits's everlasting friendship by holding her down to a walk.

Wolves were plentiful on Elkhead Creek and the bounty paid for them was high. One day on the circle I joined Biscuits driving in a small bunch of steers. Two of them had lost their tails—snapped off, he said, by wolves.

"Don't swaller that crap about loafers [his name for lobos] eatin' only old and sick critters," Biscuits said as he paused to reach in the breast pocket of his shirt for the yellow packet of Riz la Croix cigarette papers. "A loafer c'n tell fat from poor as well as any man, an' them two steers was lucky to git away."

Lucky for Jim Norvell, I thought, not for the lobos. The steers were doomed in any case, so perhaps it was better for them to die under a slaughterhouse sledgehammer than by sharp wolf-fangs tearing open their flanks and throats.

On another afternoon two bulls that had never met out on the range happened to be gathered by our roundup. Jim Norvell was in the herd selecting the beef he wanted to ship when the bulls saw each other. They roared defiance and pawed the ground, throwing pebbles higher than their backs. Growling in deeper tones, the bulls locked horns—two tons of infuriated flesh in terrible combat. Jim rode quickly out of the herd. Passing me at the herd's edge, he said, "Watch out for those bulls. When one gives up, he'll bolt like an express train. With both eyes shut he'll knock down any horse or man on his track."

For some minutes the beasts struggled. Then, as Jim had said, one bolted and we let him go, glad to see him retreating up the valley. The champion still grumbled and pawed pebbles into the air, but Jim dared ride back into the herd and continue cutting out the beef.

After another day or two, if I remember correctly, Jim had selected the cattle he wanted to ship, and we trailed them along the Bear River road to the bridge, crossed it, and drove up Hayden's main street. A man we met asked Biscuits if he had heard the news: rustlers had driven off a herd of horses and were said to be going toward Wyoming. Horses were easier to steal than cattle; with the opportunity to change mounts constantly, thieves could travel faster than any pursuer. Since we were not going north Biscuits showed little concern.

We turned our herd east at the hotel corner. The pretty Bowman girls stood on the second-story balcony watching us, and Biscuits, riding Pegasus, waved his hand and gave them a shrill cowboy shout—one of those blood-curdling yells that had cost Chick Bowen his life. I was proudly riding beautiful Queenie, and if Biscuits dared wave and shout I repeated the wild cry as well as I could. Chip saw us both wave and shout so he added his hand and voice to the salute, but neither of the girls paid us any attention. Perhaps, like Molly Wood in the *Virginian*, they wanted a formal introduction. But—also like Molly Wood—they had not needed one a few days earlier when they served us supper in the Oxford Hotel. Their failure to respond preyed on Chip, and that night when we whittled shavings to start the supper fire he said, "Them pretty Bowman girls must be deef."

"They's not deef," Biscuits retorted with a knowing wink to me, "ner dumb neither. They's smart. That's all that's wrong with them."

The cattle were to be loaded at Toponas, the terminus of a new railroad being built into the country, only seventy-five miles away. For such a short drive we needed no cavy and instead rode the same horses all the way. A mare like the spirited Queenie I rode would not have been permitted on a regular roundup. Mares always caused the wranglers trouble. They disturbed the geldings and kept an entire cavy in turmoil, and might escape with a few hopeful Lotharios. As saddle mounts, mares—even showy ones—usually sold cheaper than geldings, although Mexicans had a sentimental attachment to mares, *igual la Virgen*, and might pay more for them. Biscuits had purchased Queenie in Montana, probably at a bargain price, where Mexicans were scarce. Her beauty served his purpose well.

Jim Norvell was a man who watched expenses carefully. He found it cheaper to feed a few horses oats than to pay wranglers for herding twice as many out on the free grass where rustlers might steal them at night. He had also learned that by feeding ground oats only half as much was necessary to keep his horses fresh and strong. (Ground oats would help me greatly in an adventure with Indians later that summer.) Norvell carried all we needed on his buckboard, along with our beds and the mess box. Only four incidents on our drive to Toponas cling to my memory.

First: Shortly after leaving Hayden we picked up a bull where the road was fenced solidly on both sides. The brute insisted on smelling and grumbling over every steer in the herd. The barbed wire held them solidly and I rode through the herd to drive him out. Remembering the two bulls' frantic fight at the roundup, I watched this one closely, and so did Queenie, but he paid no attention to us. I whipped him first with my rope and then, riding behind him, I kicked and stamped on his rear with the sharp heels of my new boots. I knew that Queenie was agile and quick to turn. She could dodge that bull if he wheeled toward us, and I hoped that I, kicking the bull with one foot out of the stirrup, could stay on her back if she ducked away. A fall under the hoofs of the trampling steers and I'd be a "goner." To this day I wonder why the bull didn't attack us, but he did not, and I drove him to the tail end of the herd. There he sauntered away down the lane, mumbling to himself, while we continued our drive to the railroad.

A few miles farther on we turned off the road and drove up a magnificent grassy valley with steep slopes topped by ocher rimrocks resembling castles like those I had seen on the Rhine. The spectacular cliffs brought to my mind a line I had read somewhere: "Castles builded by no human hands." I could not remember the source of that quotation—Perhaps it was in Lewis and Clark's journals; I was not sure. I also noticed that the slopes were a tangle of mahogany and service-berry bushes.

The flat bottom of the brush-walled canyon was a poor place to bed cattle but the grass was good, so Jim Norvell called a halt. We camped beside the grazing cattle and the second event I remember on that drive occurred here. The sun set early over these castled walls and it was still broad daylight when we ate supper. The air, chilly at an elevation of almost eight thousand feet, made Chip shiver in his cotton shirt but he was ashamed to admit it. He wanted to be tough like a cowboy. Jim Norvell put on the jacket he carried in the buckboard, and Biscuits and I buttoned the vests we wore unbuttoned during the day. Chip always watched what we did, so now he dared to put on his sweater. Jim Norvell, eating from the plate in his lap, said, "When it gets dark, each of us must stand a two-hour watch. I'll take the graveyard guard."

Chip's eyes sparkled at the prospect of night herding. Hardships challenged him. Already he liked cowboy life, instead of detesting it. With his mouth still full of baked beans, he began to recite a familiar cowboy song:

> Last night as I lay on the prairie
> Looking up at the stars in the sky,
> I wondered if ever a cowboy
> Would see that sweet bye and bye.
> They say there'll be one great roundup
> And the cowboys like cattle will stand
> To be cut through by the riders of heaven
> Who are posted and know every brand.

We all knew the song, and Biscuits, a true extrovert and salesman of his own personality, complimented Chip for reciting it well, concluding, "I alus knowd you'd be a man before your mother."

Chip pondered this remark for a moment, then chuckled.

Our cattle bedded down before the stars came out. We crawled under our blankets and Biscuits rode off on the first watch. In two hours he would call me. Then two hours later I was to call the boss, who after another two hours would arouse Chip for the last, or daylight trick. The cattle seemed to lie quietly all night but at dawn Jim awoke us shouting, "We've lost some cows. Look yonder on the bushy sidehill!"

In the dim light we could see the animals dotting the slope, grazing and certainly no longer in the herd. Biscuits, always good in an emergency, was up first. His usual smile trembled a little in the chilly air. My boots felt uncomfortably cold when I pulled them on, and for warmth I tightened the silk muffler around my neck. We never knew which one of us had let those cattle get away. We three riders hoped, of course, that it was the boss, and he probably blamed one or all of us but, being a seasoned cow man, he kept his mouth shut. He knew only too well that a trail boss is at the mercy of his hands. If he is unjust or makes them angry, they can ride away, losing only a few day's wages, while he will lose the entire herd and go broke.

Without a word of complaint, Jim Norvell told Biscuits and me to bring in those cattle from the brush while they were still in sight. He and Chip would tend the main herd. Our job was difficult. Those strays wanted to remain in the thickets but Queenie understood this business. She would even nip a steer with her sharp teeth when the brush was so thick I could not hit him with my rope. Quick as a weasel, Queenie darted here and there after any animal that tried to hide or escape. My feet were still cold and the knotty mahogany brush whipped them unmercifully. Half a century later I still remembered how that hurt. At the time I wondered why Colorado cowboys did not put tapaderos on their stirrups, but few riders used them.

The next day we had a hard uphill drive over a divide thick with quaking aspens. We pushed the cattle hard to keep them from scattering and worked our own way through the trees beside them. Often we had to lie flat on our horses' backs to ride under the limbs. Aspen wood is brittle. When the limb was small we could snap it off, but if it did not break the horse would go on without the rider. It was unpleasant work until we reached Oak Creek.

Here I experienced the third incident I recall on that drive. The Moffat Railroad was being extended to Steamboat Springs. I had read about the Casement Brothers building the Union Pacific Railroad some thirty years ago and remembered the workmen's song:

> Drill, ye tarriers, drill,
> And it's work all day
> Without sugar in your tay,
> When you're working for the U.P. Railway.

I knew that Dan Casement's construction camp had contained a hundred draft horses and five times that many men, with tents for lodgings, tents for meals, and picket-line tents for the draft horses. Flatcars loaded with rails and ties had rattled in and unloaded constantly. Three to five miles of track were sometimes laid in a day. The vice-president of the Union Pacific, Thomas Durant, was said to have lost ten thousand dollars in 1869 betting that his men could lay ten miles of track in twenty-four hours. Now this exciting construction technique was being repeated here in Colorado, exactly as books had described it in early-day Wyoming.

We drove past the construction camp and I saw the circus big-top where music attracted workers who had pay in their pockets. An Irish "tarrier" walked out across the grass to see us. We permitted our cattle to graze after the fast push through the timber and I had time to talk with him. He told me their wages were fabulous—eight and ten dollars a day. The sums sounded tempting in comparison to the one dollar we made on the trail, and I considered coming back after we loaded the cattle. The tarrier did not encourage me, and from him I heard for the first time the cliché repeated so many times by common laborers in elaborate construction organizations.

"Faith an' Bejabbers," he said. "De pay's high, sure enough, but it's not so good as yours. De ducks gets it all. Day deducks for sickness whether you're sick er not, f'r horsepittal insurance, f'r union dues, f'r unemployment insurance if it rains, alus f'r sumthin until de ducks gets it all. Day even wants ta take a percentage of the little a man c'n steal."

I rode on with the cattle, a wiser man, I thought, but in college I learned that I was mistaken. An economics professor told the class that complex labor-benefit deductions began when the age of machinery replaced horsepower. I stupidly referred to this experience, but the professor did not seem to like it; he said it was not in any textbook he knew.

On the day we passed the railroad construction camp we nooned, or "shaded-up," although there was no shade, beside Finger Rock, a gigantic stone pillar in the open grass country. I wondered if Alpine climbers could scale it. After starting from our rest the cattle shied back at a wolf that may have been creeping up on them for a kill. He saw me and trotted away, tail in the air, a proud animal, and disappeared over the ridge behind Finger Rock.

Norvell owned a ranch nearby. We corralled our cattle for

the night, and Biscuits, playing High Five, took some spending money from the ranch hands. Here we enjoyed some fresh fruit purchased at Yampa, a nearby village we never saw. In cow country fresh fruit was scarce.

Toponas, where we planned to load the cattle, was only some ten miles beyond, and my fourth memorable experience on the trip occurred as we approached the railroad. Trees kept us from seeing the terminal, but we knew it must be close. Jim Norvell led the way in his buckboard. We saw him stop and wave for us to come up front. We trotted around the herd and Jim, always figuring how to make or save a dollar, told us, "Let the cattle graze. Let 'em put on an extry pound or two before loading. I'll go ahead to arrange for the railroad cars."

Jim clucked to his team and drove off across the green sod. The three of us started back to our positions around the herd, but we never reached them. A sudden shrill whistle from a locomotive stampeded the cattle. They had never heard anything like that before and fled in panic. We cowboys were behind them, so no one was in front to check the rush.

I had read about stopping a stampede on the plains by turning the leaders until the whole herd milled in a circle. Then the running cattle would soon tire and stop. The valley we were in, however, was much too rough and narrow for such a maneuver. The best we could do was race with the herd, outrun it, get ahead of the leaders, and try to stop them. This required fast riding, sometimes through that painful mahogany. Queenie seemed to enjoy the race, but Pegasus laid back those fuzzy ears of his and passed us all, showing how a really fast horse can run. I noticed that Biscuits rode loose in the saddle, so that if Pegasus turned a somersault he would sail away like a flying squirrel instead of being crushed under the horse's body. I envied that loose seat but never succeeded in copying it. Biscuits had drawn his six-shooter and carried it high over his head. I wondered what he planned to hit but believed he knew what he was doing. I was too busy ducking under tree limbs and dodging badger holes to watch. He was far ahead of me when I heard two shots, which evidently checked the cattle because as Chip and I galloped around the front of the herd to Biscuits, the cattle stood bunched together, their heads up, watching us. Chip, astride his sweaty horse, shouted with delight, "We sure stopped 'em. Didn't we!"

Slapping our quirts and rope ends against our boots and yelling shrilly, we turned the herd around and started back toward Toponas at a walk. In close formation, the cattle's backs reminded me of logs I had seen in a raft floating down Lake Memphremagog, but that Canadian lake was blue, not green like the sod ahead of our cattle here. Beyond them I saw the tiny figure of a horseman coming toward us. The figure rocked, so I knew the rider must be galloping. It was Jim Norvell. He had saddled one of the horses in his team and raced after us, hoping to save his cattle. As the herd approached him he checked his horse and rode at a walk around one side. When he came to me he paused a moment, and I remember his first words.

"Hang me for a horse thief," Jim said. "I hoped to gain two pounds on every critter by that rest, but the stampede has cost me at least ten pounds on every one of them."

All of us hoped that the whistle would not blow again and it didn't. We penned the cattle at the yards and with long poles punched them into the cars. I shall never forget the obvious relief on Jim's face when the last car door slammed shut with a bang and was sealed. Jim left his saddle and one horse at Scott Teague's ranch to ride home on when he returned by train from Chicago. He paid us off, allowing us each fifty cents per day for the ride back to Hayden. We went first to Yampa, the town near Norvell's ranch, which had one street, a block long, and a very good general store operated by a very English Englishman. Biscuits and I luxuriated in a haircut and shave, one of the first shaves of my life. I felt now, at the age of seventeen, that I was a man.

On the trip back to Hayden I drove the buckboard carrying our beds and grub box. Chip sat on the seat beside me and Biscuits followed with Pegasus and Queenie. The weather was fine and we clipped along on an easy downgrade, breathing the crisp mountain air. I noticed that Chip kept looking at my foot on the brake. Finally he blurted out, "Some day I want boots like yours, yes, and a six-shooter like Biscuits's."

I was sure now that Chip's father would be disappointed. Whether he liked it or not, his son was going to be a cowboy. We camped only one night driving back, and fed our horses the last of our ground oats. Late the next afternoon we drove into the big Hayden livery barn and put the team in a stall and

Biscuits's horses in the corral. The three of us slept that night in the barn and next morning Biscuits said to me, "Jimmie, I'm goin' to Meeker. Over there, where Pegasus ain't known, a man can make good money. Doncher wanna ride with me on Queenie?"

Meeker was on the way to the railroad at Rifle. My return ticket to Philadelphia from that town was still sewed in my pants pocket. The summer was over, and I must go home, so I said yes.

Chip's face saddened. I shall never forget the way his lips tightened with suppressed emotion. He obviously wanted to go with us, and tears glistened in his eyes when we mounted our horses. I felt sad leaving him. He was a good horseman, a brave rider for a kid, and I, like Chip, was going reluctantly back to school, ending a vacation that had meant so much to me. My biggest Wild West adventure of the whole summer was yet to come, but I could not foresee that!

7

Renegade Indians

I have some kinship with the bee,
I am boon brother with the tree;
The breathing earth is part of me.
—J. Frank Dobie

"Don't tell nobody we're headed f'r Meeker," Biscuits cautioned me as we rode out of Hayden. "People might suspicion our purpose, send word ahead and spoil the game."

It did seem better not to go by the main road. Besides, it was shorter "as the crow flies." We estimated that riding about fifty miles up the south branch of Williams Fork and across the Sleepy Cat country would put us at the forks of White River. From there Meeker was only another twenty-five miles downstream. A few roads and trails crossed some of the country ahead of us but much of it was wilderness—good, hospitable wilderness—especially between Pagoda Peak and the Sleepy Cat. Grass would be stirrup-high for the horses, and trout in the streams would feed us. None of the Indian stories we had heard all summer put them in this "neck of the woods" but by a strange coincidence our ride led directly to my unexpected camping with the renegades.

We had no packhorse. Anyone who saw us would consider us itinerant riders, not men on a long trip. I had taken the blanket out of my sleeping bag and folded it for a saddle pad. I wrapped my slicker around the light bag cover and tied the roll behind my cantle. On the saddle horn, opposite my lariat, I hung what cowboys, to show off their Spanish, call a *morral*. Farmers call it a nosebag, and in mine I put a tin cup, tiny frying pan, a Union Leader tobacco sack full of coffee, some hardtack, and a chunk of bacon. Biscuits's camp outfit was equally primitive.

"If we had some peaches," he said, and his round smiling face warned me to be ready, "we'd have peaches and cream—if we had the cream."

On this trip our horses would get no oats. At night we planned to hobble them so they could graze. Instead of heavy chain hobbles we tied a short piece of soft-twist rope around each horse's neck. When we camped we would use this soft-twist to tie each animal's front legs together. This let them walk but not trot or run. Biscuits's Pegasus carried a bell on his neck to help us find the horses if they strayed out of sight in the woods. To prevent the bell from ringing in daytime as we rode along, Biscuits stuffed it with grass.

The weather was fine; even the horses seemed to sense that we were going into a lush land of grass aplenty. Scotch thistles were in bloom. Those showy purple heads with prickly bracts seemed to be the worst imaginable tidbit for a horse's sensitive mouth, but both Pegasus and Queenie nipped every one they could reach as we rode by. Long before noon we came to aspen woodlands. The trees stood sufficiently far apart for us to ride among them, and we frequently rode across flower-dotted meadows. At this elevation—almost eight-thousand feet— autumn had arrived. The aspen leaves were now bits of twinkling yellow gold, and when we looked up through them the mountains became a deeper blue. On the smooth bark of one tree I noticed some fresh claw scratches about six feet from the ground.

"A bear done that," Biscuits said, turning in his saddle to point with the quirt in his hand. "He wants to tell other bears this is his country, an' if they wants to fight he'll accommodate 'em, an' ken lick 'em good."

In the lush meadows we often saw does with fawns, sometimes twins. Already these youngsters had lost their spots, reminding me that winter was coming and school was close behind. The deer bounded away, all four of their feet striking the ground at the same time as mechanically as toys. Their gait was certainly not graceful, but excellent, no doubt, for crossing rough country. On one steep hillside I saw my first columbines—Colorado's state flower—and I stopped to examine them. The blue blossoms brightened an open spot in a dark clump of spruce trees. The sun never penetrated that nook and

the soil remained damp and black. The tender blossoms swung
at the tips of slender, bending stems. "Them posies," Biscuits
said, "is too purdy to pull"—that rural western verb, meaning
"to pick," was new to me.

At noon every day we rested for about two hours, letting the
horses eat their fill of grass in place of the oats we had fed them
when on the trail. We fished, ate a snack, then lolled on the
ground with our backs against our saddles. Biscuits's favorite
topic was horse trading, and he told anecdotes well. One of
them concerned an expert horseman who carefully examined
the mount he was purchasing, looked in its ears and spoke
sharply to be sure the horse heard, flashed his hand past the
animal's eyes to be sure its sight was clear, rubbed its cannon
bones, feeling for splints, felt its back for saddle sores and
fistulas.

"He even lifted that horse's tail lookin' fer gofers," Biscuits
said with a knowing smile.

I did not know what Biscuits meant by "gofers," but he
ended the yarn by saying that the expert pronounced the horse
sound and purchased him. While leading the horse away the
salesman called to him: "Here's four feet of hose and a funnel.
That horse has no tongue so you have to water him with these."

Biscuits's horse-trading stories prompted me to ask if he
would sell Queenie. I wanted that beautiful mare if she was for
sale.

"Everything I've got is for sale, except my wife," Biscuits
replied as he looked absently up into the merry aspen leaves,
"and I'll give her to you."

Biscuits was not married, I felt sure, so I suspected his reply
was the standard western salesman's cliché. I found him to be a
shrewd trader. He priced Queenie at much more than I could
pay, but I knew that a mare in this cattle country was not so
valuable as a gelding and we had plenty of time to bargain. I
lacked the cash to buy Queenie at even a reasonable price, but
I did wonder and hope, as we rode along through the brilliant
aspens, if I might persuade Father to buy Queenie for me and
let me come back next summer and ship her home. This was
still in my mind when we rode into the White Bear Ranch at
the forks of White River.

After supper that night I talked to Jay Card, a cowboy I had met when working in Harp's stage station. He was a character to remember, a young man with a strangely old, deeply lined face. The lines were somehow attractive. They deepened when, with a solemn look, he made a roguish remark. He was a horse trader like Biscuits, and the three of us concocted a complicated deal. I do not remember the details, but knowing those two men I suspect I was "took and outsmarted." I paid twenty-five dollars—a goodly sum in those days when cash was scarce and horses plentiful—for which I was to get Queenie for a ten-day trip down to the legendary "lower country." Then Jay was to keep her with the White Bear horses until spring, when I could purchase her at a price we agreed upon. The three of us shook hands on this deal and I planned to leave in the morning.

Queenie had been fed no grain since we left Hayden. I knew grass to be scarce in the lower country so I would need some feed to keep her strong. A sufficient amount of whole oats would be too bulky to carry on my saddle, but fortunately I found some of the ground oats Jim Norvell had shown me how to feed. I balanced two small sacks of this on opposite sides of my saddle horn. These and the morral did not make a heavy load, but I would have to ride at a walk to keep the sacks from bouncing. Queenie's single-foot, however, was smooth and we could cover many miles in a day.

There was a road down White River, but I preferred going by the open country on the ridge to the north. At our first noon rest I gave Queenie a small feed of ground oats; it was important not to founder her with too much too soon. Early that afternoon I came to a patch of good grass below some spruce trees and decided to camp. The sun was still high in the sky, and I wanted Queenie to eat her fill because I planned to tie her up at dark without food lest she stray away during the night. I unsaddled, hobbled her front feet with the soft-twist from around her neck, and walked over to the spruce trees for a rest. On the way some grouse roared up into the nearest tree. As I looked up at them a hawk struck one of the grouse and both fell flapping to the ground. I ran toward them. The hawk released the grouse and flew away, screaming at me. I examined the dead bird and noticed that the hawk's talons had struck the grouse just below where the neck joined the body.

The heart had been pierced, killing the bird. The breast of this game bird, fried in my little pan, tasted good for supper.

Next day, in order not to founder Queenie, I fed her only twice, once in the morning and again in midafternoon when we came to some water for her to drink. Many of the cattle hereabouts were branded UCC—the Keystone brand—so I knew that I was not far from the ranch where Theodore Roosevelt had stayed at the beginning of his midwinter lion hunt in 1901. The sun was still high but the shadows had begun to lengthen when I came to Coyote Basin. The ranch house had been built at a break in the western rim where icy springs bubbled from the ground. I felt a little embarrassed to be a cowboy riding a mare, but with a bold face I stopped at the house. Four or five men, evidently washing before supper, clustered around me. As was customary in this part of the country, nobody asked me my name or where I was going, but someone said, "Get down and rest your saddle."

"What a horse," exclaimed another man in cotton shirt and galluses, who seemed to have authority. He stroked Queenie's arched neck, looked at her eager eyes, and continued, "This horse must have been cut proud. A skillful man can do that."

As a guest I wanted to be polite, but I had to say that my horse was a mare. When nobody laughed I assumed that the speaker who made this mistake must be the boss—perhaps foreman Tug Wilson himself, who had entertained Roosevelt on his lion hunt. I did notice some covert smiles, and one fellow turned his back to suppress something. After an embarrassing silence the man said, "Your mare is shore ganted up. Musta been tied up last night without feed. Turn her out in the fenced horse pasture and come to the house f'r supper."

I admired the man's ability to tell by looking at a horse's flank whether it had eaten any roughage in the last twenty-four hours, but his cowboys were less sympathetic. That night in the bunkhouse as we pulled off our boots and rolled our britches for pillows the men repeated again and again how Tug Wilson—the great Tug Wilson—had called my mare a gelding. Even after we all lay down I heard, "Huh!" from a bed. "He ramrods the biggest cow outfit in this county, and can't tell a horse from a mare."

"That's nuthin'," replied another voice. "Boss on the Lazy Y—a eastern millionaire—was really good. After workin' fr them two years one of the boys made him feel extry good by buildin' him up, sayin' how quick he larned western ways, then washed him out sayin' that he could almost always tell a horse from a cow."

The next morning after breakfast I rode into the broken country west of Coyote Basin. The terrain was uninteresting. The cedars had grown so high I could not see the mountains that I knew must be in view. Without them a man might lose his directions, even ride in a big circle, or as Mark Twain would say, "be lost or as good as lost." The only diversion in this monotonous scenery was watching the sage chickens, which were plentiful. Sometimes these big, round-bodied birds flew up at Queenie's feet. I remembered Hawkshaw's success in catching them and hoped to get one for dinner. To chase the next birds that flushed I fixed slipknots to enable me to drop instantly the clumsy oat sacks and morral on my saddle horn.

Before long I enjoyed a fast chase. Queenie ran like the wind, jumping the sagebrush, but I caught no chicken. They were all full-grown now. Their flights were still short but when they landed they ran well or flew again. The experiment proved a double failure because I found it difficult to backtrack Queenie's trail to the place where I dropped the oat sacks and my scant cooking utensils.

I spent more than an hour hunting them and realized I would be in a bad predicament if this was Wyoming where those uncertain Utes were being taken home by the United States Army. At last, after I found the morral and sacks of oats, the sun was so high it was impossible to tell directions. I was really lost now but I rode toward what I thought was west and soon came to a patch of good grass. I decided to let Queenie rest here, roll to brush her sweaty coat, and eat her fill. Hobbling her, I lay down to rest myself. I knew that it must be afternoon because I was very hungry. There was no water here so I could not brew a cup of coffee, and I wished I had learned to chew tobacco because that seemed to help cowboys when they missed a meal. I did not foresee a near calamity worse than missing lunch which lay immediately ahead.

This possible disaster had nothing to do with the Indians I had heard so much about. Instead, while Queenie ate the grass, a dark cloud appeared overhead, and a sudden shower caused her to turn her hindquarters to the slanting silver lines of rain. To protect myself, I untied the slicker on my saddle and huddled beneath a cedar until the storm blew over. Then I walked out to catch Queenie and saddle up. She snorted at me and bounded away, galloping awkwardly with her hobbled front feet. She stopped soon, looked at me, snorted, and bounded away once more. I realized that to be left on foot in this featureless wilderness would be a real calamity. Then something in her actions told me that she did not recognize me and was frightened by my bright yellow, rustling slicker. I took it off, spoke, and then walked up to her easily. With the bridle safely on her head, I put on the slicker again and made it rustle as I led her to the saddle. Henceforth, she had no fear of slickers.

Saddling up, I rode on, hoping I was going west. Suddenly I came to the brink of a precipice that dropped vertically some three or four hundred feet straight down. I remembered watching a mummers' parade from the high window of a Philadelphia skyscraper on Broad Street, and this cliff seemed about that high. Sitting on Queenie's back, I could see a sagebrush desert below me that stretched from the foot of the cliff to the horizon. This desert was bounded on the north by a flat-topped mountain at least two thousand feet high, and on the south by hills that skirted what I believed to be White River. Here at last was the beginning of the fabled "lower country" I had wanted to visit all summer.

I noticed a spot of green at the foot of the mountain—green trees, surely. Where trees grow there must be water. If I could possibly get down to that desert, I would camp tonight under those green trees.

Hoping to find some trail off the bluff, I rode along the brink, looking ahead, and at last I saw the tip of a talus slope where part of the bluff I was on had spilled down on the desert. If that talus slope began at the base of a ten- or twenty-foot rimrock I could not get down, but if the slide had started at the top and Queenie was willing, we might coast in a cloud of pebbles and dust to the desert.

We did! And the sun was still a hand's width above the horizon when I rode into the shade of those box-elder trees. Here I found a dirt-roofed log cabin, a natural meadow, good

grass, an abundance of firewood, and a small pond with polliwogs along the shore. I wondered how these creatures ever
came to this isolated spot in the desert. A road of sorts, really
just wagon ruts, led away out of sight to the east and west.

I hobbled Queenie in the meadow and was collecting wood
for a little fire when I saw some wagons a mile away. I wondered if the residents of the cabin were coming home. Watching them, I changed my mind. Four or five wagons meant too
many people for such a small habitation, and in addition I saw
three or four mounted men behind them driving a herd of
horses. Certainly I would not camp alone tonight.

The little wagon train disappeared, evidently crossing a
wash, then came in sight again, a size larger. There was something strange about the riders driving the loose horses. I had
already learned to recognize cowboys by the way they rode,
and these men were different. As the wagons came closer I
noticed that all the drivers on the wagon seats wore identical
black hats, and it suddenly dawned on me that these must be
Indians. I remembered a storekeeper who told me that
whenever he received a shipment of oddly shaped hats he
could not sell, all he had to do was give one of them to the
best-looking Indian on the reservation and the whole'lot would
be sold within twenty-four hours.

Were these Indians the renegades I had heard so much
about? Certainly there were not three hundred of them, and I
saw no soldiers. Their later actions, however, convinced me
that they must be a small detachment separated from the main
group, probably because there was insufficient feed and water
for all of them at one campground. Queenie sniffed the air
nervously. I had read somewhere that in the early days horses
warned their masters about the approach of red men; here was
a true example. I watched them carefully as they drove by. No
women sat on the wagon seats beside the drivers, but I saw
plenty of women and children sitting on the loaded duffel.
Neither the men nor the women paid any attention to me. I
was prepared to smile at the drivers but to my dismay the
copper faces beneath the stiff black hats did not respond.

On the flat beyond the little pond they unhooked their teams
and, gabbling like grackles, started to pitch their tents. In
books I had learned that Indians were silent people, grim and

dignified, but these Utes chattered back and forth, bantering constantly, keeping the women in happy giggles. Years later, when I knew the Utes better, I was told that it was part of a man's duty to keep his women laughing, sometimes with music, while they worked.

The men wore oddly designed, gaily colored cotton shirts, evidently handmade by their women. Some wore unbuttoned vests, but no one wore a coat. Their trousers were mussed and dirty. A few had shoes but moccasins seemed more popular. The women dressed in calico, and both men and women had long braids of hair hanging over their shoulders in front. One man was wearing a stained and greasy buckskin shirt. His leggings and moccasins were the only other clothes he had on his body except for a blanket folded like a skirt around his waist. He probably unfolded this blanket for a cover when he slept. He was old, and having lost all his teeth, his head looked flat like a lizard's. His reptilian eyes were hard and fixed, and I saw character and courage in his shrunken mouth. He stood on the other side of the pond, defiantly erect, not looking at me, but watching, like a storybook Indian, the sun sink toward the western horizon.

It may have been my imagination but I felt certain that unhappy meditations marked the cold, proud face of this relic of the Stone Age. He must have lived when the desert before him and the mountain at one side supplied the only food he knew, and when every stranger he met was an enemy who might kill him on sight. What memories had he kept of that brutish life? Did he look back on those gone days as bad adventures—or very, very good ones? Did the firm lines of character in his mouth disclose the glory he felt in having had the strength and fortitude to survive?

Children's excited cries attracted my attention. Little Indians were splashing along the pond's edge, catching the polliwogs, torturing them with little sharp sticks, and screaming with childish delight when the tiny creatures' humanlike hands reached out to stop the pain. My face must have registered disapproval because the children turned on me. With sinister faces they scowled, and one of them blurted out, "All white mans die someday, like frog!"

"We kill 'em white mans," another piped. "All die like frog!"

Several shrill, childish voices shouted, "O-ah! O-ah!" This was the first time I had heard the Ute word for "yes," and I never forgot it. I also noticed that the beadwork on one of the little boy's moccasins was excellent in design and workmanship. It seemed incongruous that such delicate artistry, with sensitive appreciation of design and color, could go hand in hand with insensitive brutality.

The children ran back to their encampment. I waited apprehensively, fearing that some adult Indians might come and punish me for abusing their children, but nobody came. I smelled fragrant wood smoke and the sweet, rather pleasing odor of red skin that I would learn to know so well during the years ahead. The old man remained impassive, standing straight as a saguaro cactus, watching the sun go down.

I fed Queenie her oats and tied her to a tree lest she run off with the Indian ponies. The night seemed chilly, and to conserve my body heat I wrapped my slicker around my unfolded saddle blanket and put both in the sleeping bag cover. Then I crawled in and soon fell sound asleep. The next thing I remember was being half dragged by two big Indians toward their camp. I did not want to go but was afraid to fight lest they hurt me seriously. As we approached the Ute tents I noticed many teepees among the canvas tents I had seen earlier. This was strange, and the open area in front of them was larger than I remembered. The scene reminded me of Henry Farny's painting, "The Captive," which was doubly famous since Theodore Roosevelt had praised it. The picture showed a white prisoner staked down on his back—spread-eagled—in front of an Indian village, awaiting the torture to be given him. Farny knew Indians, and the horror of this captive's situation made the painting memorable.

Here before me was a scene identical to that picture, lacking only the captive staked out on the ground. Surely these Indians did not plan to use me for that individual, but to my horror that was exactly what they did. Both my wrists and my feet were lashed to stakes that the two big Indians drove with heavy rocks into the solid ground. Then the ancient red man who had watched the sun go down appeared with a big rattlesnake. His firm mouth, which I had admired under those reptilian eyes, sneered triumphantly, or so I thought, and I wondered why any man—any human being—could exult with such pleasure in watching another man suffer.

I had read somewhere that one form of Indian torture during the rainy season was to tether a rattlesnake by a buckskin thong close to a captured victim, but not sufficiently close for the snake to reach him. Then, when it rained, the moisture would stretch the thong and the snake could hit the prostrate victim. To my horror, I noticed that a six-inch buckskin thong was bound to the rattles of the snake being carried by the ancient red man. I watched other Indians measure with a string the length of the snake and its thong. Then they tethered the serpent to a firm stake just far enough away for it to be unable to strike me.

Behind my prostrate body a little Indian boy, wearing the beaded moccasins I had admired, crouched down so close I could smell him. Holding a willow switch, he reached over me and teased the rattler. It coiled in trembling fury and struck, hitting the ground with a sickening thud less than an inch from my body. The Indians had, indeed, measured the distance accurately. I tried to talk to the boy, to plead for my life, but my tongue was strangely numb. In spite of every effort, I could not speak, and to make the situation worse, I saw in the sky behind the crouching boy a black cloud exactly like the one that had appeared before the rainstorm that afternoon. The cloud was sure to bring the rain that would stretch the buckskin and permit the rattler's poisonous fangs to sink into my flesh. Overcome now by abject terror, I struggled desperately, twisted and kicked until I hurt my toes against the side of the sleeping bag. That awoke me. Looking up, I saw the steady desert stars above my head and realized with relief that this had been a dream—a very bad dream! No sound came from the Indian encampment, and my terror during the past moments soon vanished. With assurance, I dozed until dawn turned off the morning star.

Before sunup I heard the cackle of female Indian voices across the pond. In their encampment a new day had begun. I fed Queenie her morning oats and while she ate I drank my cup of coffee. Then I saddled up, mounted, and silently single-footed away, really in a hurry now because classes would soon start for my last year at Friends Central School in Philadelphia.

Besides, the breeze at sunrise smelled sweet. Big flocks of horned larks were on the wing, disappearing with a flash of white breasts and reappearing as they turned and wheeled around. I had lived through a very bad dream that was very good to remember. In addition, I had peeked over the edge of the "lower country" I had been hoping to see all summer—a famed country beyond the law, where wild mavericks tempted any man who was skilled with a rope.

8

The White Bear Land & Livestock Company

Ill fares the land, to hastening ills a prey,
Where wealth accumulates, and men decay.
—Oliver Goldsmith

"Excuse me," the Pullman porter said, after stopping me for my ticket as I walked down the curtained aisle of the sleeping car on my way to breakfast in the diner. "Oh, I sees now, you's de gem-men who got on las' night in de rough clothes."

The porter was half right. I may not have been a "gem-men" but I had boarded "the 10:45" at Rifle the night before, carrying a suitcase containing the city clothes I had left all summer with the station agent. My rough clothes, boots and all, were now packed out of sight in the suitcase. I had checked my saddle, in the conventional gunnysack, through to West Philadelphia.

The trip home was uneventful, but when I presented the check for my saddle in the West Philadelphia railroad station it had not arrived. A few days later it was still missing. I requested a tracer, and the saddle finally turned up in a freight room at Broad Street Station. I made a special trip to get it and had to hire an expressman to take it home.

The railroad men who located my saddle asked me questions about the distant West. In those days Meeker, Craig, and Hayden were a different world from Philadelphia—farther away in time than Vietnam and Kuala Lumpur would be in the 1970s—and a trip to the West was an experience to talk or write about. My friends or their parents had all traveled in Europe, but only a very few had gone West, and then only to Colorado Springs for their health or to Yellowstone Park on a tour. One of the baggage men asked me seriously if all men carried guns Out West and must be quick on the draw.

This ignorance of the West was common in Philadelphia. When I took my boots to be repaired at the Wanamaker store, the man in charge asked if they were for "theatrical purposes." One day at the Philadelphia zoo—the oldest zoo in the United States—I watched a bull elk rubbing the velvet off his antlers. A shabbily dressed boy, younger than I, joined me, saying he wanted to go West and see wild elk. His uncle lived out there, he said, and had come back once for a visit. The boy demonstrated how that man had worn his hat low over his eyes and had walked with a certain swing of shoulders to challenge a stranger. The boy acted well. He peeped out sideways, suspiciously, from under his hat brim and gave a half nod of recognition.

The character that boy impersonated I knew well. I had seen him driving the Meeker-Rifle stage and clumping in high-heeled boots along the wooden sidewalks in Meeker, Craig and Baggs. I had worked, slept, and gone hungry with that man on long rides, and had found him strong in his lonely wilderness world but a stranger out of place in the smallest town. On the street or at a dance he wanted to appear ready for a fight, but in camp that roughneck would share his last biscuit with a stranger—and steal his spurs if he could get away with them.

Father generously agreed to buy Queenie, and I waited eagerly for spring, when I might again feel a western horse between my knees and breathe that Rocky Mountain air.

I remember an incident in 1909 during my last year at prep school. With the class, I marched across the brick-paved school yard to the quaint Quaker meetinghouse at Fifteenth and Race Streets to hear a lecture by the well-known Colorado author, Enos A. Mills. He showed us how to make a fire by rubbing two sticks together, saying it was easier to do outdoors where there was a breeze and more oxygen in the air.

The picturesque Quaker meetinghouse always appealed to me. Sitting on the wooden benches there I heard Frederic L. Paxson, the noted historian of the West, recite, in his impressive voice, the Quaker marriage ritual. I had planned to hunt rabbits that day out at Newtown Square, but Paxson was marrying my "Cousin Helen" and my parents insisted that I attend the ceremony.

All that winter I rehearsed my trip to the West to get Queenie, and on July 6, 1909, I stepped off the train at Rifle, Colorado. The stationmaster greeted me with "Back again from Pennsylvany." My saddle, in its gunnysack, had already arrived, and I sent my city clothes home because I planned to ride Queenie to Denver and ship her in a stock car to Philadelphia. At the Rifle livery barn the owner had a team and wagon he wanted delivered in Meeker. I agreed to drive it, thus saving the expensive stage fare. I knew very well how rough the "government road" was, but I drove fast through the ruts and crossed in a single day.

Going from Meeker to the forks of White River where I had left Queenie was another problem. A man at the Meeker livery barn had an unbroken colt he wanted somebody to ride. The colt was very fat, round as a sausage, with no spine or withers to hold a saddle in place. Balancing in a saddle on his slippery back made me feel like a tightrope walker, but we reached the ranch without a mishap.

Jay Card did not seem glad to see me. No smile deepened the wrinkles in his face, and he offered no arch remark. In fact, he seemed almost too agitated to speak. I feared something had happened to Queenie, and hoped he had not kept my twenty-five dollars and sold her, thinking I would never come back. He glanced absently down at his boots, and ground one high heel, then the other, in the dirt. With obvious nervousness he looked over my head at the side of the barn.

"What's up?" I asked.

"Up, your eye-balls," Jay exclaimed, and I saw those familiar lines deepen in his face. "We're all in f'r it. Ol' Man Husted, J. D. his own self, is bringin' a passel o' bloods from back East to sell 'em shares in this and his other ranches. Each ranch is about fifty miles from the next—two on White River, two on the Bear. He's organizin' 'em as one outfit to be called the White Bear Land & Livestock Company. He wants to show these gulls the open range, the free grass, between them ranches and get 'em to stock it with cattle—thousands of cattle. Them dudes all got money—more money than brains—and they may do it. The trip will take maybe two weeks. The men here is all busy hayin', every man an' team on the job, an' the boss'll be glad I've found you. Your time starts in the mornin'. You an' me'll begin gatherin' horses on the range *right now*.

We've only got a few days to catch and break 'em. We'll need four good horses f'r the chuck wagon, four more f'r the bed wagon, an' twenty saddle mounts f'r the bloods to ride f'r pleasure. J. D.'s bringin' 'em from Rifle in two wagons and a four-horse tallyho, whatsoever that may be. It seats a dozen men. The dudes'll ride on it when they get saddle sores. For a roundup cook, we've got Ed Rholm. He savvys the burro, cooked f'r President Roosevelt on his Divide Crick bear hunt in 1905, an'll be good. I'll wrangle the cavy, an' the man bringin' the gulls in the tallyho'll drive it. Now, with you as second cook drivin' the bed wagon, thank God we're fixed.

Before supper that night the foreman, "Lantern Jaw" Jake, hired me as Jay said he would, and in the morning Jay and I rode off to find some horses. At the forks of White River the mountain above the cottonwoods and quaking aspens becomes a great dome of high grassland topped by a rimrock that prevents horses from climbing out into the spruce trees above. We rounded up some fifty head, Queenie among them. She had wintered well, looked sleek and fat. We drove them down to the ranch corral and spent a day or two matching teams to pull the wagons. I selected four I would drive. Jay knew them all by name, and said the ones I had picked for wheelers were Dot and Eagle. My leaders were Moon Eyes and Spike-You-Son-of-a-Bitch, a name not to be abbreviated, but Jay smiled as he said it. For the bloods we selected mounts that had saddle marks indicating that they were "broke." To make sure they were also "gentle" we lassoed each one and rode him in the corral. I turned Queenie out with those we did not keep. I wanted her to be fit for the hard ride over the Continental Divide before I took her to Pennsylvania in the fall.

In the ranch kitchen there was a wall telephone, and one morning after breakfast it gave the three-bell ring that was our number. A voice on the other end said that the capitalists were on the way. We estimated that it would take them a good half day to drive the twenty-five miles from Meeker, and Jake told the cook to serve our dinner early so that all hands would be finished in time to view the strangers. Later, phone calls from ranches along the way kept us posted on the visitors' progress. Shortly after noon Jay propped a long ladder against one end of the barn and climbed it. Straddling the ridgepole, he could watch the road. I had never seen that usually phlegmatic man so nervous. In a few minutes he waved his broad-brimmed hat and yelled, "The great moguls is a-driftin' up the crick."

Jake and I climbed up the swaying ladder. He was as nervous as Jay—I could hear him champing the dentures in his lantern jaws. The road below us was shaded by cottonwood treetops but in a gap we saw a wagon loaded with men appear. A second followed, then a third. We waited for more but none came. We climbed down and Jake mumbled as he rubbed his chin, "I guess thar ain't no mo' gulls a-comin'."

Jake was eager to get his haying crew back in the field, but dude ranching and dudes were unknown in those days and he let us line up behind the fence at the main gate when the visitors arrived. We counted twenty-six. Those bloods paid absolutely no attention to us. Laughing and joking about their rough trip, they walked into the ranch house for a late dinner, but no soldiers were ever inspected by their commanding officers more critically. To pass judgment on them we congregated at the barn.

"They ain't he-men," one of the hay hands announced.

"They may have the makins," a cowboy said, "but they're shore a long ways from bein' prime."

"They have the good looks," said the teamster who brought them in the tallyho, "but not the brains to punch cows. I'll bet there ain't one o' them is smart enough to pull on his pants, putting both feet in both legs at the same time, unless he lays flat on his back."

"Didja see their fingernails?" another man said. "Jus' like a row o' tombstones."

Next morning Jay and I brought saddle horses to all the dudes who wanted to ride. We suppressed our laughter when a man tried to mount by putting his right foot in the left-side stirrup, or referred to a horse's "stomach." After they rode away Jay turned to me. I saw the lines in his face begin to deepen, and he asked, "Didja hear that high-collared blood tell his horse, 'Canter a little now, please'?"

That evening at supper Jake lost his temper when he learned that three dudes had galloped off, trampling down some of his alfalfa that was ready to be cut, and others had raced their mounts across a field of oats that was almost ready for harvesting. Jake would have created a scene at the table but J. D. displayed the magnanimity that made him a successful promoter. With soft, genial salesman's manners he contrived to make the guests punish one another for the damages. To establish informality, he had insisted from the beginning that every man be known only by some nickname. One was called Ginger, another Sandy, a third Squire, and J. D. became the Governor. He insisted on a sheriff who must arrest the miscreants and have them tried by their peers. Ruining Jake's hay crop was a real offense, and the sheriff made the mistake of arresting Sandy for the crime. Sandy happened to be Lucian Hugh Alexander, a prominent Philadelphia attorney, and instead of submitting to arrest he pushed the sheriff into an irrigation ditch. He was tried for this offense, not for destroying Jake's crop.

We all attended the trial that night. Several of the bloods were lawyers, and two or three were ministers—men used to speaking before a crowd. I learned later that the Governor recruited his victims from wealthy eastern churches, never inviting more than one from the same congregation. Members of our party came from Massachusetts, New York, Pennsylvania, Ohio, and Illinois. At the trial they all acted like college boys, caricaturing the dignity each assumed in real life. Sandy, with affected humility, held up his right hand and swore on Mark Twain's *Roughing It* that he would, as usual, tell the untruth, the whole untruth, and nothing but the untruth. The Squire, really Laird Dinsmore of New York City, swore that he would bear false testimony. The culprit was duly convicted and sentenced to stand up before his peers and say, "I, Sandy, am a tenderfoot."

When we went to our beds in the bunkhouse one of the hay hands said to me, "That's the first time I ever see a real pot call a real kettle black."

Next day we started on the grand trip to inspect the ranches. I drove the four horses I had selected, now hitched to a worn-out wagon. Its broken spring seat was hooked over limber side boards. During the first day I had to stop many times to patch the harness with "Mormon buckskin," the colloquial name for baling wire. The chuck wagon, tallyho, and Jay Card with the cavy passed through Meeker before I arrived. The Governor had given me a list of groceries to purchase at Oldland's store, so I stopped there. My wagon was already loaded with folding army cots—a luxury unknown in that cattle country—and gaudy quilts that the dudes had wrapped up in amateur styles; some were rolled and tied at only one end, leaving the other to bulge like a hoop skirt. A cowboy's tightly wrapped bed in its tarpaulin cover was heavy but very neat compared to these, and a crowd soon gathered where I stopped in front of Oldland's store. The moguls had been a spectacle when they passed through town, and now my wagon's colorful load gave the townsmen an opportunity to voice their observations. The barkeep at Rube Ball's saloon stood outside the open door looking at the puffy load of quilts. A broad-hatted figure with speckled face, sharp-pointed nose, and swallow-forked ears walked up to him. He looked familiar but I could not recall his name.

"Howdy, Skully," the barkeep said, and I remembered him at once.

"Hi," Skull-Creek Jones replied. Waving a gnarled hand toward the bulging rolls, he said, "If them cigareet beds don't beat all!"

"If cigareets is what they be," the pink-faced barkeep replied, "a greenie musta rolled 'em."

"I'll bet they ain't no greenies at sleepin' in 'em," Skull-Creek observed as he stepped up beside the bar man. "Anyways, I wanna wet my neck." And the two men disappeared in the saloon.

I was late leaving town. We were to camp that night at Bob Wier's ranch on Strawberry Creek. Wier was a famous hunter; some of his dogs had been used by John Goff, who guided Theodore Roosevelt on his lion hunt in January and February, 1901. The road to Wier's was reasonably smooth, and I was in a hurry to get there. With only fifteen miles to go, the four willing horses made the wheels spin, but the disreputable wagon was not equal to the speed. At almost every bump the wagon seat bounced off the wobbling side boards and threw me around. I stopped, removed the seat, and drove standing up, wedged between the front end gate and the quilts. This allowed me no foot for the feeble brake, but I made the drive without upsetting. In camp that night I cursed the White Bear Company under my breath and did my best to repair the seat.

Next morning we crossed Coyote Basin, a country familiar to me after riding through it the summer before. We ate dinner at the Keystone Ranch, but I did not remind Tug Wilson that I was the kid who rode the mare he had called a proud-cut gelding. That night we camped at a fenced pasture on the sagebrush flats where we could turn the horses loose. The capitalists adjusted well to lining up along the pot-rack for a tardy meal, and after filling their plates they scattered out to eat in small groups. Unlike cowboys, when each blood finished eating he set his plate on the ground wherever he happened to be and strolled off, talking with friends.

"Put them plates in the roundup pan," Ed shouted with a roundup cook's authority. "Any bastard who don't will go hungry next meal."

The Governor tried to shush Ed, but our cook knew his power. He knew the quotation from Bulwer-Lytton that English stockmen had brought to the West:

> We may live without friends; we may live without books;
> But civilized man cannot live without cooks.

Ed was too important to be fired, but the gulls were also too important to have their ancestry questioned and be told where to put their dishes. Fortunately, they were also too genteel to hear a word of Ed's profane language, and after every meal Jay and I searched the hillsides for plates and "reloading tools." We hands all got revenge by criticizing the bloods. Jay said that the gold in one man's teeth was a richer deposit than Cripple Creek, and he spotted another who brushed his hair over the bald top of his head in an attempt to conceal where the natural growth stopped. When Jay called him "Hidden Timberline," the cook knew at once who he meant. We cowboys said another dude talked so fast a man couldn't keep up with him on horseback. Another's mustache was a back-slider; still another, who was putting on weight, had a chin with a "grass-belly," and we were sure that the dude who was thin would have to stand at least twice in broad daylight to make a shadow.

"What'll we call the Boston bastard who always runs when we walks?" Ed asked.

"If he runs when he walks," Jay retorted, "what in hell does the fair-haired son-of-a-bitch do when he runs?"

We enjoyed making up descriptive names, and thought they were much funnier than they really were. They were very different from the names the Governor had given his guests to generate good fellowship, but by the second night, when the last plate, cup, knife, and fork had been stowed in the chuck wagon drawers and Ed slammed the cupboard door shut, we had a name for everyone.

The next day we drove to Husted's Lily Park Ranch, where we witnessed one of the Governor's spectacular displays designed to dupe the gulls. Just east of Lily Park, where Bear River cuts a canyon through Cross Mountain, the walls are perpendicular. J. D. explained that it would be very inexpensive to blast down one wall to dam the river and thus store sufficient water to irrigate thousands of acres on his ranch. To impress this on the capitalists, we heard a loud boom as we drove in, and a small landslide of displaced rock cascaded down the wall. More blasting would certainly have dammed the river, and the prospective investors may have been impressed—but evidently not sufficiently to finance the project. So far as I know, the great irrigation development was never carried out.

On Sunday, Minty (really the Reverend Henry C. Minton of Trenton, New Jersey) preached outdoors between the chuck wagon and the log ranch house. Neighboring ranch families were invited. Not many lived there, and when the few who came hitched their teams along the fence Jay greeted them with a loud voice everybody could hear: "These bloods is the damnedest fools I ever did see. A just God 'ud give ever' one o' them a Waterberry watch and the seven-year itch. Then, when they ain't a-windin' they'll be a-scratchin'."

I never envied J. D.'s problems with these cowboys and don't recall Minty's sermon under the spreading cottonwoods in that magnificent western weather. I was more interested in swimming across Bear River, which appeared to be several

hundred yards wide at that point. Water was scarce in the
West, and the cowboys I met seldom swam, so I ventured to
cross alone. It was a long swim, and I decided to wade back as
far as I could. To my surprise, I waded all the way. No
swimming had been necessary.

That night the bloods baptized the ranch foreman's baby,
Eva. In the morning we started for Craig, with my bed wagon
at the end of the procession. The bulging quilts were noticeably soiled now. We camped for noon dinner at an irrigation
ditch just beyond the Seven Ranch. After eating at the chuck
wagon the moguls separated as usual. One group sought the
"best water" to drink; the ditch looked muddy. Another group
climbed a nearby hill, seeking the "best view." A man with a
notebook studied me as an example of the picturesque cowboy,
and I did my best to play the part, even asking asinine questions about the east, especially Philadelphia; he smiled eagerly
while jotting down my quaint language. As we talked, the
Governor strolled off with a prospective investor, as usual—
J. D. always thought it best to sell stock to one man at a time.
A Mr. Lucas came back to the wagon where we skinners were
washing dishes and asked us to tell him where would be the
best place for him to bathe. He did this at almost every camp,
and Ed, the cook, waved toward Bear River.

As soon as Mr. Lucas' back was turned, Jay, who was drying
dishes with an empty flour sack, said, "When this trip is over
that blood won't even smell like a man."

Before we broke camp a strange cowboy rode into camp, and
after talking with us rode away full of stories about a new brand
of odd men who rolled their sleeves up to their elbows in the
scorching sun and seemed proud of the sunburn on their faces.
"I hear'd tell o' such folk," he said, lighting a smoke before
mounting, "but never believed such stories till I seed 'em with
my own eyes. When will some folks get sense?"

That night we camped at Maybell—a post office, store, and
house or two. The next day as we forded Bear River I made a
big mistake. I stopped my wagon in belly-deep water to let the
teams drink. Jay came along close behind me and his horses
surrounded mine. While they all drank we chatted. The current was swift, and watching the water made a man feel he was
going upstream. As we talked I looked ahead for the place on
the east bank where I could drive out, but while my attention

was away from the milling horses, my leaders jackknifed with the wheelers. Moon Eyes and Spike-You-Son-of-a-Bitch stood facing me in the swirling water. This kind of a mix-up is impossible for a man on the driver's seat to straighten out, especially with belly-deep water swishing by. I had been caught napping and did not like to admit it. Fortunately, Jay drove his cavy away and then took Spike-You-Puppy (my contraction of the name) by the bridle and swung the lead team back in their place. I drove off, climbed the east bank, and rumbled on behind the chuck wagon and tallyho. My worst experience with Spike-You-S.O.B. was yet to come.

With no more delays that morning, we passed the Two Bar horse camp where I had spent the night the year before, and stopped our teams at a town called Lay, in the center of a vast sagebrush desert. It was only a neat log cabin, a few sheds and a post office in a false-fronted store.

A. G. Wallihan, a noted big-game photographer and author lived here. His wife, who managed the lunch room, had a local reputation for backing her opinions with a gun. While waiting for her to fix dinner, Wallihan showed us a very handsome book he had written. Entitled *Camera Shots at Big Game*, it had been published by Doubleday in 1904 and had an introduction by Theodore Roosevelt. These pictures were noteworthy at that time because western big game was supposedly doomed for early extinction. The book's frontispiece showed a mountain lion in midair, leaping toward the photographer—an exciting picture! I questioned it as a possible fake, and the author turned the page quickly.

Wallihan seemed to be an elderly gentleman with a long white beard, but I learned later this was a disguise. After the bloods sat down for dinner he told me in his quiet way that he had once built a blind out on the range to photograph deer. While waiting, camera bulb in hand, the cattlemen's hired assassin, Tom Horn, had spurred past on a dun horse, making his spectacular escape after shooting Isam Dart. "Wally" thought it fortunate that the blind had hid him well.

As a young girl, Mrs. Wallihan had been courted by many men in this womanless country. Even tough Hi Bernard, the Two Bar foreman, who was believed to have marked the victims for Tom Horn's rifle, had once, in a playful mood, spurred his horse into her kitchen. She failed to enjoy his joke, missed with her first shot at him, and publicly declared an open season on Hi Bernard if he ever came to Lay again. Hi believed that she meant every word of it, and on future trips to the horse camp dared not ride past her house.

Wallihan showed me a picture of his wife which I wish he had included in his book of vanishing wild life. She was wearing a black silk dress, laced bodice, bustle, high-heeled shoes, and a big hat decorated with both egret and ostrich feathers. Rifle in hand, she stood beside three big bucks she had killed. When she died a few years later, "Wally" cut off his beard, and we learned that he was a comparatively young man who had masqueraded for years to match her age.

We must have talked too long in Lay because it became dark before we drove the twenty miles to Craig. I disliked driving fours at a fast trot when I could not see the road, which was merely wagon ruts. The tallyho led the way, followed by the chuck wagon and my bed wagon. I remember one place where we spun down a steep grade with the ruts only two feet from the edge of a ten-foot-deep dry gulch.

In Craig we pitched our tents on the vacant lot across from Mrs. Webb's "eating house." She had cleaned up the supper dishes, and we found her sitting in the kitchen quietly knitting. The Governor asked her to fix meals for all of us; without looking up from her work she refused, saying she was tired. This was a predicament for the Governor, but he displayed his usual salesman's persuasion. The performance was a sight to behold. The faster he talked the faster Mrs. Webb's knitting needles clicked together, but eventually the Governor won. "I'll do it," she said finally, brushing a lock of hair back from her perspiring forehead, "if you'll send somebody to Ledford's saloon for my meat cutter."

The Governor told me to go at once—and hurry. I hoped it would not be too heavy to carry. The saloon, at the next street corner, was the one I had sat in front of the summer before. Being unaccustomed to going alone into a saloon, especially a wild-western saloon, I assumed a bold face and pushed through the swinging doors. A line of broad-hatted roughnecks stood along the bar. The barkeeper looked down at me with curious disapproval, I thought, and asked me what I wanted. I shall always remember his inquiring face and the display of fancy bottles shelved in front of a broad mirror behind the bar.

"Mrs. Webb," I said in my best determined voice, "has sent me to get her meat cutter."

"Her what?" the barkeep replied, swabbing the bar with a towel. "We ain't got no meat cutter of hern here."

"She told me you had her meat cutter," I replied, "and she wants it."

The barkeep straightened up and called to the man tending bar at the other end, "Oh, Mack! What's this about Ma Webb's meat cutter? There's a kid here says she sent him f'r to fetch it."

All the drinkers along the bar stopped to listen, and the saloon became very quiet. The man at the other end replied, "Ma Webb's meat cutter! I know nuthin' about no meat cutter here!"

In the silence I heard a voice at the gambling tables back in the room say, "I guess she means me."

At one of the round tables, an angular, hatchet-faced man named Kilpatrick slapped down his cards and stood up. Amid a roar of laughter he and I walked out the swinging doors and up the street to Mrs. Webb's.

Next day our caravan stopped for dinner at the Two Circle Bar Ranch, certainly the most lavish spread in northwestern Colorado. I had passed here last summer driving the Norvell cattle. Five miles farther on, the road crossed a bridge, and the tallyho, full of bloods, led our procession through Hayden, making the turn at the hotel; this time no pretty girls stood on the porch.

The railroad had reached Steamboat Springs now, so instead of following last year's cattle trail, we stayed on the river road. I remember one place I would like to relocate because Spike-You-S.O.B. almost wrecked our outfit there. The road, too narrow for wagons to pass one another, rounded an ocher bluff on a shelf about twenty feet above the river. I did not want my leaders to pull on the turn, so I watched them carefully, which was fortunate. Otherwise, I would not have seen the singletree hook, for the off-leader's tug, slip loose and fall to the ground.

"Whoa!" I shouted, quick as a flash.

The horses knew my voice well and they all stopped before anything went wrong, but I never came nearer having a bad accident while driving fours. Had we gone a step farther Spike-You-Puppy, being only half hitched to the wagon, could have mixed up all the teams and the confused horses might have pulled each other and the wagon over the bluff. As it was, I jammed down the brake, wrapped the reins around the handle, and walked along the edge of the bluff until I came to Spike-You-Male-K9's tug. Wiring it back to the singletree, I drove on to a safer place for a better repair job.

That night we pitched our last camp in a fenced meadow on Bear River near Turner's roadhouse. The country was beautiful. On the steep-pitched slopes around us, the pale-trunked aspens' leaves quivered as the sun went down. After dark the bloods sang college songs around a campfire, and in the morning they packed their valises. I sneaked a final furtive look at Lucian Hugh Alexander; I wanted to be sure to remember his face because I was the uncouth cowboy who planned to surprise him in his Philadelphia law office the next winter wearing my civilized clothes.

We loaded all the bloods and their baggage into the chuck wagon and tallyho. They rumbled away, with the Governor leading them in a farewell song he had written to glorify the White Bear Land & Livestock Company. For two days I tended camp alone with nothing to do but cook my meals, watch the horses, and fish for cutthroat trout that could not resist a grasshopper on a No. 8 Abby & Umbrie snell hook. Studying the mountain skyline, I saw for the first time the profile of a gigantic nude woman lying on her back—Steamboat Springs' famous Sleeping Lady.

When the hired hands returned, we started with the horses and wagons for the distant ranch. On the way we stopped at Craig, and Jay said, "Let's get a copy of the weekly *Craig Gimlet* and read about our great expedition."

I noticed the wrinkles in Jay's face deepen, and I asked, "The *Weekly Gimlet?*"

"Yes," he said. "We call their paper the *Gimlet* because it bores folks."

The paper did not bore me. A front-page banner announced HUSTED "BOOSTERS" HERE, but the date at the top—August 5, 1909—gave me a shock. I feared I was in trouble. We had to drive these horses and wagons almost a hundred miles to the ranch, and then I had to find and catch Queenie, cross the Rocky Mountains where there was no road, load her in a stock

car in Denver, and ride with her to Philadelphia. My parents
were in their summer home at Buck Hill Falls in the Pocono
Mountains, and I planned to ride Queenie up there—another
hundred miles—and still be ready for my first year at Swarthmore College. How could I ever do all that in so short a
time?

9

Flat-Tops and the Continental Divide

Gie me ae spark o' Nature's fire
That's a' the learning I desire.
—Robert Burns

The map indicated that I would have to ride 175 miles from the ranch to Denver. By hill and dale, it proved to be 248 miles. I knew I must sleep with no camp for two or possibly three nights at high elevations, but my ride to the "lower country" made me feel at home in the wilderness. To keep warm at night I took a newspaper. The Meeker weekly *Register* was too small—only one double sheet—but the *Denver Post* was a multipaged paper, and I carried a copy to spread between my blankets. I had learned on the White Bear expedition that newsprint between blankets provided more warmth than an extra quilt, and also helped start a fire the next morning.

On my first night out I planned to camp at Trappers Lake. This was the source of White River's north fork, upstream some twenty-five miles from the White Bear Ranch. The distance was sufficiently long for my first day but nobody lived there. I was told that a road ended a few miles below the lake at Sam Hime's ranch.

Sam, a transplanted Scotsman, knew his Robert Burns. On the barn he had written in big red letters: MAN'S INHUMANITY TO MAN MAKES COUNTLESS THOUSANDS MOURN. I had found that an interest in literature was brought to the West more often by British working people than by eastern Americans. Sam, with his Bobby Burns, seemed independent and happy in this wilderness. A very pretty girl helped serve dinner at the ranch. I had reached the age when boys begin to notice girls, and I wondered whether she, too, was happy in this lonely, beautiful spot, whether it could be beautiful in the eyes of a smiling, fun-loving girl.

After a good meal, I asked Sam the way to Trappers Lake. He pointed, with an arthritic finger, to the forest wall where he said the trail began. It led me through dark pines that seemed very quiet after my sunny half-day ride coming up through aspen groves and mountain meadows. In the hushed silence of the cathedral gloom I could hear only the rhythm of Queenie's dancing feet in the soft black earth and an occasional murmur overhead when a breeze disturbed the pine tops.

The first open meadow after the gloomy forest seemed bright, fresh, and very green below the dark mountains ahead with their towering peaks. I marveled at the view, but Queenie jumped to one side so quickly she almost threw me. Her high spirits, watchfulness, and fancy footwork had their dangers. Far ahead in the meadow I could see an odd object crawling snakelike from under the forest wall. Although still some distance away, it crept toward us. It was a long line of packhorses—some fifteen or twenty, if I remember correctly. Queenie had never seen bobbing white packs before and they frightened her as much or more than the smell of Indians. She tried to bolt. I curbed and turned her around to face the cavalcade. At a safe distance of fifty yards we watched it pass us and disappear along the trail we had taken from Sam Hime's ranch.

The cavalcade contained two or three sportsmen with guides, wranglers, cooks, and packers hunting and fishing in the mountains before automobiles on hard-surface roads spoiled the West for many of us. Fortunately, I had not met them in the dense woods where Queenie might have been hard to manage.

I followed the trail on which the sportsmen had come and soon emerged at Trappers Lake, a magnificent body of water 10,500 feet high in the bottom of what appeared to be the crater of an extinct volcano. The crater slopes were carpeted to the lake's edge with evergreens that looked as soft and lustrous as velvet. At one side, in a small park, I saw a dirt-roofed cabin and rode through the pines to investigate. It was deserted and had no door, but promised shelter for the night. Nearby a small stream splashed down the grassy hillside and out into the lake.

I unsaddled and hobbled Queenie, cut a willow for a fishing rod, and tied to it the line and leader I carried around my hatband. Attaching a gray hackle and royal coachman to the leader, I cast along the riffle made by the brook in the still waters of the lake. Trout struck both flies instantly and, as every fisherman knows, two trout on one line are easier to play than one because the fish play each other. I dragged the gleaming beauties out on the sandy beach and cast again on the far side of the riffle. I caught only one this time, but with one trout for supper, one for breakfast, and one to take along for lunch, I decided to quit.

At this elevation I knew that water for coffee boiled at a low temperature and fish required more than the usual time to fry. A cook must watch a frying trout's eyes; they turn white when the fish is done. After supper I decided not to sleep in the cabin. Queenie was grazing contentedly, but in the dark she might hobble back down the trail toward home and leave me helplessly afoot. To prevent this, I unrolled my bedding on the trail where she could not pass without waking me. Unfolding the *Denver Post* between my two light blankets, I slept soundly, lulled by the whispering of the pines and the lake waters lapping on the shore.

Sam Hime had told me that a trail from the lake led almost due east over a flat-topped divide and then down Yampa Creek to the town of Yampa, which I had visited after shipping the Norvell cattle the year before. In the morning I found this trail, and after a two-thousand-foot climb through the pines I emerged on gently rolling grasslands well above timberline, known as the Flat-Tops. Drifts of everlasting snow lay white and cold in the hollows. On these semiarctic moors the trail disappeared and to get lost up there with no shelter or wood for a fire would be serious indeed. I noticed a little pile of rocks, rode to it, and saw another pile beyond. I decided that somebody—probably forest rangers—had built them to mark the way across this half-frozen moor to the eastern rim of the Flat-Tops where the trail down would become visible.

To avoid getting lost, I decided to keep one of these little stone piles in sight so I could backtrack to the lake in case they led nowhere across this featureless tundra. Riding along, I noticed little groves of dwarf willows only six or eight inches tall, and in them I saw my first ptarmigan. I recognized the plump, stubby-billed, arctic grouse at once—freckled, grayish brown on their backs and white underneath, with warm white stockings on their little legs. They are true Eskimos of the bird world. Very tame, they preferred to run rather than fly. Forgetting my caution about getting lost, I followed them from one matted willow thicket to another. Some of them would nestle on the ground to escape detection, then leap into the air, fly a few yards, and land tantalizingly close to me. I remembered how Hawkshaw had pounced on the young sage chickens and was glad he was not here to kill these rare birds.

Circling this way and that while following the ptarmigan, I failed to keep track of my directions. Suddenly it occurred to me that there was no stone-pile marker in sight. Nothing on the monotonous tundra indicated where the trail crossed this inhospitable country. I had done exactly what I was afraid I might do, and the sun was now too high in the sky to tell east from west. I would not admit that I was lost. Instead, as Indians would say, "the trail was lost."

This predicament was similar to my experience in the lower country the year before, but much worse. To be lost at an altitude of 12,500 feet without firewood or shelter could be rugged. I knew that the one thing a lost person must not do is to ride away bewildered and excited. I was sure of at least eight more hours of daylight, and in that length of time I could certainly find some way over the rim and down to the timber, where I would feel safe with firewood, game, and fish.

As helpless now as a navigator at sea without a compass, I decided to make one for myself. Of the 360 points on a compass, 359 would not lead me to the lost stone marker. I must find the one point that would, so I built a stone pile of my own and started to ride around it in the widest circle I could plot without losing sight of it. This plan worked. Before I finished my circle I spied one of the real stone markers and followed the line of them until I came to the trail down the east rim. The view from the edge was magnificent. I saw, in the forest of pines below me, the crooked line of the stream I would follow to Yampa. A half dozen beaver dams, like a flight of stairs, mirrored the blue sky, and I felt strangely at home once more.

The twenty miles down Yampa Creek were pleasant—

fragrant with the smell of pine trees and splashing cold water. At every park in the forest, a woodchuck or two whistled a shrill alarm, then, without another remonstrance, sat up solemnly to observe Queenie and me ride by. I remember one mother with four little ones, all watching us as they stood in a straight military line. When she turned her head to the right all the little ones turned theirs. When she turned to the left their little heads turned too.

Yampa had not changed since Biscuits, Chip, and I had been there. This year I stayed all night, enjoyed a good meal in the "eating house," and for the first time in many weeks slept in a bed. The next ten miles of my trip were across familiar country. At the railroad construction camp I found only a disfigured landscape—broken boards and bottles, empty barrels, worn-out harness, rotting horse collars, and discarded clothing. The railroad tracks now terminated at Steamboat Springs, where the White Bear dudes had boarded the train.

At Toponas I crossed the tracks and headed east on an uncertain mountain road. During the next two days I rode sixty-five miles, taking many shortcuts across open country. The Gore Pass I remember as scenery superior to that in a Thomas Moran painting. Later, on the third day, I came to a neat-appearing cabin on a little used road. If the owner had a horse pasture where Queenie could eat her fill, I hoped I might stop for the night. Without dismounting I called at the door, got no answer, and called again. Then a face appeared at the window, a real human face but as horrible as any false face imaginable. That face shocked me more than the sight of bobbing packs and the smell of Indians had disturbed Queenie. This was my time to shy, and I galloped down the road into the timber, on and on for at least an hour before I came to a newly built cabin in a green meadow. Riding up to the door I felt a little apprehensive, but when I called the face that met me at the open door was fresh, pretty, and unafraid.

"Sure you can stay with us." The young woman smiled. "But all we ken give you fur supper is bread and milk, unless you'll shoot us a buckskin."

"I'd get me one for you," I replied, using her vernacular, "if I had a rifle."

"I'll loan you George's .30-30," she replied, reaching up over her head for a gun inside the door. "The buckskin begin to

move at sundown," she continued, "an' if you ken hit one we
ken surprise George with fresh liver fer supper. He'll be here
tonight with boughten store victuals from Kremmling, all we
ken afford—but be kereful of his gun. We saved ever' cent for
over two year and done without things we needed to buy it."

The Winchester, a '94 model carbine, was the prized posses-
sion of these homesteaders. It had become a pet, a member of
the family. Never before had I seen such tender care given a
rifle. George's wife had stitched a thin leather cover over the
stock to keep it from being scratched, and she handed it to me
with the affectionate pat she might have given the head of a
small boy starting on an exciting hunt.

With the pet gun I walked up a brushy draw, watching for
the deer that "begin to move at sundown," and I soon experienced a strange hunting adventure. The sun had set, and at a
fork in the draw where I could look two ways I wet my finger in
my mouth and, holding it up, learned that a draft came down
both draws. This meant that deer up either one could not smell
me and might graze in my direction. I sat down to wait and
hope for a shot.

The light was fading fast. I turned my head to see the half
moon and when I looked again along the draw I saw in the
fading light what appeared to be two horses plodding up the far
brushy slope. One was plainly a packhorse; I could not see the
rider on the lead horse, but as I watched, both horses stopped
and the moon glistened on what I thought might be a swinging
rifle barrel. Had the rider I could not see drawn his rifle to
shoot? In the feeble light he might suspect and fear me. The
possibility was unpleasant.

"Hi," I shouted, and the horses I had been watching suddenly turned into what they really were—two deer. Already
their summer coats had changed to the winter "blue," which in
the moonlight looked like white pack tarps. The glint on the
gun barrel had been moonlight on the lead deer's antlers,
which were hard and shiny now since the summer's velvet had
been scraped off. It was too dark for me to shoot, and the deer,
with stiff-legged jumps, topped the ridge and disappeared. I
walked back to the cabin by starlight. George had arrived.

"Sairy says you're bringing us liver for supper," he shouted
in a cheery voice from the corral. "Old .30-30 never comes
home without meat."

Evidently .30-30 was a member of this family, but the gun and I disappointed our elders. That night I slept in my blankets at the pasture gate where I had turned Queenie loose. It was a hundred yards from the cabin, and at midnight a porcupine, evidently smelling the salty leather on my Thompson saddle, began chewing its skirts. I drove him away, but he came back, so I killed him with my six-shooter. The homesteaders heard the shot, and when I went to the cabin for breakfast George bubbled with laughter.

"So you killed a porcupine without .30-30!" George beamed as we sat down for a breakfast of humble "boughten victuals"—store prunes that had been soaked in water overnight to soften them, oatmeal mush with milk, and slapjacks hot off the griddle. In the center of the table Sairy had arranged wild delphinium—cowboys called them common larkspur—in a Sego milk can for a vase.

"How do you know it was a porcupine?" I asked.

"I'll show you," George said. "Come here, Snips. Here Snips!"

The puppy romped to the table. On the tip of his nose a porcupine quill stood out at a saucy angle.

"Snips must have been curious," George said. "He must have investigated your shot, and I'm glad he didn't bite that dead porky. Them quills is barbed, you know. They keep workin' in, never work out. I'll hold Snips—he won't bite me—if you'll pull that quill out with these tweezers. An' mind you, do a better job than you done with .30-30."

After a jolly breakfast I rode away from this happy couple wondering why Hamlin Garland and other writers considered homesteaders such dreary drudges. For this couple every day seemed to be a new delight. Perhaps it was mutual good health or cheerful dispositions. Neither complained about the sparse food or humble surroundings. I could see genuine satisfaction, no wistfulness, no longing in Sairy's face as she glanced from time to time at the product of their two years work and savings—George's lifelong dream, the Winchester, .30-30.

That day I had another shooting adventure on one of the little-used roads. Riding across a short-grass park in the timber, I saw a tall lone pine in the center. As I approached it a very large squirrel bounded to the trunk and disappeared behind it.

The creature had a magnificently broad, feathery gray tail that undulated in graceful curves as he jumped away. I knew gray squirrels back East but this one seemed much larger and different. In a few moments he appeared on a lower limb and bravely scolded me. His conspicuous gray tail arched over his head, making an awning edged with white-tipped black hairs that danced nervously as he chattered. That squirrel looked plump, good for my next meal, but too far away for a pistol shot. The tree was easy to climb and I decided to chase him to the top where I could get close enough to hit him.

I dismounted. The squirrel immediately circled the tree trunk out of sight. I always carried my six-shooter in a light holster tight to my body. This prevented it from slapping me when Queenie trotted, and with both hands free I could climb easily. As I started up, the squirrel appeared again around the trunk above me, scolded, then disappeared once more. I feared the clever little animal might escape by running down the trunk where I could not see him. To prevent this, as I climbed up I repeatedly wrapped my arms around the trunk to drive the squirrel farther up. An occasional flash of that magnificent tail reassured me that my invisible prey was scampering up ahead of me. Sooner or later the tree trunk would become too slim to hide his body and I would get a shot. The squirrel evidently foresaw this too, and once or twice he ran out on a teetering limb, where he made an uncertain mark for my pistol, so I did not shoot. We were much too high up the towering pine for the squirrel to jump to the ground. Instead, he always bounded back to the main stem, which tapered more and more as we climbed. The trunk began waving with my weight. To go much higher would certainly be dangerous, but now I saw him plainly. At this dizzy height he seemed to be frightened and quit scolding. He was so close that I noticed for the first time his long, black ear-tufts—very different from the squirrels I knew. His white belly made a good mark but I could not shoot so beautiful a creature. Abert squirrels lived in Colorado and nowhere else, so I left this one on his lofty perch, climbed down, and rode away.

I spent the night at the little town of Tabernash. Ahead of me, ten miles farther, the Great Divide I must cross loomed up bare and dull green in the eastern sky. The man in charge at the livery barn told me there was no marked trail over the crest. A work road led from town to the west portal of the recently finished Moffat railroad tunnel, and from there I must find my way for about fifteen miles up over the Divide and down to Coal Creek on the eastern slope. Most of the country was above timberline, and a rider who kept his sense of direction would have no trouble unless it stormed—but storms came quickly at that elevation. When sleet and hail hisssed along the summits even old-timers who knew the country worried. "If there's a cloud in the sky tomorrow," the man said, "I would not start if I were you."

The morning dawned bright and clear. With only twenty-five miles to ride I delayed starting. I wanted to be sure of good weather. Watching the sky, I rode the ten miles to the tunnel entrance. An excursion train full of eastern tourists had just arrived from Denver. They spied me, and some girls, with excited screams, began snapping pictures of the cowboy.

"Why do you wear those chaps?" one girl asked. She pronounced "ch" as in "chicken."

"He's not a real cowboy," I heard a young man who wanted attention say. "He's riding too good a horse."

I thought, that fellow may be right, but his premises are wrong—the cowboys I've known ride good horses.

I had seen no city people for three months and would have enjoyed hearing the latest news from back east but dared not stay. Instead, I had to find my way across the Continental Divide before sundown, so I reined Queenie toward the slope. It was always difficult to keep her from charging up steep timberline grades, but I held her down. Once or twice I dismounted to rest my arms and let her nibble grass on the alpine hillsides. Strangely enough, I remember very little about crossing the Divide. Certainly there was no sharp crest, but the wind, which blows across banks of perpetual snow, has an unforgettable tang—cold, free, invigorating. From the crannies in granite outcrops "Little Chief Hares" barked shrilly at us. Always difficult to see, their sharp cries seemed to come simultaneously from different places. An occasional hawk sailed overhead almost at hat-brim level. I felt sure the settlements west of Denver must be close, but I feared that the eastern slope of the Divide might become a precipice with a village in plain view below and no way to ride down to it before dark. I did not relish the prospect of a night above timberline with no shelter or bedding.

Riding northeast along the bare mountain crest, I finally saw a cabin at the timber's edge and reined Queenie down to it. A hospitable prospector let me sleep in his powder house, and I must have slept soundly because he came in at daybreak and gave me a real scare when he began tossing dynamite sticks into piles across the cabin floor. This seemed dangerous to me but he smiled and said, "Powder won't explode without a spark."

Eating bacon with coffee that morning, I realized I had entered a new world where the language was different from that in the cattle country. Men talked here about shafts, drifts, and stopes—all terms new to me—but I tried to learn their meaning. Proud of my new knowledge, I followed a road of sorts through the very tall ponderosa pine trees down the mountainside into a third new world that differed markedly from the mining camps. The men here talked about skidways, timber, cant hooks, and peaveys. They pointed out a logging road that led down a Gothic aisle through the pines. This was a pleasure to traverse but ended nowhere. I knew that the town of Golden, on the main road to Denver, must be near, but under the tall trees I could not keep my directions without a compass. None of the methods I used in open country helped me in this rough, densely forested terrain. A traveler here was absolutely dependent on roads built by other men, and I wondered as I rode along the gloomy trail if this dependence on others affected a forest dweller's character. William Jennings Bryan had become famous for not following other men's roads. He was called "the boy orator of the plains"—not of the forests.

My soliloquy lasted for many miles as I rode aimlessly until I trotted into the mining town of Toland, where I ate a good dinner and slept in a rooming house. A sign over the proprietor's desk told me:

My friend did come and I did trust him
I lost my friend and lost his custom
To lose my friends it grieves me sore
So I've resolved to trust no more.

Next day, making suggested short cuts to Golden, I got lost in the forest again but before dark I arrived in the town, and Queenie saw her first automobile—a noisy, sputtering machine. She shied badly at first, and the next day on the way to Denver she was still afraid of the few we met on the road. At the Denver stockyards I engaged a cattle car, bedded one end of it with straw for Queenie and the other end for my blankets and saddle. With baling wire I fastened the slat door so that it was open just enough for me to squeeze through, but so close I hoped no hobo could enter. I was ready now for the trip to Philadelphia.

I forget how many days Queenie and I rumbled eastward across the Great Plains and farmlands of the Middle West. Lolling luxuriously in the clean straw, I looked through the stock car's horizontal slats at the passing world. Railroad stations, country crossroads, big barns, and rural villages flicked by. Each, like the one before it, sped away over the horizon and disppeared. At one stop for the locomotive to draw water from a roadside tank, some hoboes peered in my car door. They evidently envied the elegant traveling accommodations of the decadent upper class. Like a true plutocrat lounging in my sumptuous baled-straw bed, I did not encourage them, but I did not threaten them with my six-shooter. The slat door was wired solidly and the hoboes sought other accommodations on the bumper, I suppose, or on the rods, or in a "gon-dó-la"— hobo pronunciation of their word for an empty coal car. Several times on the trip "shacks" (brakemen) roused me at night to see if I was harboring "stiffs" (hoboes). The schoolboy had learned these names from Jack London's book, *The Road*.

Arriving finally in the West Philadelphia stockyards, I thought that Lucian Hugh Alexander, the White Bear blood, would probably recognize me now, but I was sure he wouldn't when I changed clothes and called at his office downtown.

10

Dinner at Delmonico's

Others may go to mount or sea,
The summer show at Keith's for me,

This couplet amused Philadelphians who disliked sitting in
Keith's vaudeville theater during the sultry summer season
when palm-leaf fans were standard equipment. When Queenie
and I arrived in Philadelphia, my family were at their Buck Hill
Falls cottage in the Pocono Mountains, a hundred miles north.
Since I had only ten days left before I had to register at
Swarthmore College, my ride up there and back would have to
be fast. After that I planned to surprise Lucian Hugh Alexander. It never occurred to me that my visit with that attorney
would lead to a dinner at Delmonico's in New York.

Our Philadelphia house was closed, but I had a key. I rode
there on Queenie and tied her to the hitching post at our front
gate. Then I took a bath and put on clean clothes. When I
came out two neighbor boys who had spied my western saddle
and rope were waiting for me. They watched me tie my slicker
behind the saddle and I heard them give a little gasp of
pleasure when they saw me put my Colt .45 in a saddle pocket
out of sight. Mounting, I waved good-bye, and the wistfulness
in those boys' faces reminded me of Chip back in Hayden,
Colorado.

Riding on city streets was new for both Queenie and me, and
I did not know what route to take to the Pocono Mountains.
Some streets were paved with bricks laid on edge, others with
stone Belgian blocks that made milk wagons rattle and were
bumpy for passengers in hansom cabs. Broad Street had a
smooth concrete surface and led north, the direction I wanted
to go, so I decided to start my ride on it. This was a mistake. As
I rode along, an urchin threw a potato at me. Instead of

ignoring him I decided to catch the rascal with my rope. Queenie understood this sport, since she was skilled at catching calves. She was quick to turn at the slightest pressure on the reins but, being unused to smooth concrete, she fell flat!

Neither of us was hurt, but I felt safer when we found solid footing on the dirt roads north of the city. Queenie made good progress except near the larger towns, where macadamized roads impeded us. The small surface stones on these newly constructed raods sometimes became wedged between her frog and shoe. Then I had to dismount and pry them out.

To let Queenie regain her strength after the long trip from the West, I rode only fifteen miles the first day. The September weather was magnificent. Leaves on the trees had turned red, brown, and yellow. Corn shocks in the fields resembled Indian teepees, and the big yellow pumpkins among them reminded me of Halloween. In those horse-and-buggy days this Pennsylvania Dutch country was new to a Philadelphia boy, and I enjoyed riding past the neat farmhouses and gigantic barns. Villages along the way offered clean bedrooms and ample food, but the language had peculiarities. In one restaurant I asked for a second waffle.

"I'm sorry," the waitress replied, "but the waffles are all."

"All what?" I wanted to ask. Later I learned that "all" in Pennsylvania Dutch meant "all gone," a translation of the German *das es alles*.

On the afternoon of the fourth day's ride I saw the long, level ridge topped by what is now called the Appalachian Trail for hikers. Two notches, the Water and Wind Gaps, were both visible. A hotel in the Water Gap had been a honeymoon retreat for generations. The lesser known Wind Gap was a pass into the Pocono resort country where the Buck Hill summer community had been established. There were no buildings in the Gap but I felt at home in the woodlands although they were different from western forests. Here the underbrush was so thick it hid the tree trunks. A horseman would find it difficult to ride through these woods. Long walls of rhododendron, as tall as a man on horseback, were absolutely impenetrable. Pioneers, I thought, must have explored this country on foot instead of on horseback as they did in the West, and this may have given them the different point of view that still persisted.

North of the Wind Gap I stopped at a farmhouse for the night. The woman who opened the door was as hospitable as Sairy had been in Colorado and, also like Sairy, her husband was away but would return before dark. She said they could feed me and my horse but had no sleeping accommodations. In the West I had learned to say, "It don't matter about me so long as my hoss is took good care of," and this woman served me an ample supper spiced with sauerkraut and *schmierkase* (cottage cheese). After eating, I untied my slicker from my saddle and walked down to the garden, looking for a little dry gulley like those in the desert where, wrapped in my slicker, I could sleep fitfully through the night. The ground here, however, was soft and clammy. I was not as tough as I had told her, and when her husband returned he found me still hunting for a dry spot. He asked if I smoked. I said no, and he told me to go to the barn and sleep in the hay. That was an old western custom, and I enjoyed a good night.

Although I had spent many boyhood summers at resorts with my family in the Poconos, these were the first Pennsylvania Dutch mountaineers I had met. In the morning they served me *pawnhass* (scrapple) and apple pie. Pie for breakfast was as routine with these Germans as orange juice would be for later generations. While eating, I learned about folk heroes of the eastern woodlands who were new to me. Instead of Tom Horn and Butch Cassidy, the legends here concerned a Tom Quick and Bayard Taylor's Sandy Flash, both of whom had survived in legends of the old, wild-Indian days. For some reason James Fenimore Cooper's Natty Bumppo had not been adopted by these Pennsylvania woodsmen.

That afternoon I crossed the Delaware, Lackawanna, and Western Railroad track at Cresco where passengers for Buck Hill got off the train. To publicize the cleanliness of travel on this railroad the company advertised that:

> Miss Snow may scan on journey's span
> Each keen and faithful tower man
> Whose levers bright are swung aright
> Upon the Road of Anthracite.

A few miles farther along I came to the road through brilliant autumn woods that led to our cottage. As I rode up to the side porch Queenie's feet rustled in the fallen leaves. I drew my six-shooter and, being young, announced my arrival by firing, cowboy fashion, into the air.

It was September 18, 1909, and I had to be back in Swarthmore on the twenty-second for registration day. Queenie had regained her strength and I made the hundred-mile return ride easily in three days. At West Philadelphia I put Queenie in the livery stable and took the train to Swarthmore. Students were registering at small tables in the gymnasium, and there I learned that I lacked the necessary entrance credits. My work at the school I had attended in Vevey, Switzerland, was not recognized, although that school year was probably more educational than any other in my life. I was, however, permitted to enter Swarthmore as a special student, and my beginning courses postponed my surprise call on Lucian Hugh Alexander.

I registered for economics, French, and English—three courses prescribed for all beginners. After a fortnight of lectures and study, we freshmen took examinations that determined whether we could remain in Swarthmore. I received an A in economics from Scott Nearing, a B-plus in French from Dr. Isabelle Bronk. Professor Pace gave me an E in English, a low mark in the one subject I had enjoyed so much I took the curb bit out of my mouth—always a great academic mistake! The average of my grades permitted me to remain in college but "Sparrow" Pace did not recommend that I specialize in his discipline.

I liked Scott Nearing. He was the first teacher I had known who talked to his students as equals, man to man. After one lecture an upperclassman said to me, "I approve of socialism as Scott Nearing explains it, but I can't learn to like the kind of people who like it, and I do wish that girl who is so dedicated would wash her hair."

Freshman remember odd academic trivialities. In Isabelle Bronk's French class the boys got a big kick out of the remark she repeated every morning. We courteously stood up when she entered the classroom, then suppressed our laughter when she invariably told us in French, "Asseyez-vous."

I felt sufficiently well established now to call on Lucian Hugh Alexander but Queenie delayed this second proposed visit. A new whiskey named Baltimore Rye was being advertised extensively with pictures of a rider on a spirited black horse. The livery stable men complimented Queenie by calling her Balti-Mariah, but I was not happy when they told me she was with foal. Out West stallions ran loose with the range horses, and this colt might come within a month.

A college friend of mine owned a farm on the Delaware River in Bucks County, and I took Queenie there on a steamboat. She survived "the blessed event" but I was not in the horse-raising business. She passed out of my life forever but I always associate that little black mare with big snow-capped mountains, and I hope she accepted, with better grace than I did, a new life that fenced us in.

At last I had time for my call on Lucian Hugh Alexander. His office was on the seventh floor of the Arcade Building at Fifteenth and Market Streets. His secretary asked the purpose of my visit. I was embarrassed. Just what was my purpose? I could have told her that I wanted to discuss her employer's trial and conviction for pushing the sheriff into an irrigation ditch in Colorado. I don't remember what I said but it confused her. She went into his office and closed the door. Finally she came out and, leaving the door open, beckoned me to enter.

Lucian Hugh Alexander looked at me across the neat blotter on his desk. He was dressed in a tweed business suit and I immediately noticed his collar. It was the latest style and I had spent hours hunting for one like it. The turned-down front edges came so close together the knot of his necktie barely showed. I had finally found collars like this at Jacob Reed's expensive haberdashery on Chestnut Street.

"I drove the bed wagon last summer for the White Bear gulls," I told him—rather abruptly, I fear.

The name seemed to light a spark in his eyes but he did not ask me to sit down.

"That was not an attractive investment," he replied, leaning back in his chair and glancing up at the ceiling.

"We cowboys wondered whether the high-collared bloods had more money than brains," I admitted.

"You see," he continued, ignoring my flippant statement, "two interlocking companies claim all those ranches. There is a bewildering complex of ownership. Each company holds mortgages on the other company's land, and it is difficult to be sure which one has real equity. What did you say your name was?"

I told him.

"Write it down," he said. Standing up, he handed me a pen and watched what I wrote. "That's the name of the compiler of these books." He waved toward a shelf behind him.

I had already noticed the name in gilt letters on the spines of the *Supreme Court Reports* and *Annual Law Digest*. "He's my father," I replied.

"Do sit down," Mr. Alexander said, and I felt more at ease in a chair facing him across the desk. Something was on his mind, and he said abruptly, his eyes twinkling, "We gulls are planning a reunion dinner at Delmonico's in New York. Can you join us? It will not be formal—no ladies. Just black tie. I believe you might surprise some of the high-collared bloods."

At Swarthmore we did not wear white tie and tails until the senior year, but I did have a tuxedo, and as a college freshman I considered Delmonico's the *ne plus ultra* restaurant of the world. For three generations Delmonico's had stood for elegant eating. Owen Wister, in *The Virginian*, devoted a whole chapter to *Frogs' Legs à la Delmonico*. Van Biber in Richard Harding Davis's popular fiction dined at "Del's" with people who were who. The great British connoisseur, Oscar Wilde, dined there as the guest of the internationally known gourmet, Samuel Ward, brother of Julia Ward Howe, author of half a dozen popular books and "The Battle Hymn of the Republic." When Lily Langtree visited New York, Samuel Ward was her escort at Delmonico's. The fabulous New York financier, Diamond Jim Brady, ate there regularly, and O. Henry, whose short stories were very popular with college students, was wined and dined by his publisher at Delmonico's.

The Waldorf-Astoria and Sherry's had both tried and failed to exceed Del's. In 1900 a *nouveau riche* millionaire had given a horseback dinner at Sherry's. The ballroom was overlaid with real sod, and thirty-six guests in white ties and tails, seated on real horses, were served by waiters in pink coats and riding boots. Delmonico's never stooped to such vulgarity but remained, as always, a bastion of conservative good living, proud to appeal only to the upper four hundred, to personages who had arrived. The printed announcement of the White Bear banquet that I received a few days later listed the guests as

Top: *The schoolboy at the tiller. A sailboat and a chimpanzee gave him an abiding interest in mathematics at Cornell.* Bottom: *In 1911 a little mare called Pearl of Great Price carried the camp from Colonia Pacheco on a Sierra Madre pack trip that was stopped by Yaqui Indians. She did not buck or kick, but it was necessary to put a twitch on her lip while packing. The man wearing glasses and "Democrat gloves" is the Mexican spy in this book.*

Facing page, top: *The author sitting in Theodore Roosevelt's favorite armchair on White River Ranch, Colorado—"a chipping sparrow in the eagle's nest."* Bottom: *The summer range on upper White River, Colorado. Cattle will not stay above timberline even when the grass is good, but they get fat at lower elevations. (The man in black hat is the author.) Photo by Lloyd Lewis.* Below: *Longhorns preserved as an endangered species in the Wichita National Forest in Oklahoma. The cowboy in this book tells about driving a herd of longhorns from Rawlins, Wyoming, to the summer range in Colorado. Photos by author.*

Above: *Green River just south of the Ferry.* Facing page, top: *The ferry, sufficiently long for a four-horse rig. Note the wire overhead which permitted the ferryman to point the boat up or downstream so the current would push it across the river.* Bottom: *Crossing badlands south of Dead Man's Bench. The roads were not hard-surfaced. Pictures given author by railway agent W. A. Banks in 1913.*

Facing page, top: *A short hitch as teamster for the 4th U.S. Cavalry on the Mexican border gave the author a lifelong respect and affection for mules.* Bottom: *An insurrecto's prestige often depended on the number of his cartridges. One man, swimming the Rio Grande on horseback, slipped from the saddle to help his horse, and the weight of the ammunition dragged him to the bottom, where he was drowned.* Above: *Machine gunners behind the hidden loopholes along the side of his camouflaged freight car enabled Díaz to send soldiers and supplies past sharpshooting insurrectos on the desert, but this did not prevent the tracks from being torn up after the train passed.*

Mr. and Mrs. T. E. Sickles. Mr. Sickles is sitting beside an enlarged picture of the first bridge across the Missouri River. He designed and built this for the Union Pacific Railroad. The schoolboy's family and the Sickles' were close friends for three generations. This gave the schoolboy an interest in the construction of railroads across the Plains described in this book.

Facing page: *Insurrectos did not wear chaps. For protection when riding through desert thorns, many wore leggings. Some resembled the tops of Wellington boots.* Below, top: *The bullet-riddled Guadalupe Mission. During the entire battle the "spy" in this book was across the street from this building. He thought that the padres were defending their building but heard later that a company of soldiers was with them.* Bottom: *Making deals behind Madero's headquarters. Photo by author.*

Above: *Mexican flags fly in front
of Madero's rebel headquarters.
Photo by author.* Bottom: *Taking
this picture of a Diaz soldier
caused author's arrest for spying.*
Facing page: *Madero's
headquarters stood on this level
bit of land below the Rio Grande.
To capture him the enemy had to
come along the narrow trail
giving him time to escape to the
United States, across the river.*

Facing page, top: *An insurrecto encampment out of sight of the main road. Blankets on mesquite bushes furnished shade during heat of day, and could be pulled down for a cover at night. From El Paso Public Library.* Bottom: *A guerrilla bivouac. Note sentry at upper left-hand corner spying over top of ridge for possible approaching enemy. From a distance these camps were difficult to observe. The bedrolls looked like big rocks and the picketed horses might be grazing animals. From El Paso Public Library.* Below: *Hermann Hagedorn on his trip to Meeker, Colorado, in 1908, took this never before published picture of the stagecoach passing a freight outfit on what was called the "government road," although it was not much of a road. The schoolboy worked at a relay station for changing horses that year and he describes his experiences.* Middle: *To interest investors in the White Bear Land & Livestock Company, twenty-six Eastern capitalists came to inspect the properties and surrounding range. Many horses were driven in for them to ride and each horse had to be saddled to be sure it was broken. This one failed to pass the examination.*

Bottom: *Theodore Roosevelt said that one man he wanted to meet in Colorado was A. G. Wallihan, the photographer who took this picture of a mountain lion leaping toward him. Roosevelt accepted the picture as genuine and wrote an introduction for the book in which it was published. The cowboy-author of this book knew Wallihan well and was not so sure. Nature faking was popular and common in those days.*

Top: *The schoolboy photographed several genuine western pioneers. This is Red-Wash Jones. A snapshot of Skull-Creek Jones might have broken his camera lens.*
Bottom: *This elkhorn pyramid photographed during Custer's 1874 expedition was reported to be 12 or 15 feet high when built, but it had settled to 5 or 6 feet. Photo from South Dakota State Historical Society.*

"Minty," "Sandy," "Squire," "Ginger," and all the rest, adding as a surprise "Casey's Unknown," who would read a short paper at the dinner.

A trip to New York was almost as exciting for me as a trip to Colorado. I registered at the Waldorf and enjoyed watching the lobby full of college boys in bulgy raccoon coats. They were talking about the Yale-Harvard game. It was already dark when I walked up Fifth Avenue, passing young townsmen wearing high silk hats. They tapped their walking sticks in a manner that attracted attention and I suspected that most of them were impersonating their idea of New York aristocracy. At Forty-fourth Street I entered Delmonico's. An ornate marquee extended to the street so that guests could alight from hansom cabs without getting wet on rainy days. From the well-lighted entry hall a side doorway led to the darkened café. I glanced in, smelled rich cigar smoke, and saw white shirt fronts behind many small tables. It occurred to me that I knew western saloons quite well, but had never before looked inside an eastern one.

"Good evening, Mr. Phillips," a dignified voice in the darkened room greeted a customer.

In the gloom I saw the white muttonchop whiskers of a pompous barkeeper greeting a guest. I thought to myself that this sounded proper for Mr. Van Bibber in the storybook, but was very different from the Meeker, Colorado, barkeep's "Howdy, Skully."

A voice at my side, courteous but positive, told me, "Sir, the White Bear dinner is served on the second floor."

A servant showed me upstairs to a room that resembled what one might expect to find in a well-to-do private home rather than in a public restaurant. It was not large. Handsome drapes hung at the windows. Between them the marble mantle over a fireplace was adorned with two artificial candles on each side of a Ming statuette. Above it the portrait of a woman in balloon-sleeved dress looked down on me from an elaborately ornamented picture frame. Black-tied White Bears were already greeting and talking to one another around a long table set with ornate plates and ranks of forks, knives, and spoons in military order.

Mr. Alexander spied me at once and introduced me to group after group as "Casey's Unknown." "You are already acquainted with him, I'm sure. He was on the trip with us."

The men looked at me with puckered eyebrows. Finally one said, "My word! He's Jimmie of the bed wagon, and I took notes on the things he said because I wanted to tell my children how a real cowboy talked."

Our dinner started with littleneck clams in chipped ice, followed by soup. Somebody across the table said, "Our wives would be glad to know we are dining at Delmonico's without wine."

"Tut! Tut!" I heard the Reverend "Minty" say.

I'm glad I do not remember the names of the men seated at my right and left because their conversation was peculiar. The one at my right began. "Did you notice the dinner plates trimmed blue and gold, featuring the British royal crest? They were removed before the fish course was served."

"Yes," I replied as I leaned back so the man at my left could join us.

"I looked J. D. Husted up in Dunn & Bradstreet," the man at my left replied, "and what do you think he is worth?"

"Those plates are just for show," the man at my right continued. "They are too fine to eat on."

"Yes," replied the man on my left. "You may not believe it, but Dunn & Bradstreet don't even list J. D."

I was getting a little confused. Each man seemed to be talking to himself through me without waiting for a reply.

"Delmonico's is not what it used to be," the man on my right continued. "My father has told me that the canvasback duck they used to serve here beat anything in Paris."

"To hear Husted talk, you'd think him a man of means," the left-side man declared.

"Canvasback had exquisite flavor from the wild celery they ate in Chesapeake Bay. Wild celery, you know, is a tapelike weed that floats on the surface. It sometimes clogs the screws on steamboats. The shipping interests have destroyed the weed and with it the tasty canvasbacks are gone."

This one-sided conversation was interrupted by a waiter who served us excellent cuts of roast beef.

"Plebeian fare," exclaimed the man at my left. "The Knickerbocker bar serves this as free lunch with a glass of beer. Any roast beef, even the best cuts, lack the epicurian seasoning that makes Delmonico's famous."

Then an odd coincidence brought the two independent speakers together. For the first time they addressed each other instead of talking to themselves through me. Dishes of mousse for dessert had been placed in front of us. The flavor, evidently Delmonico's original, perplexed both men. One of them moistened the tip of his nose to refine the flavor, and he exchanged a questioning glance with the other. At last they had an interest vital to them both, and worthy of mutual consideration.

This detailed investigation of flavor, as well as the entire dinner, were experiences for a schoolboy to remember, but two events next day remain even more vividly in my mind. My sister Gertrude had received a fine award from the Philadelphia Academy of Fine Arts and I had brought a message to an artist in a studio on Twenty-third Street. Walking down Fifth Avenue in the morning, the broad sidewalk seemed strangely empty, and I turned west on Twenty-ninth Street to Broadway. This street was almost completely deserted. There was nobody in front of the long row of formal brownstone houses except two or three young fellows clustered around a streetside table. As I walked closer I noticed that a man behind the table deftly manipulated three thimbles and a white pill.

"The hand is quicker than the eye, gentlemen," he said, and I stopped to watch.

The man showed us the three thimbles, covered the pill with one of them, moved all three quickly on the table and dared us to bet, one dollar against his five, that we could not locate the pill. A bystander beside me laid down a dollar bill and pointed to a thimble. The pill was underneath and the dealer dealt the man five crisp bills.

"Bet you can't do it again, sir," the dealer said as he shifted the thimbles deftly once more.

Again the player beside me won a handful of bills. This was interesting. I watched the dealer and noticed that I could spot the pill in every shift of thimbles. Here, certainly, was a chance to make money along with the young fellow who was doing so well. Fortunately for me, I had only sufficient money for this trip and gambling never appealed to me. I walked on and, to my surprise, the dealer immediately folded up his table. With it under his arm, he and the players walked rapidly away. At the corner they stopped, looked apprehensively up the cross street, and then hurried on. For the first time, I realized that the whole performance had been planned to swindle me.

On Twenty-third Street many artists rented studios. The buildings were low and skylights on the top floors gave ample lighting throughout the day. I climbed up some three flights of stairs at the address called for on my note. The door stood open and I saw a dozen students sketching a cowboy who stood on a low platform. He wore a stiff-brimmed William S. Hart sombrero and a brilliant silk neckerchief. His chaps were strapped on backward. I watched the students, young men and women, working diligently. From time to time one would hold out a pencil at arm's length, measure something he or she saw, and continue drawing.

"Why does your model wear his chaps backward?" I asked the instructor.

"Backward," he replied incredulously. "What do you mean? They can't be on backward. Surely, a man always buckles his belt in front!"

This incident ended my New York trip. Although I wanted to go west again the next summer and work as a cowboy, I needed the extra credits to become a regular student at Swarthmore in the fall. Therefore I went to the Cornell summer school and registered for three courses: western history, psychology, and algebra. Mathematics was a specified requirement for entrance to Swarthmore. The hour the algebra course met conflicted with the western history lectures that I especially wanted to hear. This perplexed me, but I met a sophisticated student who told me to register for both, attend the history lectures, and be tutored to pass the algebra examinations without going to class.

"A tutor named Cony Sturgus," he said, and I hope I remember his name almost correctly, "conducts a tutoring class in a building down the trolley track below campus. His schoolroom contains a blackboard and long table with chairs around it. At one end he seats a chimpanzee named Al, in cap and gown. The tutor is formal. He wears a frock coat and high collar, but don't let his looks frighten you. He begins the course by saying, 'Students: May I introduce Al, your colleague—Al Gebra. At the end of this course Al will be able to pass the examinations. If you can't, don't blame me.'"

Perhaps the friendly student was kidding me. However, I did as well as the chimp—or almost as well, I hope. I passed the examination, but the western history lectures left me so numb from an excess of dates and unrelated facts I never took another history course during my four undergraduate years in college. In the final examination at Cornell I must have flunked at least one question. It asked for a list of the personal characteristics of modern Americans that could be attributed to our nation's frontier experience. Instead of repeating what the professor had told us about the traditions of democracy and political liberalism that he said were characteristic of the West, I made the mistake of analyzing the mental attitudes of Dee Wilkins, Hawkshaw, Tricky Biscuits, Skull-Crick Jones, and End-Gate Edna. These were not schoolbook westerners, but a tolerant professor, or his assistant who marked the papers, gave me a passing grade, based, I suspect, on other routine questions. Perhaps the professor hoped to discourage me from taking more of his courses.

Two other incidents at Cornell that summer stick in my memory. One was the noontime music from the campanile playing the Molly McGuire rag as we went happily to lunch, and the other a sailing experience on Lake Cayuga. I liked to sail, and with three fellow students we anchored one afternoon and swam ashore at Taughannock Falls.

"How high do you think it is to the top of that cataract?" one of the boys asked. Then, with his thumb held at ground level and his fingers pointed at the top of the falls, he estimated the degrees in the angle formed by his hand. Next he paced the distance to the foot of the falls, and with a mathematical formula in his head he wrote a few figures on a piece of paper and concluded, "It's over two hundred feet high."

This may have been a theatrical act of my sailing companion but it gave me a new interest in mathematics. Thus a sailboat has enabled me to tell fellow academicians truthfully that at Ithaca I received the stimulus that lead me to take the course in astronomy taught by "Doc" Miller at Swarthmore, a course that has given me lifelong satisfaction and delight. With my Cornell credits I returned to Swarthmore in the fall of 1910 and became for the first time a regular student.

11

Vamoose

There's a long, long trail a-winding,
Into the land of my dreams,
Where the nightingales are singing
And a white moon beams
—Stoddard King

A new national issue interested many undergraduates at the
time I entered Swarthmore. It was called "conservation,"
which later generations changed to "ecology." This concerned
the West I knew, and it had suddenly become a political issue.
Congress accused President Taft of covering up fraudulent
coal-land claims in Alaska. The frauds were exposed by Gifford
Pinchot, an officer in the Division of Forestry, and Taft dismissed him not for exposing the frauds, Taft was careful to say, but
for insubordination.

Pinchot, out of office, established a School of Forestry at Yale
and undergraduates in many colleges became interested in the
possibilities of a new profession. Forestry—certainly not the
history I had endured at Cornell—seemed to promise me a
good life in the open spaces Out West. To prepare for this I
majored in biology at Swarthmore. Professor Spencer Trotter
headed that department, and a thoughtful concession of his
involved me in a Mexican revolution.

Spencer Trotter had been a young man during the wild-
Indian days. Some of his personal friends had served in the
Wyoming Sioux wars, and he always seemed to regret that he,
in his own youth, had missed their adventures. Now, a generation later, the United States cavalry was patrolling the border
to guard against forays of Mexican *insurrectos*, and some of the
old, exciting cavalry days might be repeated. An amusing prank
by two Swarthmore upperclassmen entangled me in the border
cavalry and also in the Mexican revolution.

It is always amazing how an inconsequential act may lead to a big event. The two upperclassmen decided to steal some pies from the college kitchen. One planned to slip into the kitchen after the cooks left for the night and hand the pies out a window to the other. That night, by some coincidence, President Swain went to Parrish Hall for some papers in his office and saw the boy at the kitchen window. When Swain walked toward him, the boy fled and the one inside handed the pies out to the president.

"If thee will call at my office at ten o'clock tomorrow morning," Prexy told him, "I'll give thee back thy pies."

Strangely enough, this incident was the first step that led me into the Mexican revolution, and President Swain deserves the blame—or credit! He decided that the college should have a night watchman, and the newly employed guard decided to carry a pistol. A night or two later my roommate, Lloyd Lewis, who later became the renowned Civil War historian, walked with me up the tree-arched asphalt promenade from town to Parrish Hall after enjoying a before-bedtime ice cream soda at Vic Shirer's drugstore. We saw the watchman standing on the pillared portico of Parrish Hall and Lloyd said, "Let's have some fun. Let's see what he will do if we pretend to be slipping up on him. You hide behind the oak on that side of the walk. I'll hide on this side."

We separated, each hiding behind one of the big trees. Then we peeked around the trunks, ran toward the guard, and hid behind the next tree closer to him. The guard watched us and seemed to be nervous, so, with boyish delight, we repeated the performance, getting closer to him tree by tree. I saw the guard draw his pistol. This was really exciting. Each of us ran one tree closer, and the guard fired. The flash of his pistol showed that he shot into the ground but we raced away into the darkness around the college astronomy observatory.

"Now we can always say," Lloyd laughed when we got our breath, "that we have been under fire, just like Captain Macklin in Richard Harding Davis's book. Davis was a student here at Swarthmore, you know. Soldiers of fortune became real men to me after reading that book."

In this roundabout way President Swain introduced me to *Captain Macklin,* and that fiction made Latin-American revolutionists real men to me. I was sure the age of warfare must soon pass; civilized man would not continue to engage in such brutal and senseless destruction. Down in Mexico I might observe this phenomenon before it disappeared forever along with our forests, our wild life, corruption in government, and other calamities that we were told could be avoided by giving votes to women.

My desire to see Mexico increased as I read newspaper accounts of the revolution during the winter, and an odd event in the early spring of 1911 brought it to a climax. In those days the Swarthmore campus was mowed with a machine pulled by horses wearing big sole-leather galoshes to prevent the calks on their horseshoes from tearing up the lawn. I saw these horses coming toward me while I strolled along the boardwalk from Parrish to Wharton Hall. As they clumped past I smelled horse sweat and new-mown grass. This combination brought back to me that first day when Rhoden's longhorns reached quaking-aspen country and began eating lush mountain vegetation. In my imagination I saw Pagoda Peak's brilliant granite spire towering above the inky-black pine forest, heard the sharp bark of conies that live above timberline, and the deep howl of the timber wolf that hushed the coyote chorus while we men slept on the ground beneath the star-spangled sky. Vanished visions of that good life flicked through my mind and I decided to saddle a western horse once more and cross the Rio Grande before the revolution down there ended.

I explained this to Professor Trotter. He obviously understood young men, and he certainly felt a nostalgia for the gone days of Crazy Horse, Sitting Bull, and Rain-in-the-Face. He told me he would give me credit for the whole semester if I passed the midterm examinations and at a later date would read certain books and pass a final examination. My next problem was at home. Neither Father nor Mother approved, but they were sensible and not adamant. I remember a certain smile on Mother's face as she watched me pack my old Thompson saddle in the gunnysack for checking to El Paso.

Mother had not been an adventurous outdoor girl. She had been timid on a family coaching trip through the English lake region. Crossing the high divide from Keswick to Buttermere she and her three daughters climbed down from the four-in-hand to walk, leaving Father, me, the bugler, and the driver on the coachtop for the giddy ride and merry blast of horn while spinning down the final slope. Mother, however, had told her children about early-day experiences when the West was still Out West. Her best girl friend was the daughter of T. E. Sickles, the engineer who built the Union Pacific Railroad bridge across the Missouri at Omaha. In the 1870s, Mr. Sickles took his wife and the two girls to California in his private car. They saw wild buffalo from the train windows. At Salt Lake City, Brigham Young's favorite wife, Amelia Folsom, gave each of the girls a little gift. Mother's was a small agate jewel box. Joaquin Miller recited poems for the travelers, and on the way to Yosemite Valley the driver of the coach imbibed so persistently that Mr. Sickles sat up front beside him, hoping to curtail his drinking. These experiences, no doubt, explained Mother's curious smile as she watched me pack my saddle in the gunnysack.

When I stepped off the train in El Paso I saw no resemblance to the cow towns I remembered in Colorado. The railroad station was an imposing red-brick building with a pillared portico and a bell tower that reminded me of the campanile in Venice. I saw no indication of the revolution reported to be less than a mile away. What in this clean, modern city was the first thing for an eastern college sophomore who had come to study soldiers of fortune to do? I knew that insurrectos under Francisco Madero surrounded the established government army of Porfirio Díaz in Juárez, which was just across the international bridge from El Paso. The United States officially recognized Díaz as president of Mexico. His army, although surrounded, could get supplies from the United States. Madero, the outlaw rebel, was not recognized, and our cavalry patrolled the border to prevent smuggling of supplies to his insurrectos.

I decided to go first to the beleaguered city of Juárez. When I crossed the international bridge, the Mexican customs officer said no word to me that I remember, and I walked up Avenida Santa Fe into a strange new world. The costumes on all the men seemed fantastic. Everybody wore gigantic sombreros, some of straw, some of soft felt. Years later, in the Orient, the crowd wearing *geebalees* in a native market caused me to say, "This reminds me of my first day in Juárez, Mexico, back in 1911."

A rider on a prancing white horse attracted my attention. His

sombrero, embroidered with silver and gold, seemed to be two
feet high and three feet broad. A scarlet saddle blanket contrasted vividly with the whiteness of his horse. The man's face
was dark, his beard well trimmed. He wore Wellington boots
and big spurs. His silver-mounted saddle had a large round
horn unlike any I had seen in Colorado or Wyoming. The man
possessed real dignity, seemed unconscious of his spectacular
appearance, and obviously belonged to a culture foreign in the
United States although separated from it by only the Rio
Grande. His fantastic clothes were not a uniform. He was not a
soldier, but was clearly an aristocrat—a real hidalgo, I thought.
Here was a member of the class this revolution hoped to
abolish.

I came to the plaza where broad stone steps led up to the
Guadalupe Mission. The entrance, through an adobe facade,
was flanked by two tall niches. Each contained the statue of a
saint. A courteous self-appointed guide told me one was Saint
Peter, the other Moses. I did not know that Moses was a saint,
but on this trip I had many things to learn. A few steps beyond
the facade a square tower, topped by a roman-arched belfry,
held large copper bells corroded green with age. This picturesque church, built in 1659, was much older than Independence
Hall in my Philadelphia. Here was Captain Macklin's Latin-
American country, not the Out West I knew. Sandbags along
the Mission roof reminded me that the city was under siege
and the padres evidently intended to fight for the preservation
of the gold and silver ornaments on their altars.

At the north side of the Mission a cobblestoned street, Calle
del Comercio, sloped down from a slight elevation. I walked up
it and soon found myself between one-story adobe houses, a
few of them whitewashed. The sun was hot and the glare
dazzling in some places. This western part of Juárez, I learned,
was called *barrio alto,* and at the edge of town I came to a low
barricade where I could see the open country down the slope
beyond. I turned and, walking south along the picket line,
surprised a napping sentry. He jumped to his sandaled feet and
stood at rigid attention with his Mauser at "ground arms." In
this stiff position he stared blankly at the distant desert ridges
where the insurrectos were said to be encamped. His uniform
was of light cotton, like my pajamas. On his head he wore a

patent leather kepi with a little red pompom in front. This
Napoleonic design, its black color, and the tight-fitting nonpor-
ous leather seemed unsuitable for the tropical sun. American
soldiers, when fighting Indians, had worn broad-brimmed felt
hats with holes in the crowns to circulate fresh air. I thought, no
wonder the Mexican people are revolting against rulers who
cling to the European headgear of a hundred years ago.

Many of these soldiers, I had been told, were convicts serving their terms in the army. This small soldier's face was stolid,
dull but not unkind. I felt that he would do what I told him,
and not tell me what I must do. In the days ahead I heard
these infantrymen called *peleles* (insignificant fellows), *pelados*
(ignorant peasants), and *pelones* (a word I failed to find in my
Spanish dictionary). In the books I read they were also called
peones, but I never heard that word used in the Mexican army.
I may not have associated with the right people.

I photographed the soldier standing at attention and walked
south along the low breastworks. As I approached, each picket
snapped to attention facing those barren hills where the insurrectos were supposed to be. The performance was amusing.
The lawless frontier—the Wild West down here—I thought,
has failed to produce men like Hawkshaw, who think "sir" is a
so-and-so not yet born—and thank God for that!

From the picket line where I stood I looked down the slope
to the West and saw at the bottom a manned trench which was
the town's first line of defense. Continuing my walk along the
crest I came to two gun crews firing mountain howitzers. They
paid no attention to me, and after each shot I saw the shell
explode in the distance, making a little white cloud that scattered schrapnel over the enemy-haunted country the pickets
watched so constantly.

The artillerymen seemed to be experimenting with their
pieces. I noticed that they stooped behind each gun when it
was fired and pointed their brown hands at the departing
cannonball. I joined them and, stooping with them, noticed
that by looking along the gun barrel I could glimpse the missile
in the distance when it arched and exploded, making the white
cloud. I saw no enemies below those exploding clouds, but I
knew insurrectos were over there and thought, this is a real
battle, but it is not exciting like the pictures I have seen.

A group of horsemen rode up to us. They were neatly dressed in gray, scarlet-decorated uniforms and Napoleonic shakos. One man's white beard contrasted vividly with his suntanned face. He wore spectacles like mine, and said something to an aide. This officer rode up to me and spoke words in Spanish I could not understand. The perplexed aide returned to the handsome, bearded man who, I realized now, was General Juan J. Navarro, commander of the Mexican army in Juárez. The General turned to a younger aide, a neatly dressed lieutenant about my age or a little older. This officer came to me and, looking down from his horse with a smile that made me like him, spoke again in Spanish. Again I failed to understand a word. The distraught lieutenant shrugged, and with a twinkle in his eyes said, "Vamoose!"

I had already learned sufficient Spanish to know that *vamos* meant "we go" or "let's go," and I suspected that was not what he meant, but certainly this was not the time to discuss the idiom with him. Instead, I vamoosed promptly, glad I was not being taken to the guardhouse. Certainly I had no right to be there on the firing line. My lenient treatment was an example of the old army maxim: "It's better to be caught doing wrong by a major general than by a newly graduated second lieutenant."

Some of the pickets down the line may have suffered for letting me pass. I shall never know. I liked the young aide who spoke to me, and a few days later I hoped he had not been killed when I saw General Navarro surrender alone before a mob shouting for his immediate execution.

To vamoose I walked back downtown along a street between low adobe houses. Children's bright-eyed, smiling faces appeared at open doorways and disappeared as I approached. At some entrances I glimpsed a green patio and heard water splashing. This, I thought, is like Pompeii come to life again. The heat in the street seemed terrific but I was too interested to feel it—much. I soon came to the mission and sat on a bench in the plaza. Overhead, birds in the mulberry trees squawked like quarreling parrots, but I could not see them well enough to be sure. After a short rest I walked past the elaborately advertisied Big Kid Saloon and on to the bullring, where a detachment of soldiers were camped in the arena. They had

been shipped north in a train composed of coaches and boxcars
curiously painted with black and white squares like checker-
boards. These squares were designed to deceive the enemy.
From a distance, a square porthole with a machine gun behind
it resembled one of the harmless black checkerboard squares,
and the machine gunner could fire without being detected.

Back in El Paso that afternoon I went to the Sheldon Hotel
to write my family about the wonders I had seen. A writing
room adjoining the lobby was empty, and I sat there at a desk
never imagining that a new experience in the revolution was
about to occur. I had noticed in the lobby a short man about
my father's age who spoke with a British accent. The clerks
showed him noticeable deference, and I was told in an awed
whisper that he was the war correspondent for *Colliers* and the
New York World. Being unacquainted with journalists, I had
never heard of the famous Jimmie Hare, and in my letter home
I called him "Mr. Herr." I said he was remarkably short-legged
and I would plan some way to outrun him getting a better story
about the war.

While writing my letter, a United States artillery lieutenant
and a man wearing civilian clothes glanced in the door, then
went on, apparently seeking a vacant room. They soon returned and, standing at a table with their backs to me, they
spread out oddly cut slips of paper that each had brought
separately and now matched together to make what appeared
to be a large single sheet. The civilian pointed to spots on the
paper and said something so low I could not understand it. The
lieutenant replied but all I could hear was numbers that meant
nothing to me. Perhaps they noticed my eagerness to overhear,
because the lieutenant nudged the civilian and each man hurriedly rolled up his share of the long slips of paper on the table
and walked briskly to the doorway. Before going out, the
lieutenant paused briefly and looked quickly up and down the
hall, exactly the way I remembered the shellgame gambler had
done in New York after the White Bear banquet.

Obviously I had interrupted some secret communication between Madero's insurrectos and an officer in the United States
army. I, a twenty-year-old stranger in town, was not apt to be a
dangerous informer, but they were taking no chances and
hurried away. In their haste one of the long slips of paper had

dropped behind the table. I retrieved it and left the room as quickly as they had. Safe in the privacy of my own bedroom, I studied that paper carefully. It was part of a hand-drawn map that had been cut up. My piece showed the Díaz gun emplacements on the barricade I had walked along that morning. From these two positions ruled lines were drawn to places not on my section of the map but evidently to proposed sites for insurrecto cannon out in the desert. I was sure now that the man in civilian clothes was an insurrecto artilleryman secretly consulting the professional about setting the elevations on his guns to destroy the howitzers I had watched on the barrio alto. The portion of the map I had found, or any of the other separate segments, would not be incriminating, but the United States artillery officer obviously did not want to be seen communicating with an insurrecto. I wondered, and still wonder, whether he was personally sympathetic with the revolution or had confidential Army orders contrary to the Taft administration's official support of the Díaz regime. Perhaps he was merely a peacetime professional eager to observe from a distance how artillery performed in combat.

This gave me an idea. I might beat Mr. Hare by revealing federal double-dealing with the insurrectos, or I might get war secrets from the insurrectos which Mr. Hare would never have. I knew that one of the cavalry troops patrolling the border was stationed at Old Fort Bliss, only about two miles west from town. Perhaps I could learn something from a trooper there which would beat the famous war correspondent. The fort could be reached by a city trolley to the smelter.

Next morning, with a light blanket from my sleeping bag draped over my left arm, I rode the streetcar to what the conductor called "Old Fort Bliss parade ground." I got off. The conductor pulled an overhead cord signaling the motorman, who tapped his bell three times and drove away, leaving me where the trolley tracks crossed a hot, dusty flat lacking vegetation of any kind. The fort, less than a hundred yards away, consisted of two low-roofed adobe buildings separated by a breezeway.

I did not know just what information I wanted or where to go for it. One of the fort buildings was obviously the troopers' kitchen and mess hall, the other their one-room sleeping quarters. Inside the open door I saw folding army cots and a locked

gun rack. The long gallery on both buildings faced the parade
ground. Off-duty soldiers sat along the floor, their legs, in
canvas leggings, dangling over the edge. A sentry stood in front
of a small house beyond the mess hall. This was obviously the
commanding officer's quarters. Certainly I could not get the
information I sought there, and it would be unwise to consult
the off-duty soldiers loafing along the porch. On my side of the
dusty parade ground I saw two army wagons. At the tongue of
each one, four mules were eating from an attached feed trough.
A teamster stood beside the nearest wagon and I walked over
to him. He seemed willing to talk and I learned a great deal.
Yes, Troop E of the 4th Cavalry, stationed here, patrolled the
border, but occasionally was sent on errands to town. On those
days wagonloads of supplies were smuggled into the insurrecto
camp.

Evidently the artillery lieutenant at the Sheldon Hotel was
not the only army officer who sympathized with the revolution.
This interested me. Using the vernacular I had learned in
Colorado, I asked, "Who in hell drives them wagonloads of
supplies?"

"I dunno," the teamster replied, pushing his broad-brimmed
hat low over his eyes. The gesture seemed to imply something
clandestine, and he added, "But they's a speakeasy on the river
this side o' the smelter. Insurrectos cross a foot-stick there.
They come for beer and they probably knows."

I was not sure what he meant by a "foot-stick" but I was sure
I could cross on one if insurrectos did.

"I wooden go no furder if you got money on you," the man
said, spitting thoughtfully on the ground and covering it pen-
sively with his foot. "They's no law—Mex' ner 'Merican—in
them bastards' camp. That's a rev'lution. Ever' man fer his own
self. Dog eat dog."

Here was the real chance to learn something about Madero's
plans and operations that Jimmie Hare would never learn in
the Sheldon Hotel. Most of my cash was hidden in a money
belt like the one Captain Macklin had worn as a soldier of
fortune, and I was glad I had brought my light blanket. With it
over my arm I walked away.

The speakeasy on the bank of the Rio Grande was a ten-by-
fourteen-foot shack so fragile a few men could carry it away. I
stepped inside, saw a plywood bar decorated with a painting of

a matador teasing a bull, and thought what a grand souvenir that would make for my room at college. The barkeep nodded reassuringly, and I saw a lone man sitting on a bench across the little room. I sat down beside him. He was big, strong, and silent. Dressed in Levis and cotton shirt like a cowboy, he answered my attempts at conversation with monosyllables. I suggested a beer. He seemed grateful. We stood up and he towered above me at that fantastic bar. Here was a genuine soldier of fortune—not quite like Captain Macklin, but surely authentic. After our second beer he agreed to take me to his camp, where I could join Madero's American Legion—really a foreign legion commanded by Giuseppe Garibaldi, grandson of the Italian Liberator. What an opportunity to scoop Mr. Hare by learning military plans!

This saloon must have been quasi-legal. The back door was only a few steps from the "foot-stick," which I learned was a suspension bridge with a few loose boards for a narrow floor and a single wire for a handrail. A marshal in plain clothes stood there on guard. My companion greeted him with a nod toward me and explained, "He's one o' us—newly 'listed in 'Merican Legion."

The marshal looked at me carefully and let us pass. I did not realize until later that, by becoming a soldier of fortune, I had given up my United States citizenship, might never be able to return, and was certainly due for plenty of trouble ahead. Out on the swaying boards I found it a bit dizzying over the creeping brown water of the Rio Grande, but I remember more distinctly stepping down off the bridge onto foreign soil, ground that knew no law: *"Mex' ner 'Merican, ever' man fer his own self. Dog eat dog."*

It dawned on me for the first time that here was a community of brigands, pirates, outlaws. Some called them idealists fighting for the freedom sought by all mankind. I was also sure that I would get a better story than Mr. Hare could ever find in El Paso. Besides, my money would not last forever, and living here would be cheap.

12

A Soldier of Fortune

There is rock to the left and rock to the right
And low, lean thorn between,
And ye may hear a breech-bolt snick
Where never a man is seen.
  —Rudyard Kipling

My new friend led the way along a well-beaten path that skirted the Rio Grande. The horse tracks in the loose dirt reminded me of roundup cow ponies. I saw no shod hoofprints. Our trail circled up a wash onto a bench that appeared at first to be flat but was really cut and crosscut by intricate depressions, all excellent hiding places where I suspected the insurrectos must be encamped. I knew that the so-called American Legion was commanded by Garibaldi's grandson. To make conversation I asked if he was in camp.

"That son-of-a-bitch dassent come to our camp," my friend replied, as he kicked a sticky black greasewood stalk out of the trail. "We take orders from no man. With us it's strictly business. We get what we can get when the gettin's good. 'Tween times we live light."

This remark put an unpleasant idea in my head. I did not want to be "good gettin's" for him come night. Then, as we walked farther into the confused complex of rocky, brush-dotted draws, I realized that in this lawless country no robber need wait for night. We came to a boulder as tall as a man, and my companion led the way around it and over a brush-covered ridge into a wider but apparently uninhabited draw. I hesitated to show my fear, so I followed him with apparent confidence. Looking ahead, I saw two men walking toward us. They carried no guns—but three men, all bigger than I was, needed none. As we came closer I noticed that their faces, under horizontal hat brims, were grim, not smiling. When face to face we all stopped. There was no introduction, no names were mentioned. This was like the good manners I had learned in Colorado cow camps. My friend said simply, "He's joinin' us."

We shook hands solemnly. One of the men said gravely, "We'll see yez at mess."

That remark was encouraging, but I was still suspicious. I felt like an intruder in a strange community. Without another word, the four of us walked on until we came to a black man sitting on the ground beside a low mesquite. I shall never forget the whites of that man's eyes, set in an unusually square black face. Over his head a *sarape* draped the bush shading his *petate*, or tule bed mat. At this latitude a man seldom needed a blanket at night. When he did, the sarape shade could be pulled down for a cover. On other mesquites beyond the black man I saw many more sarapes on the bushes and rolls of bedding I had supposed to be rocks. Men lay on the ground among them, and it dawned on me that I stood at the edge of an invisible insurrecto encampment. The scattered horses I had supposed to be foraging on the rocky hills were really picketed near fighting men. I thought of Sir Walter Scott's description of James Fitz-James when his enemy, Rhoderick Dhu,

> whistled shrill,
> And was answered from the hill.
> Every tuft of broom gave life
> To plaided warrior armed for strife.
> That whistle garrisoned the glen
> At once with full five hundred men.

Here on the Mexican border full five hundred equally warlike guerrillas were bivouacked, enjoying a siesta while waiting for a whistle from Francisco Madero. I had read about a Spanish smuggler hideaway in Prosper Merimée's *Carmen*. Richard Harding Davis, in *Captain Macklin*, described a Honduran rebel rendezvous. The genuine encampment before me, not a writer's imaginary scene, filled me with wonder and excitement.

"I suspect you think I'm an Englishman," the big square-faced black said as he extended his hand to shake.

Considering his color, this was the last thing in my mind but I did not contradict him. He evidently wanted to talk and his accent was English—very good, high-class English. "I'm a Honduran," he said, swelling out his big chest with pride, "not a Britisher at all."

I nodded agreement and he seemed eager for an audience. Obviously a talkative, uneducated man, he was well informed superficially and showed no sign of subservience. He looked me over, up and down, and continued speaking with his unusual accent: "William Walker was a great filibuster, about your size, a little man, no larger than yourself but brave and active. I was about to observe," the black continued in his stilted English, "Walker might be a good man for you to emulate. He became president of Nicaragua until Vanderbilt's shipping company euchered him out of office, but he would not quit. Finally got shot in Honduras. Those were great days!"

The black man paused for a reassuring look from me. My three silent companions had walked away and I felt a little safer without them. The black, evidently convinced that I was an attentive listener, beamed with friendliness. His remarkable eyes sparkled as he continued. "I fought with Zelaya, really a great soldier on Mosquito Coast. You've heard of him? Good! Two years ago the United States Navy butted in, like Vanderbilt did, yes. Zelaya disappeared, but he's still alive, and he'll return. Then I'll fight for him once more. In the meantime, I fight here, Viva Madero! You understand?"

A lean, lanky white man joined us. His petate lay under a nearby mesquite. He seemed as anxious as the black to talk, and began with a complaining southern drawl, "We-all a-bin a-settin' here, stock still f'r thirty days, with Juárez a-lay'n thar in plain sight, ready f'r us-ens to pick. If li'l ol' sawed-off Madero don't do suthink right now, quick, Orozco'll learn that Frenchified ignoramus how to run a rev'lution."

This was the first complaint I had heard about Madero, the first hint that his whistle would not produce an eager insurrecto behind every tuft of sage, give fighting life to every mesquite, and garrison the badlands. The name Orozco was new to me, but in the days ahead I would hear Pascual Orozco mentioned often. The black man, having lost his audience, began reading a tattered book.

"If Orozco don't," the newcomer drawled, "I'm a-quittin'.
We-all 'av stood about all we k'n stand. No use a-wastin' mo'
good time a-settin' here jest to hep him. They's two better
revlutions in Cent'l Amerikee right now, both bettern this un.
I'm f'r goin' thar. Yes, pronto!"

I never knew this man's name and always called him "You,"
but I somehow felt safer with him and the black than I had with
the silent man who "enlisted" me. My judgment, I learned
later, was not valid. At this time, however, I decided to camp
here with these talkers, and I spread my little blanket over a
nearby mesquite where the ground seemed level enough for
sleeping. In the blanket's shade I found the dry air surprisingly
cool. A third man walked past us, going toward the river with
an empty bucket. He clumped along in rundown cowboy boots
that resembled mine. In a monotone he sang to himself:

> Viva Madero y Orozco *también*
>   We're gonna take Chihuahua
> But we don't know when.
>   Come all ye insurrectos
> Who can raise a white man's thirst
>   We're gonna take Chihuahua
> But it's Juárez first.

The complainer I called "You" looked at the singer's retreating back and with a superior smile drawled, "Hark that no
'count blabber-guts."

His description sounded somehow more devastating than the
usual profanity. The black, engrossed in his tattered book,
made no comment. I was curious and wondered what a professional soldier of fortune liked to read. Looking sharply, I saw
that this freebooter was studying Buckle's *History of Civiliza-
tion in England*. Certainly brigands, bandits, and pirates, I
thought, are as unpredictable and as different from one another
as the rest of us.

If there was any regimentation or discipline in Madero's
encampment, I saw no sign of it. During the long days ahead I
was never challenged. No picket ever stopped me. Was this
the equality, the democracy promised by his revolution? I

wandered at will through the scattered bivouacs under the vast
sky—picturesque days sweet with the smell of creosote bush,
wood smoke, and horses. The only uniforms on Madero's insurrectos were cartridge belts. Men who could afford it wore three
outside their nondescript jackets—one around the waist and
one over each shoulder, making a cross on the soldier's body.
When loaded with cartridges, called *balas* by insurrectos, a
man carried quite a load. One rider dressed in this fashion
tried to swim the Rio Grande. In the deep water he helped his
swimming horse by slipping from the saddle. The heavy balas
dragged him to the bottom, where he was drowned.

I found the rank and file insurrectos were friendly fellows
wearing gigantic straw hats and sandals. They did not care for
my Bull Durham or the Lorillard's Beechnut chewing tobacco I
carried in a heavy ten-cent paper package. Instead, they carried cotton sacks filled with crisp brown tobacco leaves that
they crushed with their hands and wrapped with cornhusks
into *cigarros*. I marveled at their skill in cutting these wrappers
with quick strokes of razor-sharp knives. Most insurrectos carried *esclarajos* (a word I could not find in the dictionary), which
consisted of pieces of flint and steel used to ignite a bit of
cottonlike fluff they carried in empty .30-30 cartridges for lighting their smokes.

These sociable insurrectos let me examine their rifles. Most
were .30-30 Winchesters, but I saw .45-70's and one
hexagonal-barreled .45-90. Unlike the "humane" cupronickel-
jacketed projectiles used in the United States Army Krags and
Springfields, the bullets for these insurrecto guns were "soft-
nosed," designed to dilate on contact with flesh, making ugly
wounds. One insurrecto who called himself a *Jesu-cristero* (fol-
lower of Jesus) showed me with religious pride how he had
filed a deep *cruz*, or cross, on the tip of his bullets so they
would flatten out and make a deadly tear on the body of an
enemy.

Filled with curiosity, I prowled through Madero's entire
encampment, even through the *vivaque* of the almost naked
Tarahumara whose only weapons were bows and arrows. These
Indians were very different from those I had seen in Colorado.
They did not braid their hair. One man wore a pair of pants

with the legs tied around his neck. All the men's feet were bare and calloused like horses' hooves. I was told that a match could be struck on the soles, but am not sure about that.

Members of Madero's American Legion dressed and looked like the cowboys I had met working for the big outfits in the western United States. Biscuits would have felt at home with them, but none I saw gambled or played cards. A legionnaire told me in blunt-tongued English, "We got no money, none of us, until we take Juárez. Playin' cards on credit ain't no good. The winner, ever'body owes money to, is sure to get shot in the back come the first fight. Get me?"

"No fight, no loot. When will Madero get goin'?" I heard this complaint many times.

Two English-speaking artillerymen showed me their cannons with pride, and said they were handmade in a captured railroad shop. Steel axles from a locomotive had been cut and bored to take three-inch cannonballs. The guns were mounted on the running gears of sturdy farm wagons. I was sure I had seen one of these artillerymen with the United States lieutenant in the Sheldon Hotel, but thought it unwise to renew a questionable acquaintance. He had evidently not learned how to sight his pieces accurately and seemed to have little confidence in them. Instead, he showed me hand grenades he had made. Each one was a stick of dynamite with a half dozen thirty-penny nails tied around it. He had wired this explosive assembly to a light board shaped like the back of a hairbrush so it could easily be thrown.

"With these," the man said, glancing confidently at his companion, "we'll drive the greasers out of them trenches at the foot of the slope. When we get to the edge of town, we'll blow a hole in the side of the first adobe house. That's easy done! We're *scienced* ever' bit as good as them *cientificos*." (That sarcastic Mexican nickname for the better-educated, better-armed Díaz men had puzzled me. Now I understood it.)

"Instead of runnin' up streets where soldiers on the roofs can shoot us," the second artilleryman said, "we'll tunnel from house to house. That way a man can pick up a little spending money, and when he comes to a store the gettin' is really good. But if Madero don't let us go soon, every white man here'll quit and head for Central America."

Always I heard that complaint about Madero. He was a man of peace who wanted to negotiate for the surrender of Juárez, but his army wanted to fight and prosper on the loot. I decided to go see Madero, if only from a distance. His headquarters was west of our encampment, separated from it by a precipitous ridge five or six hundred feet high. The trail to it followed the Rio Grande, traversing the bluff where the river cuts that ridge. As I walked along the trail I met parties of insurrectos carrying guns slung over their shoulders. They were coming back after visiting Little Sawed-Off. Others, going in my direction on horseback, passed me, whipping their mounts with the flats of their swords. The path was so narrow I stepped aside to let them by, and I noticed that their horses were small compared to northern cow ponies. Few stood twelve hands high and none I saw weighed a thousand pounds. They all seemed thin and underfed. One that shuffled along the trail ahead of me was so weak its hocks knocked together.

Where the trail rounded the bluff I looked down on the peculiar geography that had prompted Madero to select this place for his headquarters. Here the Rio Grande, which flowed south through New Mexico, turned east, becoming the boundary between Texas and Mexico. Across the river from where I stood I could see the office buildings and brick furnaces of an American smelter. On the Mexican side of the river, just beyond the bluff, I saw half a dozen or more square adobe houses on a flat of about a hundred acres. Here was a tiny bit of Mexico isolated from the rest of that country by the bluff. A wire fence across the flat marked the border of the United States.

This small area of Mexico below me was alive with men and horses. On one adobe residence, larger than the others, I noticed half a dozen flats—red, white, and green. They decorated an awning at the front of Madero's "White House." From that building he could watch the trail on which I had come, and if he saw the enemy's army approaching, a few steps would enable him to escape through the fence into the United States.

I walked down to the little flat. Mingling with the men and horses, I came to the decorated house. The front door was two steps above the ground and there was a window at each side. Adjoining the house I saw a low adobe hut with a dirt-roofed

pórtico, evidently for Madero's servants. The equality cham-
pioned by his revolution did not rule out menial help.

Insurrecto chieftains wearing gigantic hats and crossed cartridge belts rode up frequently and dismounted at Madero's
door. Some knocked and went in. Others were met at the
doorway by Little Sawed-Off himself, in a white suit. Guests
who stood on the first step up from the ground did not tower
above him. Once or twice Madero stepped down and walked
past me on his way to another house. He reminded me of a
professor at Swarthmore, a thoughtful, unassuming man.

Here at headquarters I first saw Pascual Orozco, a leader
very different from Madero. His clothes were not distinctive
but he stood almost a head taller than the other men and his
voice had authority. The Spanish language I had heard at
Swarthmore was soft, lisping, often musical, lacking the rugged
strength and masculinity of the Germanic tongues. Until I
heard Orozco, I could never imagine Spanish being spoken by
the cutlass-carrying soldiers and crossbowmen under Cortés,
Balboa, and Pizarro. Such a ladylike language seemed out of
place in the mouths of brutish sixteenth-century fighting men
who had conquered the world. Orozco's Spanish was coarse,
vigorous, ungrammatical. He accented the wrong syllables, but
when he spoke the men around him listened. I understood why
the soldiers of fortune I had met hoped he would take command away from Little Sawed-Off. I also thought that if I had
to choose one or the other as a permanent companion, I'd take
Madero for congenial company but not for an immediate military victory.

In front of Madero's house some boys, many of them
younger than I was, raced their horses back and forth. The roar
of their hooves must have disturbed Madero. To attract attention, each rider whipped his mount into a furious gallop. Then,
with his wicked spade bit, he would jerk the frantic beast to a
sliding stop, whip him to run again, and jerk him to a stop once
more. Bloody foam hung from the sweating animals' mouths. I
had never seen horses abused quite so badly. Hawkshaw was
brutal with horses, but he seemed gentle compared to these
youthful revolutionists. For them I could not yell "Viva!" and I
was glad to start back to my bivouac. Luckily, I got there at an
opportune moment.

Walking toward the bushes where I had established my petate, I saw five or six horses saddled with the curious big-horned Mexican rigs. The men standing at the horses' heads wore gigantic embroidered sombreros, and cartridge belts crisscrossed their bodies. My black Honduran friend was talking to them in rapid Spanish. I noticed the whites of his eyes.

"Cheese it!" a nearby voice whispered to me. The man I called "You," with a sly movement of his head and eyes toward the strangers, murmured in his Arkansas accent, "That's Pancho Villa!"

I already knew of Pancho as a dangerous man, an outlaw *arriero*, or muleteer, who murdered for fun, wanted people to laugh when he killed a man, and hoped to get an extra laugh by shooting any observer who remonstrated. He had joined Madero with fewer than a hundred of his fellow bandits but now commanded a regiment. I wondered what he might be seeking at our petates. Had we done something wrong? I could overhear the black talking to him quietly and fast but understood no word. Dumbfounded, I hesitated, too fascinated to run. Finally I decided to act. Pretending unconcern, I walked boldly around the horses to my petate. The black man's remarkable eyes were dancing. He had mastered the situation. From a private cache he had dug up a can of tomatoes and two or three cans of sardines. His hospitality and the delectable food intrigued Villa's companions. They hesitated, looking to Pancho for leadership. Pancho burst into an explosive laugh and started to take off his leggings.

I had never seen any leggings like those—they resembled the tops of Wellington boots—certainly hot to wear although good leg protection when riding through creosote bush or mesquite thickets. The lower ends covered the laces of Villa's shoes and were cut away in the back for the shanks of his big-roweled spurs. A thin steel band along the back of the bootleg held the two sides together.

We all sat down on the hard desert ground. Pancho pushed his magnificently embroidered sombrero back on his head, ate rapidly, and laughed loudly, evidently enjoying both the food and company. I thought, at last I have met Henry VIII, not in a schoolbook but on the hoof. One of his men helped him snap on those fantastic leggings before they all mounted and rode away. I noticed that Villa "packed" his rifle on the offside of his saddle with the stock to the rear so that he could dismount with it in his right hand. This attracted my attention because I liked guns and had found carrying one on the offside of a horse to be clumsy, especially on a tall horse.

When they were gone, the black man, looking over his shoulder to be sure nobody was listening, explained that the American Legion, eager to get rich sacking Juárez, had planned to attack without orders from Madero. Orozco had learned about the scheme and told Madero, and they had sent Villa to investigate, quash any disobedience, kill if necessary, and no questions would be asked. "I warrant we're stopped now," the black concluded in his strange British accent, "but, 'pon my honor, mate, if we don't fight soon most of us'll quit and go to Central America."

"What does Giuseppe Garibaldi have to say about this?" I asked.

"Have you heard him say anything since you've been with us?" the black replied, as he rolled his petate back over his grocery cache. "He's in El Paso at the Hotel Sheldon seeking publicity with newspaper men."

To placate the restless troops, Madero planned a great celebration for Cinco de Mayo, Mexico's national holiday commemorating a decisive victory over the French army in 1862. For this occasion Madero and the científicos declared a truce, which permitted Diaz to ship in food for his troops but no munitions or reinforcements while they discussed a peaceful solution for the siege of Juárez. To shelter the participants a big circus tent was pitched along the river. Here Madero, Orozco, and Villa met with a delegation from the city. During the conference hopeful politicians organized meetings throughout the rebel encampment and, being politicians, they shouted promises of everything to everybody.

I found the best entertainment nonpolitical. Insurrecto cowboys had rounded up and stolen a herd of cattle from the great *hacendado*, Luis Terrazas. They had driven them to the open desert beyond our bivouac and invited all lovers of liberty and equality to come and play with and kill these cattle at leisure. What could be more democratic than that! Also, a few Americans slipped through the United States cavalry's border patrol with wagonloads of groceries to be traded for the Terrazas beef we were going to slaughter. Obviously some commanders in the United States Army were negligent or sympathetic with the insurrectos, otherwise the wagons would have been stopped.

When I arrived at the bunch ground amateur matadors were already teasing the cows to fight and skillfully evading their sharp horns. The narrow escapes made everybody laugh. We ate the fresh groceries, had a good time, and repeated the popular couplet:

> Mucho trabajo,
> Poco dinero,
> Poco tiempo combate.
> Viva Madero!

This was not grammatical Spanish but every man understood it and that was all that mattered to these

> Compañeros of the plow,
> Hungry, tired and dirty,
> Each would acquire his own wealth now
> With a trusty thirty-thirty.

Back at my petate that night of Cinco de Mayo, the black man was disconsolate. "Madero settled nothing in the big tent today," he said, "and wants another conference tomorrow. The wool is being pulled over Little Sawed-Off's eyes. Truce or no truce, the científicos will use these delays to ship reinforcements in by train from Chihuahua and ammunition from the United States hidden in tubs marked 'manteca' [lard]. Mark what I say."

The man I called "You" agreed. "That Madero," he drawled in his Arkansas accent, "we kaint l'arn him nuthin'. In every camp here the men is riled, all in a sweat to be off, oilin' their rifles, sightin' at 'maginary científicos. I suspicions suthinks sure to happen, sure as shootin'. Yes, pronto!"

Next day "suthink" was obviously happening. The whole encampment seemed disturbed by Madero's delay. More riders than usual whipped their scrawny horses past our bivouac. Before noon a stranger stopped. I had never seen him before but the black knew him.

"Villa has ordered his men to march tonight after dark," the stranger said. "It's secret, breaks Madero's truce, but the enemy is breaking it, too. Villa says he's gonna stop that train bringing the reinforcements. Orozco's men are packing to help him."

I saw the whites of the black man's eyes sparkle. He spoke quietly, his British accent very precise. "You can believe that if you wish," he said, "but I'll wager that Villa is not breaking the truce because the foeman is doing so. Villa does not need Orozco to help stop that train. Mark what I say, mate! Orozco's force is bigger than Villa's. He will circle the city and attack from the east while Villa strikes along the railroad route. Something will surely happen at dawn tomorrow. Then, our American Legion has a chance. The científico army will form to oppose Orozco and Villa. We can surprise the enemy with an attack in the rear. I say 'Viva Madero' now, whether or not Little Sawed-Off knows we have already started the battle."

Here was my opportunity at last. Jimmie Hare would be in the Hotel Sheldon when the battle started. I was going to be in Juárez, watch the insurrectos come in from three sides, write the first authentic account of the battle, and "scoop" the great war correspondent. I had only one problem. How could I get into Juárez by tomorrow morning?

13

Arrested as a Spy

But when it comes to slaughter
You will do your work on water
An' you'll lick the bloomin' boots
Of 'im that's got it.
          —Rudyard Kipling, *Gunga Din*

If I got back safely to the United States I knew I could enter
Juárez from El Paso as I had done before, but as a soldier of
fortune I was sure to be stopped if I tried to return to Texas by
the "foot-stick" over which I had come. Swimming the Rio
Grande would expose me to sentries on both sides. I decided
to walk up the river past Madero's headquarters, drop down
under the river bank after dark, and slip upstream unnoticed
until I was sure to be in New Mexico. Fortunately, the Army
patrol at this place was not vigilant. I reentered the United
States without being challenged and next morning crossed into
Juárez by the international bridge from El Paso.

Sunday, May 7, 1911, was beautifully clear, but the shooting
I expected did not start. I waited on a bench in the plaza under
the mulberry trees, then decided to photograph the picket line
where I had surprised the sentry on my last visit. I remembered the way and walked up Calle del Comercio along the
Mission wall. When I arrived at the barrio alto a picket was
standing correctly at attention and I took his picture again. He
gazed out across the flat where the American Legion planned
to attack after Orozco and Villa "opened the ball," but I could
see no enemy in that familiar country. Instead, two Chinese
were working in a field just beyond the last federal trenches.
Those poor fellows, I thought, are going to be in the cross fire
between the insurrectos and the científicos when the battle
begins—if it ever does.

At noon that day in a Juárez restaurant I enjoyed two fried eggs that looked up at me round-eyed from a raft of spicy enchiladas. This was rich fare after a camp diet of *frijoles y carne seca*. Beans, roasted strips of tough beef, goat meat often rank in flavor, and hard tortillas with an occasional joint of raw sugar cane for dessert had been considered an insurrecto banquet. This new food tasted better, but I had come to see a battle. Had it been postponed or abandoned? Perplexed, I decided to spend the afternoon at a bullfight, a new experience for me.

Not being an aficionado, I was particularly interested in the *banderilleros* who dared place their sharply barbed, paper-frilled sticks in the withers of a charging bull. This spectacular feat seemed impossible but the performers repeated it many times, and I finally solved the trick, or thought I had. The bull must be enticed to pursue the man as he ran in an arc-shaped course. Thus when the bull's arc of pursuit met the man's arc of flight, the two-legged runner could make a final sharp turn faster than the four-legged bull. It seemed as simple as that. The man, however, must judge the time precisely and, as he rounded the bull's horns, jab the two sharp banderillas into the charging beast's withers—a really remarkable sleight-of-hand trick.

The ticket seller that afternoon had announced that the matadors would kill four bulls. Certainly, *el promovedor* anticipated no insurrecto attack on Juárez. Each bull was fought according to the usual schedule, except the last, and I have never seen anything like it since. The act was humorous. The banderillero had dressed for it like a clown, with a big sack of sawdust strapped to his stomach. He sat on a chair in the center of the arena—a lonely figure indeed.

At first the bull paid no attention to him. The man waved the fluttering banderillas until the bull noticed him and, with ears cupped forward, walked toward him curiously. When fifteen or twenty feet away the bull lowered his head and charged. The seated man dodged to one side. The confused bull, hooked where he thought the man would be, missed him so closely that one horn tore open the sawdust sack, but the dexterous banderillero placed both barbed sticks in the charging bull's withers. Amid a roar of applause from aficionados on the surrounding seats, the clown walked nonchalantly away. He even pretended not to glance over his shoulder as the frustrated bull, instead of following him, tossed its head at the swinging paper-fringed sticks in its back.

This performance terminated the bullfight. Men and boys from the sunny-side seats swarmed over the wooden *barrera* into the arena. Laughing and shouting, they swung their jackets like bullfighter capes, executing *verónicas* before imaginary bulls. Spectators from the more expensive *sombra,* or shady-side seats, walked quietly away from the ring, sauntering up Calle del Comercio toward the plaza. I joined them, marveling that this picturesque world seemed oblivious to the insurrectos camped around the city. Flat wagons carrying the dead bulls passed us. After circling the plaza a time or two, they were driven to a butcher shop where a red flag announced that meat—certainly very tough meat—could be purchased.

At supper time I noticed a sign on the wall beside an open door, COMIDAS 30¢ y 35¢, which certainly meant meals for fifteen cents and seventeen and a half cents American money. I investigated and found the tamales in steamed cornhusk envelopes quite adequate. Returning to a park bench in the plaza, I saw a long line of carefully chaperoned girls promenading in a large circle around *el quiosco de música.* The band played popular melodies—"La Serenata," "Carmela," and "Huile, Huile Palomita." One short, spirited tune—"Naranja Dulce"—caused a ripple of giggling laughter. Why "Sweet Orange" amused the girls I shall probably never know. Young men marched solemnly in the opposite direction, and I saw an occasional note passed between the lines. Some of the girls were my age and I thought them very pretty. The music was romantic and a three-quarter full moon glowed above the Mission bell tower.

Before long the merrymakers began to melt away. I wondered why the insurrectos had failed to attack all day long and looked at my Ingersoll dollar watch, a clumsy little machine—to wind it I had to open the back and use a key. The watch hands pointed to ten o'clock—time for me to seek *una posada,* or lodging for the night.

Two tall men wearing dark blue capes with scarlet linings sat down beside me. They reminded me of the gendarmes I had seen in Paris. I carried a pack of *ojo* cigarettes in my pocket. The molasses-dipped wrappers appealed to me and I offered each man a smoke. They accepted, lighting them with sulfur

matches that illuminated handsome, well-chiseled Spanish
faces. The second man put the cigarette pack in his pocket and
they both stood up, telling me politely to come with them.
Both were dressed in handsome police uniforms so I felt no
fear of being kidnapped and was rather curious about our
destination. I somehow liked the men, but did not like losing
my cigarettes.

We walked up Calle del Comercio beside the Mission and
turned to the left along Calle Mariscal. In the dark I saw a
dimly lighted wide-open doorway, the entrance to the city
marshal's headquarters, which occupied an entire block. We
entered, dodging around a large *olla* (jug for drinking water)
that hung in the entrance. The water in these porous clay pots
seeps slowly out to the surface, where it evaporates, cooling
the water inside. When the olla hangs in an open door or
hallway the evaporation is faster and the water cooler.

The room we entered was not brightly lighted, but I saw four
uniformed men seated on benches along the inside wall. At the
far end an officer sat behind a desk. My captors addressed him
as "El Jefe" and, executing a formal about-face with a flash of
the scarlet lining of their cloaks, they strode away, leaving me
standing alone. El Jefe demanded my camera, wrote something
on a slip of paper, put it and the camera in a desk drawer, and
told me in English that I would be tried in the morning.

"Tried for what?" I asked him.

"For being a spy," he replied. "Our organization here is
good, like in United States. More better, yes. Our spies in
camp of Madero see you there. Today we see you take pictures, yes, of our military positions. Your trial tomorrow will be
legítimo, legal, justo, all same in United States, yes. Buenas
noches."

My dismissal was formal, final, and precise. El Jefe had said
nothing that was not proper but somehow I disliked and distrusted him. He seemed too self-important. Constantly comparing his country with the United States made me suspect
that he felt inferior, unsure of his own importance. I was not
disturbed about my arrest. Latin-American courts and jails
were new to me. No citizen of Caesar's imperial Rome arrested
in Syria or Egypt ever felt more confidence than I did of my
status. Come morning, I would send word to the American
consul and be released.

The guards who held me must have been a constabulary of some kind, not regular police. Their Mauser rifles were stacked in a corner of the room. None of the four men got up from the wooden benches, which were eighteen inches wide. I remember the width exactly because I tried to sleep on one of them. The big room felt colder than the desert. An adobe house keeps the heat out all day and, with its wide door open at night, seems colder than outdoors. Remembering how my silk neckerchief had kept me warm on the ride with Biscuits in the Sleepy Cat country, I tied it around my waist under my clothes. This warmed me, but the bench was hard and narrow. I could not sleep. The four guards sitting along the opposite wall began to nod drowsily. El Jefe sat in his chair behind the desk with his head drooped forward, also alseep. Wrapped in his cape, the barrel and butt of a rifle stuck out at each side. I, being young and foolish, decided to play a trick on these men—a typical college prank. I would disturb them by pretending to escape. To become a real fugitive in the dark, twisting alleys of Juárez at midnight was unthinkable, but it would be fun to alarm my captors, especially the pompous El Jefe who had dismissed me so abruptly and obviously considered his chair a regal throne.

I stood up quietly and tiptoed toward the open door, hoping to be seen. Somebody gave a startled cry. El Jefe, throwing back his cape, barked a gruff order and the sleepy guards jumped to their feet. I enjoyed the commotion and turned innocently to the olla. A gourd dipper for drinking hung beside it. I filled it and sipped the cool water, pretending, exactly as I had seen the clowning banderillero pretend at the bullfight, to ignore the threatening danger. El Jefe failed to comprehend the joke, but his men smiled and I felt that they were amused and had become sympathetic friends. I liked these men who liked my joke. This proved fortunate for me on the following day during the battle which none of us foresaw. That night I strode back to my wooden pallet, lay down, and really fell asleep.

The next thing I remember was the cooing of pigeons on the Mission walls. For a long moment I wondered where I was. As consciousness returned I realized that a new day had dawned. Sitting up, I looked out the open door where the olla hung. Two men in gigantic straw sombreros passed, driving burros packed with vegetables. They turned down Calle del Comercio toward the market. I heard the banging of distant shutters as merchants opened their shops. The guards stood up, smoothed their uniforms, and beckoned for me to follow them into a back room where we helped ourselves to coffee in tin cups and sourdough biscuits, not the tortillas we ate in the rebel camp. When we returned, His Highness was drinking coffee from a china cup in solitary grandeur behind his desk.

"Can you send this note from me to the United States consul?" I asked.

El Jefe blew across the top of his cup to cool the drink. "I told you last night," he replied, "you will have trial this morning. Fair, legal trial, yes. As insurrecto, you are no citizen of United States. You have no consul. Sit down. I call for you."

This sounded final, but half an hour later two urchins stopped at the olla for a drink. When El Jefe was not looking I gave them the note with a few centavos for delivering it to the consul. They ran away dutifully on this errand but I never knew whether the consul got my message. I was waiting for him or for my promised trial when I heard distant shooting on the eastern side of the city. I suspected that Orozco was opening the battle a day late, but said nothing. The men around me seemed unconcerned. They did not even glance at one another.

The shooting stopped. A few minutes later we heard a series of fast volleys. Still the guards showed little interest. There were no shops on Calle Mariscal, so I could not tell what the citizens thought of the bombardment. After a short silence the shooting started again, louder this time it seemed to me. I wondered if Orozco was advancing, but realized that I might only be imagining that the shooting sounded nearer.

At twelve thirty, according to my watch, a new and really louder volley from the south set the Mission pigeons flying desperately overhead. My guards glanced at each other this time and smiled—still not apprehensively. I wondered if Villa was coming in from the south according to the battle plan I had heard. The shooting continued from that direction and two of the guards walked out in the street. They looked up and down, then ran back in, their faces very solemn. A few minutes later I heard a roaring thunder of hooves racing down Calle del Comercio from the barrio alto. Four horsemen rounded the corner of Calle Mariscal and stopped at our doorway. Shouting harsh Spanish that I could not understand, they stooped low on their horses' backs and spurred them into the wide-open door. Only one wore a uniform; the others seemed to be excited civilians, or perhaps they were officers in plain clothes. Their horses, frightened on the wooden floor, reared and plunged against the walls and ceiling. Somebody opened a door into the patio. The frantic horses, with their riders, ran out through it.

El Jefe remained seated regally at his desk. In a commanding but excited voice he ordered the wide street door closed. A heavy cross beam I had not noticed was swung down to prevent ramming the door open from the outside. El Jefe remained on his throne, but all the guards followed the horses to the patio. I went with them, feeling myself a comrade rather than a prisoner. At the patio's center a faucet on an upright pipe dripped water into a round metal tub. Beyond it I saw a line of men with rifles climbing a ladder to the flat roof. I joined them and found the roof was fortified by sandbags piled shoulder-high on three street sides. The front of our building, which faced the Mission, was undefended.

East of us the pigeons circled the Mission bell tower, evidently afraid to alight. Across the street to the north I saw a massive flat-roofed adobe building fortified like ours with sandbags. This, I learned later, was the city jail. At one corner a tower, the highest edifice in this part of town, loomed up a tall story above the sandbagged roof. Along the tops of the sandbags I saw the heads and shoulders of soldiers standing in formation. I recognized their familiar cotton uniforms but wondered why their kepis were white instead of the black patent leather I had seen on the picket line. Looking closer, I saw they were wearing white cloth covers on the black kepis. This certainly must have made them cooler under the semitropical sun, and keeping the covers white and clean was a good task for a soldier. As I watched, a squad of them climbed a sloping ladder to the tower's fortified top. I could not be sure what they saw from there. All I could see by looking west from our roof were the vacant housetops of the barrio alto and beyond them the distant desert ridge I had become familiar with while in Madero's encampment.

The American Legion was certainly not advancing across that desert in the manner described to me by the black—but I was

not sure. An occasional bullet hummed drowsily over our
heads. It seemed to come so slowly we could dodge it easily.
As each bullet passed, every man on the roof ducked, then
straightened up again. El Jefe had come out in the patio to look
up at us. Although he was safe down there, I noticed that he
too ducked for every bullet exactly as we did, and the men on
the roof exchanged knowing smiles. I felt that they did not
respect him and his stuck-up, timid ways—a commander who
would have little authority in a crisis.

Looking again at the ash-heap ridge far to the west, I saw
some men, the first enemy insurrectos I had seen. They were
apparently firing in our direction, but were much too far away
to be shooting at us. Certainly they were not advancing to take
the federal trenches below the barrio alto, but they might be
covering a party ahead of them that planned to take those
trenches with the hairbrush hand grenades the insurrecto artilleryman had told me they would use. As I watched, the constabulary on our roof suddenly began to fire fast and furiously. I
ducked my head behind the sandbags and dared not peep up. I
felt sure that such rapid firing could not be accurate, but it
might make a curtain of flying bullets that would stop advancing insurrectos already in town from running through the
streets.

In the patio, El Jefe, watching from his safe place, scampered back to his regal chair.

"You see-a heem run?" a friendly guardsman said to me.
"We calla heem 'El Jefe-Beega-Head' for fun. El Jefe legitimo,
hee-a go Chihuahua. Come back mañana. El Jefe-Beega-Head
have happy day now. Sit in chair like beeg-a king. Mañana, like
'lectric light, he go out, si."

I recognized the speaker as one of my guards who had smiled
when I surprised them all last night by drinking from the olla.
Pleased with the recognition, I stood up without thinking and a
bullet ripped the top of the sandbag in front of me. The flying
sand blinded me so that I could see nothing down in the street.
Across the way on the jail roof, soldiers were also firing. Volleys banged from the Mission, too, driving off the pigeons in
frantic flights. The bombardment made my eardrums throb.
The friendly rifleman beside me, stooping below the sandbag

wall, held out his Mauser for me to feel. The continued shooting had made the barrel, although insulated by a long wooden
stock, too hot to hold comfortably.

"Caliente," the man exclaimed, slapping the hot wood. "Muy
caliente."

The sand in my eyes had taught me not to look over the west
breastworks again, but I dared look east past the Mission at the
lower city. Beyond Avenida Santa Fe a cloud as white as cotton
rose above the flat housetops. A moment or two later the whole
earth shook and I heard a cannon boom—much louder than the
howitzers I had watched on my first day in Juárez. The cannonball must have passed high over our heads if the geyser of
yellow dirt beyond the barrio alto indicated where it hit.

A short silence followed and El Jefe-Beega-Head appeared
down in the patio again. Another cannon fired and he ran back
to his throne. If those shots were well placed and if the insurrectos had captured that first line of defense trench, as I had
been told they planned to do, certainly they were all dead now.
I wondered, however, if the insurrectos had already left that
trench and come on into town. Our men on the roof had shot at
something in the streets. Perhaps the big cannon were striking
behind, instead of on, the invaders.

The afternoon sun was very hot, and I made several trips
down the ladder with a bucket to bring up drinking water from
the dripping faucet. The men appreciated this. At one place on
my rounds there was a gap where the fortification had been
destroyed. The men beyond needed water and one of them,
seeking help, crawled to me on his stomach to keep safely
below the shattered breastwork. I could not crawl to his comrades on my stomach with a bucket of water but I skipped
across and was not hit.

Just after leaving that group to serve others along the firing
line, I heard a shout of pain, and looked around. A bullet had
sliced a man's forearm while he had held his gun barrel as he
shot above the sandbags. Another man gave no outcry when hit
in the hand, but he dropped his gun and climbed awkwardly
down the ladder into the patio, using only one hand. A third
man, only ten feet from me, collapsed silently into a heap. The
men beside him were too busy shooting into the street to pay

any attention. As yet I had seen no enemy nearby. The entire battle seemed more like an earthquake or thunderstorm than a combat between men.

The fusillade stopped as suddenly as it had commenced. I happened to be in the patio filling my water bucket at the time. El Jefe-Beega-Head popped into the patio with a Colt six-shooter in his hand. He evidently assumed that I had come down to escape or to let the enemy in the front door. Very excited and angry, he shouted, "Get back up that ladder. You come down again, I keel you."

I heard the click of his Colt's mechanism as he "racked" the hammer back. Only a slight pressure on the trigger now would fire the bullet straight at me. I must have been scared because the .45 caliber of his gun barrel looked as big around as the bore in Madero's homemade cannon. A Colt revolver, I knew, shot as hard for an excited nitwit as for a man who could be reasoned with, and I wondered what to do.

Somebody up on the roof fired a shot. I shall never know whether it was at an enemy, into the air by accident, or on purpose to distract Beega-Head's attention. All I know is that El Jefe, apparently terrorized, forgot me and scampered back to his lonely throne in the house while I scrambled up the ladder as fast as I could go.

When I reached the flat roof the men, who had not seen the incident, ordered me back for more water. I protested and half a dozen rifles pointed at me. The faces above them were dark with anger. Once more I wondered what to do. If El Jefe-Beega-Head saw me back in the patio he would certainly shoot, and I believed he wanted an opportunity to heroically kill an enemy. I did not know sufficient Spanish to explain this and wondered whether it would be better to die by his single bullet at the foot of the ladder or be mowed down by half a dozen Mausers on the rooftop. Suddenly it occurred to me that when this was all over it might be fun to tell friends which was the less painful way to die. Then, in spite of myself, I had to chuckle at this Irish bull.

14

Prisoner of War

Never saw a man who looked
With such a wistful eye
Upon that little tent of blue
Which prisoners call the sky,
—Oscar Wilde

The lull in the battle may have saved my life. Men who had
seen El Jefe-Beega-Head order me up the ladder told me not
to go down again but to stay where I was. They argued vocifer-
ously with those who had pointed their guns at me.

The argument ended when a stray shot wounded one of the
men. Excited marshals crowded around him and an officer
ordered them to stand back and give the fellow fresh air.

The man killed earlier that day had been covered with a
blanket and placed at the foot of the sandbag wall. Having
never seen a dead man before, I watched this one closely. A
marshal I did not know stepped up and turned back the cover.
He may have hoped to identify the victim, or perhaps he was
merely curious. The sight he exposed was truly sickening. The
man's brains had been blown out by one of those soft-nosed
bullets.

Across the street on the jail roof, soldiers were bringing a
dead comrade down the ladder from the tower. This created a
problem. The limp corpse continually folded up and slipped
into the spaces between the rungs of the ladder. Our men
enjoyed the uniformed peleles' predicament, but refrained
from shouting suggestions to them.

I wondered whether the insurrectos had really got into town
and been driven back. Three bodies still lay in the street. They
might be soldiers or insurrectos. The fact that nobody dared go
out to cover or remove them made me suspect that the enemy

might be lurking in some nearby building. With time on my hands, I dug out the bullet that had barely missed me, planning to keep it as a lifelong souvenir. It had mushroomed badly, like the one that killed the man on the roof. The insurrecto who fired it, probably a Jesu-cristero, had filed a vicious cross on its tip to make it doubly deadly. These bullets came from sporting rifles like those the insurrectos carried. Since their Winchesters would not shoot accurately from long distances, I suspected some rebels were already in Juárez. Both the artillerymen and the black had said the American Legion planned to fortify themselves in houses and move forward with stealthy attacks. I wondered whether they might be barricaded now at the edge of town, planning another advance. A curious tinkling sound in the street attracted me. I had never heard any sound quite like it before.

"Míralos!" our men shouted as they looked over the sandbag breastwork. "Míralos!"

I looked down, too, and saw a little cavalcade of mules. Two of them carried machine guns, others were neatly packed with ammunition. They all appeared to be trim and military, very different from the slouchy insurrectos. Four mounted officers seemed to be in charge and a half dozen uniformed peleles, wearing sandals, pattered along with them. They passed directly below us. Trotting down Calle Mariscal, they turned toward the barrio alto. I could not see where they unlimbered, but I soon heard their rattling fire from at least two locations. Then silence! A prolonged silence! I presumed that any rebels who had been fortified in town had been killed.

Men on our roof leaned their guns against the barricade and sat down to rest with their backs against the sandbags. Some dozed drearily, the brims of their hats over their faces keeping the hot sun off their eyes. Too tired to cheer, they murmured in Spanish, "Victory at last!"

Late in the afternoon a distant bugle sounded from across the city. A bugle west of us answered it. A few minutes later the handsomely uniformed Navarro followed by two aides in scarlet-trimmed tunics rode up Calle del Comercio. I recognized one of them as the aide who told me to vamoose. All three were handsomely mounted on bay horses whose spirited feet twinkled in the dusty street. As they passed, men on all the rooftops waved hats and rifles, shouting "Viva Díaz!" That afternoon we ate our first meal since breakfast—hardtack and sardines.

Elated with victory, one of the men on our roof spied a large group marching in ragged formation along the distant Rio Grande. A soldier on the jail roof across the street pointed to them and shouted to us that the crowd was Villa's army, all captives now. This, we soon learned, was a great mistake. The alleged captives were really a concentration of the poorly drilled American Legion preparing to attack; as darkness fell, red streaks of flame began spitting from their rifles. Where was Navarro with his machine guns now?

That night parties of men I supposed to be from the American Legion roamed the twisting streets of northwest Juárez, raiding residences. Occasional shots told us that some householders were fighting—and probably dying—to defend their property. Everything seemed uncertain and very ugly. The guards on our building moved from the outer walls to the edges of the patio where they could shoot down at rebels who might break in the front door. We were all very tired. Many of the men spread blankets on the flat roof, laying their ammunition on them so it could be picked up more quickly than from a cartridge belt or box. I saw one marshal count his six remaining cartridges, spread them on his blanket, cross himself, and then sleep peacefully, it seemed.

Another man mumbled, "Muerte a todos los gringos," as he rubbed his hand covetously over his line of cartridges.

I understood that remark to mean "Death to all Americans," and I knew these Mexicans resented Yankees' taking part in their revolution, especially those Americans who joined the American Legion, to which I was supposed to belong. However, I can say frankly that no man abused me, and El Jefe-Begga-Head was the only one of them I disliked and really feared.

A blanket was given me for the night to lie on, not to use as a covering. The coarse gravel on the roof made a rough mattress. I spread the blanket in a corner of the roof and wondered how, if we were attacked during the night, I could explain that I was

an insurrecto noncombatant. Another prisoner climbed the
ladder and joined me. I had not seen him before. He understood no English and when I spoke Spanish he shook his index
finger at me and shrank timidly away. This Tarahumara Indian,
evidently arrested before I was, had been kept in a cell somewhere in the building and now, when the fight had become
crucial, he was sent up to the roof.

We lay down together below the sandbag wall. Half asleep, I
remembered a picture in a schoolbook of soldiers with fixed
bayonets jumping on helpless victims below a breastwork that
resembled the sandbags above us. Two thoughts came to my
half-conscious mind: if my dead body is ever found, the only
name on it identifying me will be John Wanamaker, the store
label in the back of my undershirt; I thought, too, that the
three-quarter moon above the Mission's adobe bell-tower must
also be shining tonight above the avenue of oak trees at Swarthmore College where Lloyd Lewis and I had had fun frightening the guard.

Before morning a strange marshal awoke me. With him I
climbed down the ladder. Then he lifted it from the patio wall
and, holding one end, told me to take the other. We carried
the ladder through the room where El Jefe sat, as I had first
seen him, wrapped in his cloak, the barrel and butt of his rifle
sticking out on opposite sides. I felt a strange compassion for
that bigot. Temporary as El Jefe-Beega-Head knew his office to
be, while the boss was away in Chihuahua he prized his temporary position so much he was obviously prepared to die—not
fighting on the roof with his fellows, but sitting in that chair.

El Jefe said no word when a guard opened the door for the
marshal and me to carry the ladder into the street. It seemed
very dark outside. I heard the wide door slam shut and the
heavy beam drop in place again behind it. The marshal and I
were now alone, and I noticed that he carried no gun. Had I
been a venturesome young man I might have dropped my end
of the ladder and run away, but I knew the streets were filled
with looting guerrillas who might shoot at sight, so I felt safer
walking through this lions' den with the marshal than running
off alone. Besides, he was at the front end of the ladder and
would meet an enemy first.

We walked north between the front of the marshals' building

and the Mission wall. At the corner of Calle del Comercio a
voice challenged: "Alto! Quien vive?"

The ladder man up front dropped to his stomach in the
street, and so did I. Lying flat between the adobe house walls,
it seemed very quiet. I could not see the man who challenged
us. The moon was out of sight behind the walls, but a star or
two—probably planets—shone bright, steady, and very close
above the crooked street in this adobe city. The cool cobblestones under my face smelled like good earth, like the dry
desert I knew and relished. My companion, lying in the dark
ahead of me, replied to our unseen challenger, "Viva Mexico!"

This reply failed to reassure the unseen challenger. "Long
live Mexico" was appropriate for either an insurrecto or a
científico. I heard the invisible man cock his rifle. His Mauser's
bolt action sounded very different from the lever mechanism
on a Winchester. This assured me that we were not confronted
by a rebel. My companion must have noticed this too because
he stood up, speaking very rapidly in Spanish. I understood the
words *escala* and *comida,* so I knew that our ladder had something to do with a meal, but this mystified me.

"Si, a buen seguro," the unseen man said. "Vais. Ándela, mis
paisanos. Ándela!" This surely meant, "Certainly! Go ahead,
my fellow countrymen. Hurry."

We hurried with the ladder across Calle del Comercio to the
jail, where a warden opened the door for us. We carried the
ladder down a dark hall with iron-barred doors clanging behind
us. Rounding a corner, we came to a patio where soldiers
crouched around an open fire, some nodding with sleep. Above
them I saw the round, smiling face of a cook in shirt sleeves.
He was molding great white biscuits out of dough in a dishpan.
He lacked wood to finish his cooking and greeted us with words
of joy while his helper chopped our ladder into firewood. This
shortage of fuel at the end of the battle's first day indicated the
woeful inadequacy of Navarro's logistics.

A turnkey with a lantern led me down a dark aisle through
more iron gates that clanged behind us until we reached an
archway closed by double doors. The upper half of each was a
barred window, but I could see nothing in the darkness beyond. The doors were bolted together and further secured by a
chain and padlock. The turnkey undid these elaborate

fastenings, opened one door, and I stepped in. He closed the door behind me, slipped the bolt, threaded the chain back into place, snapped the padlock, and without another word walked back down the hall. In the dim light I saw him turn a corner and disappear. I could see nothing ahead and I had no idea of the room's size. The area smelled strongly of unwashed men. Fearing I might fall into a pit or down a flight of stairs, I stepped ahead slowly, feeling the floor with one foot until I kicked something soft. I reached down with my hand and found a human body, but could not be sure whether it was alive or dead.

I have read many accounts of the horror of Mexican jails, of the filth, the vermin, the brutality of the jailers and beastiality of the inmates. None of these things seemed entirely true to me in this Juárez jail. The man whose body I had kicked in the dark spread out half of the gunny sack on which he slept and without a word patted it for me to lie down beside him. Come daylight I saw tall white walls towering up some eighteen feet to a brown, beamed ceiling. On the concrete floor men were sprawled on their backs and sides. I counted twenty. The room was probably thirty feet long by twenty wide, so we were not packed together. There was no furniture of any kind—nothing but the burlap sacks used for bedding. The only opening was ten feet from the floor—a slot through the thick adobe wall a yard wide and only six inches high. Vertical iron bars prevented an escape through this narrow window. The only other way we could look out of the room was through the barred sections of the entrance doors. A porcelain toilet with no seat stood in one corner under a high, wooden water box and chain for flushing. So far as I know, it was in working order. With nothing to eat or drink there was little use for the toilet. The white walls adequately lighted the room. If there were any lice on the floor or walls they ignored me.

The men were slow to get up. There was no reason to do so. Here and there one sat up while another just rolled over on the floor. Everyone seemed to be Mexican except for two men at the far end of the room who seemed to be American, older than the rest of us, coarse, brutish, Cro-Magnon-featured cavemen. They had chinless profiles, curly hair and wore shabby jackets. I was curious to know what all the prisoners were being held for but asked no questions and no one showed any interest in me.

Breakfast was served from a big cauldron. Each man held out a broken cup, tin can, or anything he could find and got a dipper full of warm water with cornmeal in it—a very weak, flat mixture but standard Mexican fare. This was my third meal since being arrested. After swallowing this soup we hid the cans we ate from and lay down again.

Shooting soon began on the roof. We could not tell what the soldiers were firing at, but there seemed to be some action in the street outside our slit of a window. One of the young Mexicans was lifted up on the shoulders of a big man so he could look out and report to us. The window was so narrow he could see little, and all I understood from his disconnected account was, "soldados" and "insurrectos."

Cro-Magnon nudged me and, without saying a word, showed me a little copper .22 cartridge in his calloused palm. When nobody was looking he flipped this shell so that it hit the window bar beside our observer's face. That young man thought a bullet from outside had barely missed him. He threw himself back to the jail floor and refused to be held up again.

This was probably very funny to Cro-Magnon but he did not smile. Evidently a professional gambler, he displayed no emotion except for an odd expression in his eyes. The incident was unfortunate, because—being small—from now on it was I who had to perch on the tall man's shoulders and report whatever I could see outside. The bullets peppering the side of the jail made the job dangerous. Any one of them might come through the long, narrow window. I could not look down into the street where the men were fighting but from the houses across the way I saw that we were at the corner of Calle del Comercio above Calle Mariscal. The shooting soon stopped. There was nothing for me to see and I jumped down off the man's shoulders. All of us lay down on our empty burlap sacks. Nobody talked. There was nothing to say.

After an hour or more we were aroused by a squad of soldiers who marched down the corridor and turned into a patio we could not see from the barred entrance doors to our cell. As soon as they were gone two guards opened the doors and called a man's name. A Mexican at the far end of our room stood up.

"Convicted to be shot as a spy," Cro-Magnon whispered to me, and I saw in his eyes the odd expression of pleasure I had noticed when he frightened the young man at the window with the .22 shell. This time it seemed to be my possible fate as an accused spy that he enjoyed.

The condemned man walked solemnly through the lolling prisoners. Nobody offered any condolences. Instead, I thought I heard a slight ripple of satisfaction. I had heard that same suppressed self-righteous murmur in my Swiss school when a student, no more guilty than the rest of us, was caught and led to the headmaster's room for punishment. Do suffering prisoners get relief by seeing others suffer more than themselves?

The man walked out one of the double doors and the guards closed it. We prisoners sat very quietly, listening to the chain being slipped roughly back into place and the padlock being snapped shut. The prisoner and two guards walked down the corridor and around the corner into the patio where the soldiers had gone. I heard a military command and the rattle of Mauser rifle bolts cocking the firing pins. A short breathless silence. Two sharp orders. The roar of a volley. A queer gurgling sound and groan. The soldiers marched back into the corridor, their sandaled feet slapping on the hard floor as they walked away. That was all we heard; we had listened intently, and every sound was unforgettable. I have never seen a picture of an execution by firing squad since that day without hearing in my imagination these identical sounds.

I was charged with the same crime as that man! Would I be called next? My nationality had not saved me when I asked for the American consul. I might now be rolled in the same ditch with this man and no one would ever know my fate. But did that really matter, I asked myself. Why does every man seem to want some kind of gravestone? I wrote my name and address in the back of my pocket diary and in spite of myself smiled at the senseless consolation of that feeble identification. Weak from lack of food, I lay down and remember next being aroused by a rough cry: "Comida."

The prisoners all stirred.

"Let's eat!" Cro-Magnon announced stentoriously.

Our second meal in jail was one piece of sourdough bread the size of a man's fist, but it tasted good. After dinner the shooting began again, hotter than before. In addition to the rifles on the roof, cannon roared every few minutes very close to the jail walls. I was lifted up again to peer out the window slit but could not see sufficiently well down in the street to learn whether the cannon at our building's corner was manned by federals or insurrectos. A rain of bullets smacked against the jail wall with reports like rifles. Soldiers on our roof began throwing down bombs with long sputtering fuses. These drove the cannoneers away, so I thought they must be insurrectos but could not verify this. Perhaps insurrectos had captured the cannon there from the científicos. All I know for sure was that the cannon rumbled along Calle del Comercio's cobblestones to a new position.

We prisoners had been safer, I thought, with the cannon at our corner instead of up the street where a direct shot might puncture our adobe wall and bury us in the ruins. Yet, strangely enough, the cannon was not fired from its new position. The battle seemed to have ended. A building somewhere was on fire but the insurrectos had evidently been repulsed. As darkness fell the jail and surrounding streets remained silent. Men in our cell began to shout with deep agonized voices: "Agua! Agua!"

I thought those men would be less thirsty if they saved the moisture in their bodies by keeping quiet. The cries for water, however, were repeated occasionally all night. No other sound broke the stillness of the jail. I did not know that the soldiers on the roof above us were also suffering for want of water.

I learned this the next day and, being fond of books, remembered Benjamin Franklin's statement that for the want of a nail the shoe was lost; for the want of a shoe the horse was lost; and for the want of a horse the rider, the battle, the king, the country, were all lost. This would soon prove true in Mexico. For the want of water in Juárez, the nation Díaz had ruled so successfully for thirty-five years would be lost and a different Mexico would be born.

During the night of May 9 and 10, 1911, no sound but the prisoners' calls for water broke the silence. With the first gray light of dawn, rifle shots commenced again. The battle seemed to center now around our jail. The prisoners forgot their need for water. Instead, they repeated over and over that Navarro would never surrender. If the insurrectos took Juárez, he had sworn, they would take only a ruined city. The adobe buildings would be difficult to burn, but already a house near our jail was on fire and dirty brown smoke seeped through our narrow window slot. I was lifted up once more to look out and report. This hurt my eyes and made me cough, so I jumped down onto the cell floor again.

It is difficult to say how rumors start in a jail. I remembered hearing Civil War veterans blame the Confederates for threatening to kill the Yankee prisoners in Andersonville prison by shelling it down before Sherman could take it and release them. Certainly all of us in the Juárez jail feared that, if defeated, Navarro's last act would be to shell the jail. This belief, with the earthquaking thunder and smoky air, broke everybody's spirit. The Mexicans crouched miserably in a line, their backs to the wall away from the street. One man crossed himself. Three others followed. Then all sat and solemnly mumbled Ave Maria. The two Cro-Magnons lacked this dignity and I was ashamed of my countrymen. Plainly delirious, they circled the whitewashed walls, kicking any burlap mat not occupied, and recited their criminal history. I had never seen men act like this before. They whined about being driven from New Orleans, Dallas, Los Angeles, becoming outcasts even in Mexico. Lacking the fatalism of some professional criminals, these men were childishly sorry for themselves. They blubbered about dying in the debris of this prison. Their performance made me act more bravely than I felt, if only to shame them.

Suddenly the bombardment stopped. We prisoners looked questioningly at each other. The two Americans who had lost their nerve sat down on their bed mats mumbling dejectedly. In the silence I heard marching feet outside our barred doors and walked across to look out. Two prisoners joined me there. We saw soldiers from the roof marching toward the jail's front door.

"Qué pasa aquí?" ("What goes on here?") one of the prisoners called to the soldiers.

"We've whipped the enemy," a soldier replied in Spanish. "We're marching out to pursue and capture all of them."

No soldier mentioned the shortage of food and water. Perhaps none dared do so within hearing of the officers.

I was relieved to know that the battle had ended. This time the victory seemed to be genuine, not just soldier talk. Then it suddenly dawned on me that the victors would now try me for being a spy and sentence me *al muro* (to the wall)—colloquial Spanish for the firing squad.

While the soldiers were still marching out of the jail we went back to our burlap resting places. Occasional shots indicated that an insurrecto sniper was delaying the pursuit but probably not seriously. One of the idle prisoners walked over to the door, glanced out, and pointing to something, exclaimed: "Mira! Mírala!"

His voice expressed real exaltation. Several of us ran to him and looked through the grated doors. On the corridor floor I saw a crowbar. A traitorous soldier must have left it there to help us escape during the army's absence. One of the prisoners brought a small ball of twine and with a skillful cast lassoed the crowbar, dragged it to the door, and lifted it triumphantly into our cell.

We were not sure what was best to do with the bar. If we broke down the doors now the noise would attract a warden anywhere in the jail. Moreover, to escape only into the corridor would leave us with many more iron gates separating us from liberty. We finally decided to hide the bar under somebody's burlap bedding and wait until late that night when we might quietly tunnel through the thick adobe wall to the street. To me this seemed the surest way to evade being tried as a spy and sentenced "to the wall."

15

Insurrectos Capture the Jail

The combat deepens. On ye brave,
Who rush to glory or the grave!
—Thomas Campbell

The insurrectos were evidently in full retreat. Their sniper who was delaying the pursuit had stopped firing. Sudden scuffling at the jail's main entrance perplexed us. Then we heard a heavy ram pounding the front door. Voices cried "Viva Madero! Viva Madero!"

We realized now that the soldiers who had left the jail roof to pursue the insurrectos were really retreating, abandoning the building. A splintering crash told us the front door had been broken open. We all jumped to our feet. The jail corridors resounded with cheers, shouts, and the ripple of running feet. We prisoners yelled "Viva Madero" and a motley crowd wearing red, white, and green ribbons on hats, sleeves, and cartridge belts congregated at our double doors. Other mobs swarmed throughout the jail, battering open the cells. Some really ugly characters, I thought, are being freed among us.

We prisoners, using the crowbar, worked with others on the outside and soon splintered our two doors. Insurrectos jumped through the wreckage and swarmed into our cell, shouting, slapping our backs, shaking hands, calling us brothers, *paisanos, Maderistos.* Somebody thrust a battered Mauser into my hands and pointed with a smile to the red rag around the stock, which I understood, made the científico Mauser an insurrecto weapon. A federal soldier had evidently deserted with it. I learned later that thirty per cent of Navarro's soldiers had already joined the insurrectos. An army drafted from the Díaz jails could not be expected to fight hard for his Establishment. Madero's victory was inevitable.

The shouting crowd swept me through the splintered doors of our cell, down the arched corridor, out the main gate into Calle del Comercio, and around the corner into a part of town new to me. The streets were a shambles, the buildings pockmarked with bullet holes. Cannon had knocked the corner off one house. Telephone wires hung in festoons from the poles, windows in houses were smashed, doors sagged open.

Horsemen dashed recklessly through the mob of gay and ragged men firing six-shooters and rifles wrecklessly into the air. For self-protection I walked close to the house walls. At one doorstep I saw a dark, sticky pool of blood dripping into the street. Farther along a whitewashed wall was splattered red with blood and smeared where a man had fallen and still lay, an unattended, shapeless heap. In the stores and saloons cash registers rang as looters opened them.

To escape the mob I stepped into a big saloon. Two dead men lay on the floor. A newspaper covered one man's face, but the other's was uncovered and flies buzzed above a ghastly grin. On the handsome bar a line of sandaled men reached for the fancy bottles that decorate the shelves in front of barroom mirrors. Here were the fine drinks common men could not afford but had looked at covetously as they quaffed humble *cerveza* or a shot of tequila with a pinch of salt. Now these poor men reveled in drinks they had only dreamed about. They would pull a cork or break a bottleneck, swallow a drink or two, democratically hand the bottle to anyone standing along the bar, and then reach for a different variety.

The saloon floor, the bar, and men's sandaled feet were wet with spilled brandy and wine. Some generous fellow handed me an opened bottle of champagne, a wine I had read about in romantic fiction but never tasted. Being very hungry and thirsty, I grasped it. Unfortunately, it was not iced and the liquid effervesced in my mouth like a thousand sharp pins and needles. Coughing and sputtering, I cast the bottle down on the wet floor.

Two men rolled a heavy safe out past the dead bodies and chopped at it with a pick and axe. They worked desperately fast, broke the outer wall and found an inner safe surrounded by sand. They scooped this out onto the wet floor and breathlessly hacked open the inner safe door. One of the men, too tired or drunk to sit up, lolled on the floor, pawing hopefully through the papers in drawer after drawer. There was not a centavo in any of them. The owner had fled with all the money. The two exhausted men sank unconscious on the wreck.

A billiard hall next door attracted me, and here I saw my Cro-Magnon comrades. They had systematically taken advantage of opportunities in the saloon. Each had four or five bottles of rare liquor they were tying up in bandana handkerchiefs. They left by a back door, carrying the treasure to a hiding place they had established in a gulch down by the Rio Grande.

Another looter, searching the wall racks for billiard balls, was friendly. It occurred to me that a number-10 ball—to commemorate our May 10th victory—would make a good paperweight souvenir at college. I triumphantly picked one off the rack, and the friendly looter gave me an incredulous look. To be helpful and instruct a fellow soldier of fortune, he said, "Take only the cue balls."

I realized that I was not acting like a professional, and he continued, "Only the cue balls is valuable. They'll fetch you real money."

With my 10 ball, I joined a group of soldiers of fortune seeking new stores to loot. We walked down Calle del Comercio toward the plaza. The north wall of the Mission was so thickly peppered with bullet holes that we stopped to look. At two places the concentration of bullets had cut notches at the top of the adobe wall. We should have known better than to stand still, making good marks of ourselves, but the bullet-cut wall was interesting.

"From the look of them notches along the wall," one of the men remarked, "two sharp-shooting padres put up a good fight before we knocked them out."

While we watched we heard a shot and one of our men collapsed without a word. The rest of us ran fast to the plaza. Evidently another sharp-shooting padre who supported the wealthy Establishment was still on the Mission roof. When we were safely out of sight under the plaza mulberry trees I looked back at the Mission and saw that St. Peter, in his niche on the

Mission façade, had already stopped a ball with his key and another bullet had broken Moses's sword.

"Greasers beat us to the church altars," a strange soldier of fortune said to me. "They got all the gold and silver ornaments, but we beat them to the White Horse Pawn Shop."

He must have been bragging because, as he spoke, a gang of ragged Mexicans passed us wearing silver jewelry on their straw hats and lavish opal stickpins in their crisscrossed cartridge belts.

I heard shooting in the direction of El Paso and decided it was still dangerous out in the streets. A small cantina east of the plaza seemed a safe refuge, but it was there that I got my biggest fright during the battle—doubly frightening because I was the unwilling chief actor in a scene I had created by accident. The room was small and crowded with insurrectos wearing crossed cartridge belts. A short bar stood across the back wall of the room. At one end a closet had been made by boarding up the space below a flight of stairs. The closet door stood open and I saw buckets and a mop inside. The owner must have been an undercover rebel or a man greatly respected by them because there was no looting in his cantina. I elbowed my way to the bar through the big-hatted crowd, leaned my Mauser, with its insurrecto cover on the stock, against the bar and, showing off my Spanish, said, "Déme tequila."

The barkeep set a quart bottle, a tall glass, and jigger on the bar. Evidently I was to pour my own drink and pay for the number of jiggers consumed. Looking at the barman with a confident smile, I asked, "Tiene la sal?"

He slid the salt cellar, already on the bar, to me, and I filled the little depression on my wrist at the base of my thumb as I had seen Mexicans do before drinking tequila. I touched my tongue to this salt and, taking the bottle in my left hand, began to pour a drink into the jigger in my right. A man in the noisy "chingadoing" crowd gave me a thoughtless shove. Subconsciously I shoved him back, harder perhaps than I intended, and to my surprise the man fell to the floor with a thud. His head hit against the open closet door under the steps, slamming it shut with a bang.

I was embarrassed, really frightened. I was a hated gringo. Would these bepistoled insurrectos turn on me en masse, or would they stand back and allow the heavily armed man I had knocked down to get up from the floor and enjoy taking revenge on me before his comrades? I decided to ignore the incident if I could, to pretend I was not connected with it, and I began pouring the tequila into the jigger, but instead of watching the jigger in my hand I peered out through the corners of my eyes at the crowd. I soon felt the liquor pouring down the outside of the glass and I realized that I had filled the jigger to overflowing. Still hoping not to attract attention by looking at my victim or at the crowd, I gulped down the tequila, laid two bits on the bar, left my Mauser—which I was glad to get rid of—and slipped out the door into the plaza. This might have been a lucky escape, or perhaps the crowd was too drunk to realize what had happened or even that I had knocked down the man.

Sure now that I should seek safety in the U.S.A., I started down Avenida Santa Fe toward the international bridge. This street was noticeably higher than the ground on both sides and trolley tracks had been constructed along it. Ahead of me as I walked toward El Paso I saw a horse-drawn cannon bump up over the rails and down to the lower ground at the east. I recognized the American Legion's homemade three-inch cannon, but was more interested in the half-naked Indians running along behind it shooting arrows into the air. Here were the friendly Tarahumara I had visited in Madero's camp.

Wild bow-and-arrow Indians in a real battle were something I had read about in Parkman's *Oregon Trail* but never expected to see in real life. The tequila had refreshed me and I decided to follow and watch these red men. They were fleet-footed but when the cannon was unlimbered to shoot I realized that the battle for Juárez was still being fought right here, and I lost sight of the Indians.

I could not be sure what the artillerymen planned to hit but I noticed a long, official building about two blocks away. The windows were barred in the peculiar Spanish style which permits an observer inside to look along the outside wall. The door under a tall Roman arch was closed tight. A sudden volley of shots from somewhere—I could not be sure where—made the few of us who were watching duck into a patch of tall weeds between two houses. A bearded man behind me had noticeably short legs. He turned out to be Jimmie Hare, who had evidently been able to cross the bridge from El Paso. In spite of all my fine plans to beat him, he was getting the facts for a firsthand story of the battle.

The cannon fired and certainly missed the fine building, if that was its mark. Men hurriedly swabbed the barrel as I had seen them do in pictures. I watched them reload. Another shot was sure to puncture the building and kill many men inside.

"Bandera blanca!" The shout made me look again at the long building. I saw a white flag. A man in uniform ran out the door waving a note in his hand. An insurrecto carrying a rifle strode up to him, snatched the note, and wrote something on it. I noticed that he wore a mussed white shirt, high-topped shoes, and a white band around his narrow-brimmed hat.

"That's Garibaldi!" Mr. Hare exclaimed.

This was the first time I had seen our commander, who seldom if ever visited his American Legion.

The uniformed man carrying the note ran back into the building and slammed the door. A few minutes later some officers in uniform appeared. One held out a sword in his left hand toward Garibaldi, who took it and shook the man's right hand in a friendly manner. I was not close to them but I felt sure that General Navarro was surrendering his army.

"Mátalos!" ("kill them") a ragged insurrecto yelled as he ran out from a hiding place. Other guerrillas came running from various places.

"Muerte a Navarro" ("kill Navarro") one of them shouted.

"Al muro!" ("to the wall") another cried.

A man on horseback trotted down from the direction of the plaza. There were probably only a dozen of these new arrivals, but Garibaldi, with two or three followers and the uniformed officers, went back quickly into the building and shut the door in the faces of the gathering insurrectos.

Here, indeed, was an unusual situation. The rebel victors, having received the surrender of Navarro's army, were now defending it and themselves from their own men. Both high-ranking insurrecto leaders, Orozco and Villa, with their followers were busy elsewhere "taking" civilian sections of Juárez.

This form of command was perplexing, but one of the men who had hidden in the weeds with me said, as he plucked a cocklebur from his trousers, "La guerra es concluido."

Everything about the building seemed very quiet. The disgruntled guerrillas stood silently before the closed door. The only combatants who could force that door open sat on the ground beside their cannon eating sandwiches evidently obtained at a nearby grocery. The man who had spoken to me seemed to be right: the war was concluded, although the top insurrecto commanders were not in sight.

This was a victory of logistics, not of arms. The científicos surrendered because they had no food and the insurrectos occupied the town's waterworks. Díaz's peleles lacked the heart for a sortie to take the waterworks, although they had fought doggedly behind breastworks. Their defeat and the fall of Juárez soon ended the revolution. Thus the saying about the want of a nail proved true once more, as Mexico's longest regime of peace since her independence from Spain was brought to an end.

I, like Navarro's soldiers, had eaten no food since the day before. My earlier weakness had been replaced by a second wind, but I had dizzy spells now and my eyes began to play tricks on me. Indians, I learned later, purposely engendered visions by enduring hardships similar to those I had undergone. Certainly my next experience seems so improbable that I have never been able to explain it. I found myself in a Chinese restaurant, and how it had survived with the fighting all around it still mystifies me. I must have looked very disreputable in a coat, shirt, and trousers that had been slept in for three nights, but the Chinese waiter greeted me with Oriental calm and made no reference to my disreputable appearance or to the battle that had barely subsided. The dining room was empty. The waiter handed me a menu with due dignity and suggested that I drink a bottle of their choice cerveza de Tolca while deciding what to order. I wanted something that could be cooked in a hurry and I saw on the menu "rum omelette." The final "te," I thought, is for social grace and will make the omelet cost an extra peso. I remembered that Van Bibber sometimes ordered rum omelets in Delmonico's. My money belt—like the one Captain Macklin wore—had never been detected. It still held some cash, so I ordered the dish. Nice scrambled eggs were soon placed before me and I eagerly grasped a fork.

"No! No!" the shocked waiter remonstrated. With officious ceremony he showed me the "Jamaica" label on a bottle he was holding, and in my imagination I heard the buccaneer song in Stevenson's *Treasure Island:*

> Fifteen men on the Dead Man's Chest—
> Yo-ho-ho, and a bottle of rum!
> Drink and the devil had done for the rest—
> Yo-ho-ho, and a bottle of rum!

I nodded approval of the bottle exactly as I thought Van Bibber would have done. The waiter, with an Oriental bow, filled an ounce jigger, poured the precious deep brown rum onto the eggs, and flamed the tempting dish with a match. This performance was obviously for imaginary guests in the vacant dining room. I blew out the flame, began eating, and from my coat pocket took the little diary in which I had written my obituary yesterday in jail. With a stub pencil I started writing an account of the battle for Juárez—the account that failed to beat Jimmie Hare's, but did bring a sum of money that seemed large to me.

After finishing my meal, still tingling with the strong Jamaica rum, I decided to go back to the building where the insurrectos had shouted for Navarro's death. I found a few men still there, quiet now but apparently watching the tightly closed door. A horse and buggy stood across the street, its black curtains drawn. I was curious and waited with the men. Nothing happened. I became restless, wanting to go on to El Paso. I finally decided to leave but at that moment the house door opened. To my surprise Madero stepped out. I was sufficiently close to be sure. He wore a tailored jacket, riding breeches, and shabby, mud-spattered English riding boots. Beside him a man loomed up a full head taller—it was General Navarro in workman's overalls! His beard was now clipped close to his face, leaving only a very small goatee. This disguise was probably considered necessary to enable him to pass by antagonistic insurrectos. The two men walked briskly to the curtained

buggy and drove away. I learned later that Madero took the
General to his headquarters and gave him a horse and two
scouts who knew secret passages across the border into the El
Paso suburb where wealthy Mexican supporters of Díaz re-
sided.

That night I slept soundly in El Paso. The next morning the
bridge was open, so I hurried back to Juárez, hoping to get my
camera containing the pictures to illustrate my story. At the
bridge an obliging Mexican official gave me a note to the newly
appointed *jefe politico* of Juárez, an elderly, almost fatherly
man who seemed interested in my experience. He doubted
whether I would find my camera, but gave me a note to the
guard at the marshal's building and also an invitation to a
reception Madero planned for officers and all members of the
American Legion. Just a small reception, he said. "Madero
wants to meet and thank Americans who helped win the battle."

At the marshal's building the guard read the note and with a
smile let me search through all the drawers of Beega-Head's
desk. They were empty, of course; Beega-Head, the guard told
me, had been found dead in his chair, shot by the first insurrecto ghoul who entered the building. He could have escaped
by surrendering with the other marshals but stubbornly refused to vacate his exalted seat. The coward in action had died
bravely on his throne.

Complete peace seemed to have returned to Juárez. Shopkeepers were sweeping out their stores and tourists from El
Paso were taking photographs of the bullet-pocked buildings.
Two young men in picturesque western garb sat at a sidewalk
tavern sipping drinks and posing as soldiers of fortune for
tourists to photograph. I had never seen either of them in the
insurrecto encampment, but they may not have been impos-
tors. I certainly did not know all the men in Madero's army.
Another man who also sought tourist attention in town recited,
to anyone who would listen, the details of the battle and what
Navarro should have done to win.

Madero's reception was in the ornate Aduana Fronteriza on
lower Calle del Comercio. At the entrance I saw a few men
wearing elaborately embroidered sombreros loafing at the
door. They all wore coats and trousers, not the sarapes and

crossed cartridge belts worn in the field. The group was so small I feared I had come to the wrong address.

"Como se este?" I asked, to practice my Spanish.

"Una recepción para oficiales Mexicanas," I was told, "y todos los hombres en la legión extranjera."

I did not have to know much Spanish to understand that phrase, and I certainly had been in Madero's legion of *extranjeros*, but I looked in vain for the black or the man I called "You" or any of the other soldiers of fortune I had met. There were, of course, a hundred or more in the Legion, so this was not strange. A bare-legged Tarahumara Indian stood guard at the door with a Winchester instead of bow and arrows. He had probably been placed there as an ornament to give an appearance of equality and democracy to the ceremony. I doubt whether his gun was loaded.

The room inside had a high ceiling and very little furniture. At the tall, wide windows dark red curtains were parted by decorative tiebacks six feet from the floor, admitting ample light. The walls between the curtains were smoothly plastered with olive-colored burlap and on them hung handsome gilt-framed portraits of Mexican notables wearing elaborate military uniforms decorated with resplendent medals. Below these pictures eight or ten real men in civilian clothes stood in line shaking hands with a slowly moving column of visitors. Above their heads in one of the framed pictures I recognized the smooth-shaven face of Benito Juárez, the revolutionary statesman who had succeeded Maximilian.

An unfaded rectangle on the burlap wall showed where another picture had hung. It was now on the floor, upside down, but face to the room—a portrait of Porfirio Díaz. Beyond the faded square stood the man who had caused that picture to come down. Unlike the men in the ornate frames, Francisco Madero wore no uniform. Instead, he was dressed in a formal frock coat and for some reason his highly polished black shoes attracted my attention. The heels seemed unusually high, perhaps to put him more in line with the taller men beside him.

Madero had ordered all his supporters in the receiving line to wear civilian clothes. He wanted to demonstrate that his administration would be one of peace and reconciliation, with

none of Díaz's military oppression. Watching him before I
joined the handshaking line, I thought his face seemed really
friendly, and very different from the cold, stern, deper-
sonalized paintings on the wall. He shook hands in a jerky
French manner, and I may have been wrong but I felt that he
was not quite at ease with the crudely dressed guerrillas who
walked slowly toward him holding huge embroidered sombreros in their left hands. These rural fighting men also seemed
to be uncomfortable in their cheap, ill-fitting civilian clothes,
and I noticed conspicuous bulges in the backs of their jackets
revealing the six-shooters hidden in their belts. Orders or no
orders, these men had come to the reception armed. Perhaps
there was no place in chaotic Juárez where they could safely
leave their valuable guns.

On both sides of Madero stood prominent leaders in the
revolution. Beyond them, also on both ends of that line, I
noticed two or three frock-coated individuals nobody seemed to
know, but it was necessary to shake hands with them before
reaching the notables. I had gone through a similar procedure
at the White House in Washington to meet President Taft, but
in that case each man in the receiving line had repeated my
name to the next. Here this was done differently. I told my
name to the first in line and shook his hand. Then, instead of
repeating my name to the next man, he told me the rank and
name of that man. I shook his hand, and he in turn told me the
rank and name of the man beside him. This was repeated down
the line until I met Señor Governor General of Chihuahua,
Abraham Gonzales, an older man than Madero. His handsome,
square face was one to remember. He seemed to take a really
personal interest in each of us. There was frankness and hon-
esty in his friendly eyes—no scheming, no double-talk for
political approval in this personality—rare qualities in a professional politician. I liked him, and felt he was a man who
belonged to my kind of people. For the first time I felt a real
sympathy for the revolution. If this man and Madero could be
leaders, Mexico might have a real birth of new freedoms and
their country might become a model for all Latin America.

My opinion changed slightly when Gonzales introduced me
to a conceited young man as his Señor Secretary of something
or other. He appeared to be only a few years older than I was,

and I detested him on sight. He reminded me of an unctuous Swarthmore alumnus who had come back to visit college the year after graduating. That pest had bragged about his job, his importance in the commercial world, and the innocence of college professors. I wish I could remember this Mexican's name; all I do recall distinctly is that he was insufferably conceited, and pompously offered me his hand as a favor while talking seriously over my head to somebody following me.

The next man was Madero. I considered having him notice me by addressing him in French but decided that would be showing off. I liked Little Sawed-Off. His brown eyes seemed large, almost limpid, but his grip was firm. I felt there was real bravery underneath his modesty. He introduced me to Señor Pascual Orozco, Commander in Chief of his Army. Pancho Villa was obviously not present that day. I already knew Orozco by sight and had watched him in a crowd. An uneducated Mexican with a gift for leadership in battle, he appeared unsure of himself in the receiving line. He had obviously rented a black tie and hand-me-down tuxedo for the occasion. Wearing this at midday failed somehow to dress him up, and to cover his embarrassment he watched Madero constantly, smiling a little too much to be sincere, I thought. Eager to shake hands, he tested my grip and I gave him the best I had. This attracted his attention momentarily and I believe pleased him. His bleached-blue eyes, hard as marble, glanced down at mine and I noticed for the first time that his cheekbones were high and slightly broad like an Indian's.

To me the poorly attended reception was a combination of ancient pomp and make-believe play-acting, as artificial and as interesting as the half-naked Indian at the door, the worn-out magnificence of the high-ceilinged room, and the cold portraits of Mexican notables who had no representatives in this receiving line. I had seen the rebels and also the científicos in battle. Many of them I had liked personally. I had admired the black's calm courage in facing Pancho Villa, who had come to kill him. I liked the marshal who, with a smile in the battle's lull, had handed me his rifle to feel the hot barrel. I could never forget the soldier who, when going to sleep, had laid out the six cartridges he determined to shoot before being killed. Those men had faced death with fortitude, and my memory of them was not improved by this handshaking reception for a small chain of obviously embarrassed, poorly dressed fellows whose hidden six-shooters showed plainly through the backs of their cheap civilian coats. These men, shaking hands for bubble recognition, would have looked better in rough clothes.

Everything picturesque and memorable was surely over now. I returned to El Paso and went to the post office, hoping for a letter from home. The clerk at the general-delivery window handed me an envelope with a stamp canceled in Philadelphia. A letter from home! Good! I opened it eagerly and chuckled at the first line. It asked, "Why don't you write?"

16

A Hitch with the 4th Cavalry

Ho! Get away, you bullock-man,
You've 'eard the bugle blowd,
There's a regiment a-comin' down
The Grand Trunk Road.
—Rudyard Kipling

The Juárez battle gave Madero a legitimate port of entry for supplies. Food and ammunition would no longer have to be smuggled past the United States cavalry patrol. This doomed the Díaz regime, and Madero's revolution became an immediate success. The war I had come to see was obviously "concluido," and I must get a job for the rest of the summer.

I now realize that there were probably plenty of jobs for a college sophomore in El Paso, but in those days I thought that the only job I could fill was punching cows. With this in mind I walked over to the Southern Pacific Railroad station to inquire about trains to Paisan, Pecos, Fort Stockton, or any likely place the ticket agent might suggest in the cow country of west Texas. Crossing the open square in front of the baroque red-brick depot, I met Bill, the cavalry teamster who had told me how to get into Madero's encampment.

"Do you know a man who can drive fours?" Bill asked. "We need a teamster for the headquarters wagon."

To be attached all summer to the fighting 4th Cavalry—employment Tom Horn would have relished—was the kind of job I wanted. Even Spencer Trotter, I thought, would look back all his life to such a job, so I walked with Bill to Old Fort Bliss, where he introduced me to the headquarters mules—four snappy grays. The leaders were small and quick. Bill told me to watch out for Penny, the near leader. She did not like to have the crupper put under her tail and always jigged a little, threatening to kick.

"You better play safe," he said. "Stand right up agin her so if she kicks, she'll hist you offen the ground. She can't hit you if you stand agin her."

The headquarters wagon was parked beside Bill's Troop E wagon about a hundred yards from the Rio Grande where we watered our mules every morning, noon, and night. The border patrol had been discontinued but this did not change the troop's routine. Every morning shrill bugle notes commanded all of us:

> Come get to the stable
> As fast as you're able.
> Water your horses and give them some corn.
> For if you don't do it,
> The colonel will know it,
> And then you will rue it, as sure as you're born.

Soon the click of brushes on currycombs told us teamsters the troopers were busy while we harnessed our mules to be ready for orders. The Rio Grande River water was unfit for soldiers to drink, so almost every morning I drove to El Paso with a sergeant who took five big hogsheads to be filled with city water. We also made trips for groceries, and occasionally participated in practice marches out in the desert. There was a barrio between our wagons and the river. Some of the Mexicans' chicken yards were fenced with tall stalks of ocotillo cactus, which substituted excellently for chicken wire. Many of the hens, however, were loose and they frequently visited my wagon seeking the grain spilled from the mules' manger. One hen soon made a nest in my baled hay and left me an egg almost every day, a welcome addition to Army rations.

Wagon boss Brady was a gruff character, usually silent but quick to act, a man who might hit first and never explain. One day somebody grumbled about a stray puppy in camp. Without a word, Brady tied the timid little animal to a wagon spoke and beat the crying creature to death.

Sometimes Brady spiced his callous cruelty with wry remarks. We teamsters furnished our own beds but were issued

Army folding cots in the troopers' squad room. My sleeping bag attracted bedbugs.

"Put your blankets on that big anthill west of the fort," Brady told me. "That's how I cleaned the bugs out of my bed in less than an hour. An' when I lifted off the last blanket I saw the last bedbug on top of the hill. He was standin' off a ring o' angry ants, all a-whettin' their cutlasses to get him—just like Custer's last stand!"

Our first payday was quite an event for me. The paymaster, with an armed guard, came in a Dougherty wagon and set up a table on the dusty parade ground. Each trooper was trained to step forward when his name was called, salute, take off his hat, hold it out for the money, salute again, and step away. We teamsters were instructed to act the same way but instead of saluting when our names were called, we were told to say "Yes, sir!"

Before dark that payday, a third or perhaps half of the troop had acquired practically all the money by playing blackjack or twenty-one. Several of the winners now had sufficient cash for a really exciting poker game. After mess that evening I went with a few troopers to a dance at a Juárez dive. The orchestra consisted of two fiddles, an accordion, a piano, and a bass drum. The music had good rhythm and was loud. Most of the dancers were Mexican insurrectos wearing cartridge belts across their bodies, and two of them danced with rifles in slings on their backs. This looked awkward for a two-step but a rifle was so valuable the owner dared not leave it anywhere. These insurrectos also wore their gigantic embroidered hats while dancing. I noticed that one girl took off her partner's sombrero and held it in her left hand while they danced.

Only the insurrectos could afford the luxury of dancing with women. At the end of every dance each man was supposed to lead his partner to the bar where he paid a dollar for a quart bottle of beer for the two of them. A soldier earning fifteen dollars a month could not enjoy such lavish entertainment, and not a man in our group indulged. However, we did drink draft beer at the bar, costing veinte y cinco centavos (twelve and a half cents American) a glass, and we danced the foot-stamping Chihuahua polka and the hand-clapping De la Rosa with each other. I was embarrassed when my partner pulled the tablet out of my hip pocket and slapped it on the bar. I did not want to be known as a writer, or as the author of those dispatches about the battle of Juárez. For me it was honor enough to be a 4th Cavalry teamster driving the headquarters wagon. Fortunately, the other men failed to notice this incident and soon they began singing:

> Damn, damn, damn the insurrectos,
>   Pock-marked kackyack ladrones,
> While beneath the starry flag
>   We'll civilize them with a Krag.
> Then return us to our own beloved homes.

The insurrectos who understood English surmised that this Philippine war song applied to Mexicans and resented being called *ladrones*. They bunched in an angry mood. We were outnumbered four to one in the slums of lawless Juárez and I saw the ugly flash of several drawn knives. Some of our own men who were getting drunk made the situation worse by shouting insults. Fighting mad over nothing at all, they wanted to clean out the greasers, come what may. In a hand-to-hand brawl somebody would surely be killed, but this catastrophe was averted by a strange coincidence. One of our singers, half drunk like the others, certainly did not realize what his song would do when he began, with a clear resonant tenor voice, a composition new to me:

> Every nation in creation,
>   Has its favorite kinda booze:
> The French drink wine, the Germans beer,
>   The Yankees what they choose.
> The Russians go for vodka,
>   The blacks for gin, guitars, and blues.
> Every nation in creation,
>   Gets a jag on but the Jews.

Boom, boom—the drummer in the orchestra accented the rhythm perfectly. He did not know the trooper's song or the trooper but he had absorbed the tune. Perhaps the Mexicans' drawn knives put more than music into his mind; an ugly fight would hurt his business.

Our trooper began a second verse, describing drinks in England, Denmark, and Spain. The tune was catchy and easy to learn. The drummer kept time with the singer, and the fiddlers soon picked up the melody. By the third verse the insurrectos were singing, in what language I shall never know, but we all ended as good friends. That night walking back to Old Fort Bliss we told and retold the incident, laughing louder each time.

When we arrived our squad room was dark. Taps had sounded hours ago, but the poker game was still being played quietly on an Army folding cot by the light of two candles. Next morning only half of the troop answered reveille. The call "We can't get 'em up, can't get 'em up, can't get 'em up at all" was never truer, and this was still the situation when mess call sounded:

> Cof-fee, coffee, coffee, without a speck of cream;
> Sou-py, soupy, soup, without a single bean;
> Por-ky, porky, pork, without a strip of lean;
> In this he-man's armee.

Many men lay groaning on their bunks, and I thought how easy it must have been for Washington to take Trenton after that Christmas party during the Revolution.

"They ain't all down," said a trooper standing at the door when I looked in at the folding cots. "See that man on the second bed? He ain't drunk. He just moved his foot."

After that twenty-four-hour debauch Troop E became as well disciplined and trustworthy as any company I have known. I remember comparing it with drafted men in World War I. Of course, men who enlist for fifteen dollars a month in good times are very different from draftees, but those early-day regulars, when sober, were well trained and trustworthy in an emergency. Our officers were distant and exalted. The men might criticize them, as they did the weather, but, like the weather, they did nothing about it. During the summer I served with Troup E I did not see enough of our commander to recognize him in a crowd. I had expected to find a dashing young captain like those in storybooks. Instead, he was an

undistinguished middle-aged man wearing second-lieutenant
bars. The first sergeant was our real company commander.
Tall, neat, usually silent, and a little aloof, he knew every man,
horse, and mule in the troop. An excellent horseman, he was
the ideal cavalryman, a model for all his men.

Some privates, of course, looked forward to the end of their
enlistments. It was common for a soldier to say at breakfast,
"Now I have only two months, two days, and a meat ball,"
which meant he would be free after dinner on his last day.
Another favorite saying was "I have only seven days and a roll
over," which meant he would be free in one week after getting
out of bed. I remember that the enlistment of two men terminated while I was with the troop. They both went to El Paso in
high spirits and two days later they came back to tell us they
had decided to "re-up in the calvary."

The few remarks troopers made about their officers were
mildly satirical, an attitude, I suspect, of most underlings in big
organizations. A typical private in the 4th Cavalry always used
the same mannerism and whining tone of voice when mocking
an officer. I presumed that this was characteristic of privates in
other regiments, but years later I read that Ranald Slidell
Mackenzie, the 4th Cavalry's famous colonel during the
Indian-fighting days, was described by his men as "fretful,
irritable, and irascible." These words, when I read them, gave
me a mental jolt, because the 4th Cavalrymen I had known
invariably began each anecdote about a superior officer by
mimicking his voice and saying in a "fretful, irritable, and
irascible" manner, "Oh now, you men, why do you always
. . ." etc. This made me wonder if the 4th Cavalry troopers had
inherited this affected style from the famous colonel.

With the border patrol no longer necessary, Colonel E. Z.
Steever ordered Troop E to join the rest of his regiment at Fort
Bliss, a modern barracks eight miles from our encampment at
Old Fort Bliss. At the new location the troopers erected a long
picket line for the horses. Wall tents on one side housed the
officers, and we slept across from them in round Sibley tents.
This put the horses and horseflies between officers and men.
We tied our mules to our wagons at one end of the picket line,
and that first night we learned by scuttlebutt that a speakeasy
sold drinks out on the desert west of the fort. After taps a few

of us improvised a plan to evade the sentries, drink a couple of clandestine beers at a lean-to in the dark, and return without being caught. Such pranks, as was commonly said, were "the curse of the Army."

At this new encampment I saw my first Army pack train, an outfit I had read so much about in John Bourke's *On the Border with Crook.* I noticed that a mounted packer led a gray mare at the head of the pack train wherever it went, and the mules followed her as devotedly as though they were tied to her. Mule psychologists may know whether the attachment was filial or sexual; all I know is that every mule knew the sound of that mare's bell, and when it rang they all came running and followed her wherever she was led. I was familiar with the sawbuck pack saddles used in Colorado, but here in the Army the pack mules wore stuffed leather pack saddles called *aparejos.* These required more skill to pack because they lacked panniers for carrying small articles, but they were better on long wilderness trips because there was no wooden framework to break. The packers were paid more than we teamsters and new men were being sought and trained. I liked to pack a horse but knew I was too small to lift a hundred-pound sack of oats or bale of hay onto a mule's back and hold it in place with one hand while lashing it in place with the other, so I did not apply for the job.

Colonel Steever, having the whole regiment together, displayed his skillful drilling. It was interesting to watch. With plenty of room on the open desert west of the fort, he liked to march troops "company-front" to test his men's skill at keeping their horses' alignment. One day he ordered two aligned squadrons to face each other a quarter of a mile apart. He ordered both to march forward and as they approached each other it was obvious there would be confusion when the two lines met, but the colonel's judgment for exact distances was so accurate that he wheeled one line and it missed the other by a horse length.

Steever repeated this again on another day and many of us watched, wondering whether he had the skill to turn the advancing lines again, as he had done before. This time, to our surprise, he let the two advancing lines become much too close for such a maneuver. They were sure to meet face to face but again, at the last moment, the colonel ordered both lines: "Fours right." To our amusement, the two newly formed columns of fours, within a few feet of each other, marched away in opposite directions.

The colonel also drilled us teamsters to drive our wagons in single files, columns of twos and fours. The mules never adjusted to holding alignment in these formations as well as cavalry horses, but in one of the colonel's fancy drills they performed well. It was an arrangement for wagons in Indian warfare I have never seen mentioned in military books. He placed one four-mule team and wagon alone in the desert. Then he ordered two wagons to be driven up behind it and stopped on opposite sides with a front wheel of each against the hind wheel hub of the stalled wagon. Next, more wagons were ordered to drive up in pairs behind the last two and lock their front wheels against the outside hind wheel hubs of the wagon ahead of them. This was repeated until the wagons formed a long narrow V. The colonel closed this V by ordering the remaining wagons to lock their front wheels inside, instead of outside, the hind wheels of the stalled wagons. This eventually formed a diamond-shaped corral with half the mules inside where they would be safe from Indian attack.

Strangely enough, the mules inside stood quietly together in harness but if they were put in that wagon corral unharnessed they would quarrel, bite, and kick each other. The colonel and his staff rode past this peculiar formation of wagons with no word of approval or of criticism. This, we civilians were told, was praise in the Army.

Colonel Steever experimented with a new plan for a desert encampment. On the Fort Bliss plain the wind was very hot, and sand blew into the food in our mess tents before we had time to eat. The colonel, having well over five hundred men, ordered details from each troop to dig holes sufficiently deep for the regiment's mess tents to be pitched with the tops below the surface of the plain. In these holes the wind did not blow sand in our food, but the sun beat down on the tent tops, making the heat inside almost unbearable—up to 110 degrees one day. Wagon boss Brady said, in his abrupt manner, "This ain't hot. In Arizonee once, I see a dog chasing a jack rabbit and it was so hot both of them was walking."

An order to pack for a march to the Sacramento Mountains pleased all of us. Silk guidons were issued to replace every troop's bunting flag. This was the usual procedure before going into action, and it started a latrine rumor: we were marching off to police the Mescalero Apaches who threatened trouble in those mountains. I suspect, however, that the real reason for our march was the officers' desire to leave the furnace heat on the desert.

During the afternoon before leaving, Colonel Steever and other ranking officers at the fort rode out to review us, exactly the way Custer's 7th Cavalry had been reviewed three days before its fatal fight on the Little Big Horn. The schoolboy interested in western history could never forget his part in this usual military performance that preceded going into action. Each troop's gleaming silk guidon on its nine-foot staff seemed to make all the troopers sit a little straighter, a little more alert. Passing the mounted reviewing officers, each guidon dipped in proper salute and we wagon men, driving in column of twos, brought up the rear. Professor Trotter, I thought, would have understood the thrill of being in this parade.

The next morning reveille sounded before daybreak. We ate breakfast by firelight and the column started in the dark. I could not see the van, but looking back as I drove away I saw a dozen big bonfires where the rear guard was burning each troop's refuse. The march ahead of us was approximately a hundred and fifty miles with only one town, Alamogordo, on the route. I do not remember how many days we marched but most of the way was across the desert. Our guide, in picturesque pioneer costume, rode with the colonel and his staff. His clothing seemed a little cleaner and more handsome than I had seen on other western characters, but his face was hard and sharp. He knew the desert and led us competently.

A mounted regiment marching across western plains is a sight to remember. There was no road, and we zigzagged around sandy dunes that were often wagon-box high and capped with cactus and chaparral yucca. In many places these plants brushed against our wagon covers. Their seeds at this time of year were hard, green, and big as baseballs. We teamsters could reach them from our seats and a driver up front decided to have some fun. He plucked one of the buds and, standing up, threw it at the teamster on the wagon behind him, then ducked down to safety below his own covered-wagon bow. The victim, unable to throw back, grabbed the next bud he came to and threw it at the man behind him. And so it went down the long line of wagons. I happened to be at the end that day with no wagon behind for me to pelt when my turn came, but I collected a good supply of big, hard buds. When the man ahead of me raised his head above his wagon bow to throw, I beat him to the draw, and every time I saw his head rising for another try I threw a good hard bud in his direction. We teamsters from different troops were all strangers to each other; these greetings were not exactly cordial or modest but we enjoyed them as long as the yucca lasted, and we held no grudges. Life in the regular Army on a hard march Out West could be fun.

Where the desert became more open we teamsters ran out of ammunition and for the first time I occasionally saw a member of our rear guard riding fifty to a hundred yards on either side of us. It occurred to me that those troopers were trailing us the way we trailed those Texas longhorns from Wyoming to the Colorado summer range.

On our long march, water became a problem. The colonel, always thinking about equipment for campaigns against Indians, kept the pack train experimenting constantly. He had devised big rubber pack sacks that carried one hundred pounds of water. Two of these heavy bags on a mule never made the mule's back sore but they constantly sprang leaks. One side would get snagged by a cactus thorn and the water drizzled out. This usually frightened the mule, and he was often hard to catch for repacking to make the water bags balance.

The second or third day out, the blistering heat and lack of water made my leader, Penny, show signs of exhaustion late one afternoon. Her ears began to hang sideways, she quit pulling, let her whiffle tree lag, and failed to respond when I called her name. Suddenly she began to sweat severely. I hoped that a good currying might revive her the way rolling revives a horse, so I stopped the teams. With comb and brush I jumped to the ground and walked forward to give Penny a good brushing down. The sand we were driving through was ankle deep and very hot. Since my boots were loose at the ankles I was somewhat protected from the heat but I wondered whether my feet could stand it very long. Penny responded quickly to the currying. Her ears perked up, and she stretched her back, showing that she felt better as the currycomb brushed out the caked sweat. While I rubbed her down, the corporal of the rear guard rode up. He was hot and tired.

"Get back on your wagon," he commanded in an angry voice, "and keep going!"

I was hot and angry too. "Go on, yourself," I replied. "I'm not leaving four of Uncle Sam's mules and wagon behind just to let you eat supper on time. I'll get to camp with this outfit if it takes all night."

The corporal rode away. I do not know whether he waited behind, as a rear guard should, or rode on ahead, but I revived Penny and drove into camp before dark. Wagon boss Brady met me and looked over my mules.

"The officer of the day commands you to report to him as soon as you unharness," Brady said, his voice foreboding trouble.

In the Old Army that statement surely meant censure. I wondered how the O.D. had heard about the event, and I expected trouble. I found him seated on a folding army campstool in front of his tent. He reminded me of a Civil War photograph I had seen in a book, but that did not ease my concern. In a stern voice he asked what had happened. I told him, and he called for the corporal. We waited silently until he came.

"I was hot and tired," the corporal said, "and I spoke too soon. I believe this man saved the teams and wagon for us."

This was a generous confession. To admit an error instead of making a weak excuse took character, and I'm sure the officer of the day respected him as much as I did for doing so. The O.D. did not want to lose four mules and a wagon during his tour of duty. He congratulated me—an unexpected courtesy in the hard-boiled Army—and I have hoped that the corporal, if he stayed in the service, retired on a commissioned officer's pension.

Every day the Sacramento Mountains loomed a little higher on the desert horizon. We knew that the Southern Pacific Railroad tracks lay along their western slope and that we would cross those tracks at Alamogordo. On the last day before reaching the town we skirted the White Sands, established later as a National Monument. In town, as we rested one day under gigantic cottonwood trees, I wondered how we were going to climb the mountain wall that loomed four or five thousand feet above us. The villagers were hospitable. Soldiers were a rare sight for them. One kindly elderly lady told me she wanted to do something for "the boys in blue." Would we like a cake if she baked it for us?

None of us was dressed in blue, but I assured her we liked cake and that night we teamsters enjoyed a feast.

A local ranchman's son dressed like a cowboy stopped at our wagons to talk. He rode a good horse. I borrowed it and tried a trick I liked to do at a gallop. It is easy and spectacular. All a man has to do is jump off his running horse and hold tight to the saddle horn. The moment his feet hit the ground he will be thrown back up into the saddle.

The young man watched me do this twice. "You Indian-fighting cavalrymen," he said, "can sure teach us tricks it will be fun to show the girls."

I did not disillusion him by saying that I was really a city schoolboy from back east.

To drive up on the Sacramento Mountains we circled to the north where a road went up a valley to Cloudcroft, at that time a single store on the grassy mountain plateau. It was only a twenty-mile march but an accident prevented us from making it in a single day. It happened in front of me on a narrow road along the steep side of a deep gulch. Looking ahead past my lead mules' long ears I was watching the rear of the wagon ahead. Its arched canvas top prevented me from seeing the mules hauling it. At the right of the road ahead there was a bridge that crossed the gulch at a right angle to our road. I presumed we must cross it and I prepared to make a sharp turn, always difficult with fours. Suddenly the wagon ahead of me bumped, jolted off the road, and stopped with one front wheel precariously close to falling into the gulch, which was thirty feet deep. I stopped my fours, as did the teamsters behind me. We all locked our brakes and craned our necks to see what had happened.

The teamster up front must have been unskilled, and when

he came to the bridge he had let his leaders continue to pull after making the right-angle turn. This made them pull the wagon on a hypotenuse which would have dropped it into the gulch. Seeing this too late, the driver quickly jerked his leaders to the left and both fell off the bridge.

The rear guard came to the teamster's rescue, unhooked his wheelers, and with a chain around the rear axle pulled the wagon back on the road. We supposed both leaders had been killed by the fall but to our surprise they scrambled up the hillside across the gulch. Neither seemed crippled but when their harness had snapped and let them drop it had skinned the hair off their bodies, leaving long bloody stripes. Two troopers caught and led them to an open place along the road. The wheelers hauled the wagon there, and with one troop as a guard we all camped for the night.

Next day we drove on to Cloudcroft. Our camping place on the grassy mountain top was pleasant, but I was a little shocked by the colonel's order to chop down splendid big aspen trees to make temporary harness racks beside our wagons. This was contrary to the "save the forests" slogan taught us by conservationists at college. The colonel evidently cared nothing about ecology, but he continued training us teamsters by selecting difficult, instead of easy, places for us to drive. When a freight car loaded with supplies arrived, instead of spotting it at a level place he instructed the engineer to leave it on the narrow strip of rails between two deep railroad cuts through parallel ridges. To get a wagon to that car a teamster had to drive up over the first ridge, set his brake tight, coast down the other side, and stop when the wagon came abreast of the railroad car. This level space was so narrow that the lead mules had to stand on the uphill slope ahead, a position draft animals dislike. They don't mind pulling up a hill from a level place, but to start on a steep slope where a release of the brakes pulls the load back on them before they start often confuses them.

I had heard that in the early days some stagecoach drivers strapped themselves to the coach seats. Certainly I needed to be strapped to my seat for the first downgrade between those railroad cuts. The prospect frightened the soldiers in my wagon, and one of them volunteered to stand in the wagon bed with his arms around my waist. That held me on the seat and I drove the wagon safely down to the freight car. These two cuts gave the colonel an excellent opportunity to judge his teamsters' skill. The little mules and I had become so well acquainted that I hoped he would ride out and watch us.

No soldiers were permitted to visit the Indians and they never came to our camp. Although we were at the edge of their reservation, I remember seeing only one—a heavy squaw. Her hair was parted in the middle and a braid hung down beside each cheek. The sarape around her shoulders trailed almost to the ground, and I noticed that her moccasins were handsomely beaded.

Early in August the green aspen leaves at this elevation changed into golden coins dazzling against the blue western sky. To me this meant that summer must soon be ending. Swarthmore College started late in September and I decided to end my holiday with a last fling, visiting faraway places across the Rio Grande. I had read about grizzly bears in Reuben Gold Thwaites' editions of Lewis and Clark's expedition and heard that these ferocious monsters were still plentiful in Mexico's Sierra Madre Mountains. I wanted to shoot one before returning to college, so I drew my pay and bade good-bye to each of my mules with an affectionate kick in the ribs, an attention I believe they liked. It hurt me a little to leave them. They were truly what western horsemen called "crackerjacks."

17

Sierra Madre and the Land of Deseret

*Something hidden. Go and find it. Go
and look behind the Ranges—
Something lost behind the Ranges.
Lost and Waiting for you. Go!*
—*The Explorer*, Rudyard Kipling

I failed to get a shot at a grizzly bear, did not even find a track,
but I had one experience more dangerous than dealing with a
wounded bear. The incident that sticks most vividly in my
memory, however, concerns a night I spent in a big hacienda,
or Mexican cattle ranch. My room's door sagged, would not
close, and stood open to the patio. I awoke long before daybreak and in the dark outside I heard the squeak, rattle, and
splash of a windmill. Dawn must be approaching because I
heard the flapping of hands making tortillas. It was still pitch
dark when a boy entered my room carrying a tray with a cup of
coffee and big silver sugar bowl on it. I sat up in bed and took
the cup and a spoon. The boy pointed toward the sugar, and I
dipped out a spoonful. He left so quietly I knew he was
barefoot.

This hospitality on a working cow ranch in 1911 was new to
me, but I supposed it announced that breakfast would soon be
ready. I got up, pulled on boots and breeches, and stepped out
in the patio, joining my *huésped* (host), *el cacique,* and two
dark-skinned *vaqueros* washing hands and faces in basins on a
bench along the wall. We all walked together into a small,
whitewashed dining room. It was barely light enough to see,
but I recognized the big, ornate sugar bowl on a square
wooden table. The four of us sat down around it. One of my

spurs caught under the rung of my chair, embarrassing me temporarily because the other men, all wearing spurs bigger than mine, had no mishaps.

A buxom barefoot woman thumped into the room with a plate of fried eggs for each of us. Then she placed in the center of the table, beside the sugar bowl, a deep dish of beans in rich brown gravy seasoned with cumin seed. She also brought a plate piled high with tortillas fresh from a fragrant wood fire. No city oven can give such a distinctive flavor to food. With a dipper we filled our plates with these spicy beans and, folding a tortilla into a scoop, shoveled the feast into our mouths, consuming tortilla and beans in the same bite. This, with the sweetened coffee, made a substantial meal that stays with the ribs of an outdoorsman on a long ride, and the breeze that comes at dawn made a second cup of coffee taste extra good.

East of the hacienda the desert stretched away endlessly. The morning sun peeped over a distant ridge as we rode out of a round adobe corral. That morning we had a rattlesnake experience I shall never forget. Chihuahua diamondbacks are very big, and this one warned us as our horses approached. His rattles sounded like meat frying on a hot fire, a sound signaling imminent danger. The snake's head was raised more than twelve inches about its tense coils. I had never seen a snake so big before except in pictures of cobras being charmed by Asiatic flute players.

"I show you trick with Señora Serpiente. Loan me your gun," Pablo, the rider beside me, said in Spanish.

I wondered why he did not use his own six-shooter but realized that cartridges were expensive. A cowboy's wages had gone down, instead of up, after the recent revolution to distribute all wealth. Some vaqueros worked now for their board.

"Here it is," I replied, pulling out my pistol.

Pablo dismounted and, with my Colt .45, walked ahead of the horses toward the coiled rattler. "Watch me shoot," he said, "like Americanos say, 'from the heep.' Easy as pointing with finger. No time is waste sighting down gun barrel, but I blow off hees head. Watch!"

Pablo stopped in front of the buzzing snake, stooped forward, and as he pointed my gun toward the coiled serpent he glanced back over his shoulder at me and fired.

"Good shot!" he shouted without looking at the snake as he handed back my six-shooter. "I hit heem square between eyes."

I knew he exaggerated, because a .45 slug is almost as big as a snake's head, but Pablo dragged this snake toward the horses, holding its writhing body by the rattles. That snake was certainly six feet long and as big around as a man's arm. All that remained of its head was a short ribbon of dangling skin. How did Pablo shoot so accurately without looking at his mark?

This was explained to me later. A rattler, I was told, seeing the muzzle of the gun coming forward, prepared to strike it, not the man. Thus its own head becomes the bull's-eye when the gun is fired.

I decided to try this experiment myself on the next snake we met but it did not work for me. That one, as big as the previous snake, lay in long curves at the foot of a "cut bank" below a branched prickly pear. I wanted that truly gigantic diamondback's skin for my room at college. Dismounting, I stepped toward it but, instead of wagging its tail and raising its head to strike, the snake crawled rather slowly into a hole at the bottom of the bank. In no time half its spectacular body was out of sight. Without thinking, I grabbed the rattles on its tail to hold it back.

"Let go, queek," my companion shouted. "Snake, when he go in hole, turns head at entrance. Hees body circles in hole but hees head waits to strike whatever holds hees tail."

I let go, and the fantastically designed body slithered out of sight, its rattles waving me a feeble good-bye.

I have wondered since if a rattler does turn in a hole as Pablo said. Could it strike from the entrance without coiling for the blow? My attempt to pull this one out by the tail, however, was certainly foolhardy, the rash act of an eager schoolboy who did not think.

I left my friends and followed the Mexican Northwestern Railroad tracks that ran into higher country where I might find that grizzly bear. At a siding—no station that I remember—I saw some covered wagons and a herd of horses. One of the herders, a redhead about my age or a year older, greeted me with quick, dancing blue eyes and a smile.

"We are Latter-Day Saints," he said, waving his arm toward

a group of men and women clustered around several piles of supplies along the railroad siding. "Gentiles call us 'Rattle-Day Snakes,' for fun. We're hauling this plunder to our stake at Colonia Pacheco. I'm Heber Hansen. Glad to make your acquaintance.

After this formal introduction we spurred our horses side by side and shook hands. Heber was very different from the Pink Angel I had met in Wyoming four years earlier. I knew he must belong to the Mormon group who had taken their plural wives to Mexico when polygamy was abolished and Utah attained statehood in 1896. Heber's associates welcomed an additional rider to help with the horses. Also, fuel for cooking would be scarce on the trip to Colonia Pacheco, and an extra man with a lasso on his saddle could drag dry sticks for firewood from the pine groves the wagon train would pass.

On the first day we camped early for the horses to eat their fill of half-knee-high grass. At dark we corralled them in a circle of wagons. Outside the circle, each family cooked supper beside its wagon just as they did in pioneer pictures. Heber's Aunt Pachie cooked ours. "Pachie," I learned, was short for "Patience," and "Aunt" meant she was his father's plural wife, not his aunt.

Heber and I became good friends. We worked well together catching, harnessing, and hooking up the teams. He taught me how to swear in Mormon lingo, to say "dog take it" or "by damn" or "I'll be go to hell." We both liked horses and hunting. He told me where a roach-back grizzly could be found, and we planned a pack trip to hunt him after we reached Colonia Pacheco.

That Mormon settlement differed from a typical Mexican town. The houses resembled those in rural Palmyra, New York, where Joseph Smith said he first saw the Golden Plates, which he translated into the *Book of Mormon*, published in 1830. No house had been molested by the insurrectos on their way to join Madero, but they had stolen a few of the Mormons' horses. Heber took me to see his mother's residence and got clean clothes for our pack trip. We used just one pack animal, a small sorrel named Pearl. "A Pearl of Great Price" was the title of a popular Mormon sermon, and this mare "of great price" was temperamental. She did not buck or kick but she had the bad habit of bolting, especially when first caught in the morning. Even with a rope to her hackamore Pearl could drag a man around the corral, and I appreciated the high heels of my boots. They dug into the ground, making me solid like a post when I sat on a loop of the rope to her head. Every morning when we packed her it was necessary to put a twitch on her lip or twist one ear to keep her quiet.

Our camp outfit included an eight-by-ten-foot tent and a little sheet-iron stove. This seemed elaborate for two men but was usual Mormon equipment, and I found a stove better than a pot-rack and heavy Dutch oven for cooking, especially for baking biscuits. I asked Heber about coffee, and he recited a poem taught all Mormon children:

> In the Land of Deseret
>   Where the saints of God are met,
> Tea, coffee, and tobacco we despise.
>   While lik-ker we never touch
> And of meat we don't eat much
>   For we're going to grow healthy, great, and wise.

"It'll be all right, though," Heber said with the smile I liked, "to eat *meat much* if we kill it in the mountains."

We found meat plentiful. The wild turkeys we saw flew high up in the trees and stretched their long necks looking down at us. A bullet spoiled some of the breast meat, but not much. White-tailed deer were plentiful, but smaller than the mule deer I knew in the Rockies. Two men could eat one in a remarkably short time. We hunted constantly for grizzly "sign" and crossed the Continental Divide but did not know when, because there was no timberline where we were. The tall pines stood far apart, letting the sun warm the moist soil. In some places grass grew stirrup high, and I remember vivid scarlet stars in the green foliage that must have been poinsettia, a plant I had never seen before. Flocks of parakeets, strangely colorless in flight, sparkled like yellow and green jewels when they alighted on a bush or tree.

We came to several barrancas, deep gorges with almost perpendicular sides. Heber enjoyed rolling rocks into them. We came to one ravine two thousand feet deep, and as we rode

along the rim he watched for gigantic boulders too big to lift.
When he saw one that had an unsubstantial base he dismounted and, sitting on the ground, pushed it with his feet
until it teetered over the edge and crashed down through
trees, starting minor landslides, sending whitetailed deer racing away in terror. To cause such a disturbance in the primeval
wilderness evidently satisfied some craving in his isolated life.

We came to a place where the barranca's slope was less steep
and decided to ride down and water our horses. This consumed
an hour, and in the bottom we made a startling discovery. Our
noisy rolling of the rocks may have endangered our lives—or
perhaps saved them. We never knew which, but Heber
noticed a narrow game trail through the lush vegetation and
rode along it. I followed directly behind him. Suddenly he
stopped and exclaimed, "Well, I'll be go to hell!"

Looking past his horse I saw a few dirty blankets draped on
the bushes ahead. I rode up beside him and on the ground in
front of us lay a few tin plates, an unwashed spider, and the
white ashes of a dead campfire. We both dismounted. The
ashes were still hot. A few chunks of well-cooked meat remained in the spider but the grease had hardened, so these
campers had been gone for an hour or two, perhaps since we
rolled the rocks. Their footprints were plain. I had learned
during my Colorado days the importance of studying tracks.
Those in this camp were not made by cowboys' high-heeled
boots or by shoes. They were also quite unlike the moccasin
tracks I had seen in the United States. Heber recognized the
footprints at once, and I saw that he was nervous.

"Lamonite huaraches," he said, remounting his horse.
"Surely Yaquis! Let's get the got to hell out of here, dog take it
quick."

Since the revolution, the Yaqui had become dangerous. Our
rolling those rocks may have frightened them from their camp,
or they may have only been off hunting in the neighborhood.
In either case we rode back up that barranca as fast as our
horses would go. At camp we packed Pearl and traveled all
night. Next morning we took turns watching and sleeping until
noon, then hit the trail again. Two days later we rode into
Colonia Pacheco. It was good to get to a community that looked
so peaceful and so modern, but at the cottage where Heber's

mother lived a farmerish neighbor greeted us with bad news. "Orozco," he said, snapping one of the galluses that held up his trousers, "has revolted against Madero. We hope no more insurrectos come here to take the horses we have now."

I had entered Mexico with a hand-written visa signed by a supporter of Madero. Trains still ran to Juárez and a conductor was sure to examine it. Then Orozco's followers might arrest me. I did not look forward to another sojourn in a Mexican jail and wanted to return on time for my junior year in college. I had successfully crossed into the United States without a permit during the revolution when our cavalry patroled the border, so I decided to try and do this again. It was two hundred miles to the border but I had ridden farther than that from the ranch on White River to Denver. The country down here was less settled—wilderness most of the way—but I considered that an advantage. My horse, Gordo, was not fast but he had a so-called bread basket, a fullness of his flanks that indicated he might miss a meal or two without exhaustion. He had one bad trait: he would trot and gallop, but when whipped to make him really run he would never lay his ears back and do his best. Instead, he would "sull" (cowboy dialect for *sulk*) and I suspected that if I whipped him harder he might balk. This could be disastrous in an emergency, but with plenty of cartridges and a sack of tortillas on my saddle I set off for the long ride.

The first two days were in mountain country with plenty of game birds for me and grass for Gordo. There was no road but the streams flowed north, the way I wanted to go, and I had only one frightening experience. As I was riding down a grass-floored valley between two long pine-capped ridges, a broad-hatted Mexican stopped me. I had seen no man since leaving Colonia Pacheco and knew of no settlement here. The man insisted that I come with him, a request that sounded like a command. He wore no gun but on one sandaled foot I saw a big Mexican spur, which made me hesitate. Was his horse hidden somewhere, or were his armed comrades waiting to back up his order? Gordo was no good in a horse race. I did not want to follow this man but decided to play brave and do so. To my surprise, I found that he had four horses, not one. They were hitched to a load of logs stalled by a chuckhole. The near wheeler was saddled. The man who stopped me evidently rode that horse and drove by "jerk-line," which accounted for the spur that had made me suspicious. I helped get the load of logs going by giving an extra pull with the lariat attached to my saddle horn; and was glad to have been a good samaritan.

On the desert north of the mountains, grass became scarce. I planned long rides on Gordo—fifty miles a day if he could stand it. On the first day out, after riding only some twenty miles, I came to an excellent patch of bluestem. Not knowing when I would find the next horse feed, I decided to unsaddle, let Gordo rest, roll, and feed for an hour or two. As I took the hobbles off his neck, the sun went under a cloud and before I had even twined the rope around his front legs a sudden hail storm hit us like a barrage of bullets. Gordo turned his rump to the storm. My hands became so cold that I was unable to tie the hobbles, and I wondered if I could survive without a bed in the open country ahead. Ten minutes later the sun came out, midwinter turned to summer, and I warmed quickly. This was typical of Sierra Madre borderland weather.

The next day the mountains and changeable weather were far behind me, many desert miles away. Occasionally I came to country roads through the mesquite and ocotillo cactus. When they headed north I followed them, but not when they turned to right or left. New Mexico was still well over a hundred miles ahead. In the days to come, if I remember correctly, I stopped a time or two at a cluster of adobe houses for a meal or cup of coffee, but I always slept in the open, often during the warm daytime when I came to good grass for Gordo. At sunset I saddled up again. Refreshed by the breeze that comes with evening, I rode away. After dark the North Star guided me throughout the night. I had been reared on Longfellow. His Magi, I thought, really knew how to navigate the open range in hot weather because the poet wrote:

> Three Wise Men out of the East were they,
> And they travelled by night and they slept by day.

On the last day of my journey another rider gave me some concern. He acted so suspiciously I feared he was a spy who might prevent me from crossing the border. He obviously watched me constantly, reappeared after I thought I had left him behind, and seemed to avoid coming close enough to speak. Finally, when we were about a hundred yards apart, he turned his head suddenly and I saw for the first time his long Chinese queue. He was escaping to the United States as I was, and feared I might stop him. His people, being shopkeepers, were hated by the revolutionists for being capitalists, and many Chinese had been massacred at Torreón. Henceforth, we rode together across the vast land until we came to a broken barbed wire fence we believed to be the United States border.

Several miles beyond it a well-traveled road led us to El Paso, where I boarded a train for Swarthmore and my junior college year. Reluctantly, I admitted that I was growing up, must seriously continue my schooling, and prepare for my life work. I felt quite sure that my Wild West experiences had ended and from now on books would have to take me to the next adventure that beckoned.

18

Adam and Eve on Green River

In the morning up we rise,
Ere Aurora's peeping,
Drink a cup to wash our eyes,
Leave the sluggard sleeping.
—Izaak Walton

"I'm sorry but I can't recommend you for MacMillan's expedition," the director of athletics at Swarthmore told me. "I have watched you in the swimming pool. You haven't the physique and lack the bodily strength."

Donald Baxter MacMillan was advertising for college seniors who wanted to join him exploring the arctic. He had been one of six men in the elaborate expedition that enabled Robert E. Peary to achieve his lifelong ambition to be the first man to reach the North Pole. Peary's achievement had been eclipsed by Dr. Frederick A. Cook who, while Peary's expedition was still somewhere in the unknown north, cabled from the arctic that he, Cook, had reached the North Pole. Five days after this exciting message reached the civilized world, Peary cabled from Labrador that he had been to the Pole. The date he gave for his discovery was a year after Cook claimed to have been there. Thus Peary, with his complicated equipment, his carefully selected companions, and an expensive vessel especially constructed for arctic water, appeared to have been beaten by an unheralded white man with only a handful of dog-driving Eskimos. This dramatic turn of events delighted public opinion but not Peary's partisans, who immediately pronounced Cook an imposter. Charges and countercharges filled the newspapers during my college years.

The prolonged arguments created a new interest in the arctic. MacMillan proposed leading explorers to northern Greenland, the Ellesmere and Axel Heiburg islands. Eskimo in that distant land still subsisted on musk oxen, much as the Plains Indians had lived on buffalo. In my imagination I had camped with the Sioux while reading Parkman's *Oregon Trail*. Now I wanted to see the nomadic Eskimo before they vanished from the earth.

The director of athletics may have been right when he said I lacked the necessary strength, but his remark hurt. I knew I had more physical stamina than delicate Francis Parkman. In the cow country the smell of dawn air, when wildlife begins to stir, had always intrigued me. I was eager to "leave the sluggard sleeping." Horseback hardships had honed my body, and I felt sure of survival in any wilderness.

This disappointment led to a really rash and important experience. I may have been influenced slightly by a desire to disprove the statement of the director of athletics but I'm sure the real reason for my new involvement was the thrill I remembered from roughing it Out West. The new opportunity came to me in a roundabout manner. "Pop" Pearson, professor of elocution at Swarthmore, asked me to head a tent crew for the chautauqua performances he planned. His chautauqua, I presumed, would be superior to the "Chirography" mentioned by the illiterate loiterer in Craig, Colorado. Certainly Pearson's devotees would speak better English.

Pearson's plan was clever. He had six circus tents and a program of entertainment for six days. Each tent stayed six days in a village, then moved to another one. His performers made one-day stands, travelling from tent to tent. Thus each village received the full program and the performers were kept busy. After every sixth performance the tent crews spent most of the night taking down the "big top." We loaded this and all the chairs into a railroad baggage car for shipment to the next location, where we pitched the tent for another six-day run. We had just thirty-six hours to make this move; tickets had been sold in advance for the new performance so we had to be on time.

We usually got little sleep after taking down the tent for each move on the sixth night, but this was no harder than herding

longhorns at night. I liked the job but it certainly did not
provide the test of wilderness hardihood the athletic director
said I lacked. Once during the summer a cyclone blew down
our tent in Maryland, but that was a minor event. The audience saw the storm coming and, being inured to cyclones, most
of them escaped. When the wind hit our big top it lifted all the
quarter poles off the ground and started them dancing so high
they punched out the seats of nearby chairs. The top soon tore
in half and the whole tent came down over us like a big, wet
rag. Fortunately, the few people who had remained were not
hurt and I found a local seaman who had both the knowledge
and the proper needles for sewing heavy canvas. The repaired
tent was up in time for the next day's program, which was well
attended. Half the crowd may have come to see the damage
and learn how it had been fixed.

We tent men enjoyed the performances, the music, and the
speakers. Between shows we became acquainted with the en-
tertainers, who were usually interesting, as were some of the
townsmen we met in the villages. One of these lured me into
the important experience I craved. If I had not worked for that
chautauqua I would not have met Dr. Decker, and the schoolboy's life would have been very different. The doctor was a
retired Army officer who had been everywhere and seen
everything—almost everything! Full of amusing anecdotes, he
was usually the center of a laughing crowd. He looked very
much like Theodore Roosevelt, and made the most of it. Once,
he told us, he rode in a Rough Rider parade, sitting in a
carriage ahead of the President. When the crowd mistook him
for Teddy and cheered, Dr. Decker stood up and waved,
stealing the show.

I was surprised to learn that he had visited Craig, Colorado,
with a young mining engineer named Herbert Hoover, who
was interested in extracting gold dust from desert sand.

"Remember the name of Hoover," Dr. Decker said. "He's a
big shot now in London mining circles. Give him time and he
will be known here in the U.S.A."

Dr. Decker had prospected in the country west of Craig,
knew that land better than I did, and had ridden deep into the
fabulous "lower country," camping once in Pat's Hole where

Bear River flows into the Green. This was the land beyond the law—the Old West where a good rider on a good horse could build up a good herd by catching mavericks. Decker's partner had a claim there and said that two hundred and fifty square miles of grassland could be cornered by controlling a few water holes. All his partner needed was cattle to stock that range.

The temptation was more than I could resist. Immediately after graduating in 1913, I packed my saddle in its gunnysack and checked it on the train I boarded for Pat's Hole. The best way to reach that distant land was by the Denver & Rio Grande Railroad to Mack, Colorado. From there a narrow-gauge line ran north to Gilsonite mines near Watson, Utah. One more day by stagecoach would put me across the Uintah Basin to Vernal where, on the next day, I could travel by stagecoach to Jensen, Utah. From there I would have to ride on horseback thirty-five miles with no trail over Blue Mountain to Pat's Hole, in Colorado.

My transcontinental train out of Denver was so long that at the Mack stop the conductor let me off a hundred yards from the station platform. The train steamed away on a straight track across a sagebrush plain as flat and wide as the ocean. The only town I could see was a water tank and four small houses standing alone in the center of that vast sagebrush solitude. Far to the north, twelve miles away, the Book Cliffs rimmed the horizon. Carrying my heavy suitcase, I walked up the railroad ties to the station where I saw, across the track, a store, one residence, and a hotel operated by the narrow-gauge railroad company. I found the rooms modern, clean, and expensive. While eating dinner, served on fresh white tablecloths, a voice called, "Is James Monogram here? Yes, Monogram. That's sure what the telegram says."

I claimed it and tore open the yellow envelope. The message inside was ominous: "Sisters ill with typhoid probably from watercress sandwiches at wedding reception stop stay near good hospital [signed] Father."

That night I wondered what to do. Mack was no place to be seriously ill, but I could not get back to Denver in thirty-six hours. Next morning I felt well and decided to take the narrow-gauge. I knew little about typhoid fever and wondered how the approach of this illness might feel. In the train's coach I sat beside a man whose face was rugged and deeply wrinkled, apparently an outdoorsman.

"I'm Ute Osborn," the man said (an intriguing name surely). "Glad to meet you. This railroad beats any in our United States, yes, or in any other goddamn states. The grade over the Book Cliffs is seven and a half degrees. On such steep tracks a standard locomotive's piston thrust would spin the wheels, but the special Shay en-gines on this line turn the drive wheels so slow they take hold and haul the train up and over."

Ute's conversation made me forget about typhoid fever. The railroad ended at Watson, only a freight station and store built two years before on "Vac"—short for Evacuation Creek, a tributary of Bitter Creek. These names had a western twang that appealed to the Philadelphia boy. Watson also had a hotel that Remington would have liked to paint. Guests stayed here while waiting for the stage to Vernal. A big bedroom held three double beds. Two strangers often had to share one, and to accommodate a lady, the bed at the far end could be separated from the others by a sheet hanging from the ceiling.

At dinner, eight of us—all men—sat around a long table. The waitress, a full-bosomed blonde in a low-necked party gown, wore rubbers instead of shoes. She set two big platters of meat and potatoes on the table, placed a V-cut of apple pie and slice of "mouse cheese" at every place, and then plumped around to the front screen door. Opening it a crack, she used the door-jamb as a rest for her .22 rifle, took careful aim at something, and, as we ate, she fired.

"By God," she said, triumphantly slamming shut the screen door, "I got him!"

"Did you hit him in the head or in the belly?" a man at the table asked as he sopped up gravy in his plate with a slice of bread.

I knew now that I was really Out West again and this trip would be fun.

"Belly shots don't count," said another man, chewing a mouthful of beef. "You must alus hit a prairie dog in the head or he'll get away down his hole even if you've killed him dead."

Fifty miles of sagebrush flats and badlands separated Watson from Vernal. The only houses along the route were stage sta-tions for changing horses. At one of them a cable ferry crossed

Green River. By this clever contraption the ferryboat's prow could be pointed either up or downstream so the current would push it to the opposite bank.

The buildings in Vernal reminded me of Colonia Pacheco. Mormon architecture usually differed from the conventional false-fronted houses built in frontier towns. The Vernal hotel resembled a cottage in Palmyra, New York. It was operated by a Gentile with a Mormon wife. He was proud of his baby son and led him out to meet me on the front porch saying, "Tell the man what you are. Go on. Who are you?"

"I'm half Irish," the little fellow piped, "and half Mormon."

Next morning I boarded the mail stage to Jensen, where I would start my horseback ride to Pat's Hole. Jensen was only fifteen miles away and two horses were sufficient for pulling the light spring wagon. I sat beside the driver, and his wife occupied the seat behind us.

"Now, Seymour," she cautioned when the driver began to talk religion as soon as we left town.

The desert ahead promised no change of scenery so I encouraged Seymour to continue. His face brightened and his wife settled back in her seat, now obviously pleased because Seymour was pleased by my attention.

"At first there was a man and a woman," Seymour began, "a male and a female, the most natural thing in the world. And they lived in the Garden of Eden. Their name was Adam and Eve."

The level road ahead stretched straight as a plumb line through the sagebrush. The wagon's spring seat was comfortable, and crisp western air sharpens any conversation.

"A sarpent," Seymour continued, "brought a nice red apple to Eve. I think it was a Baldwin. She took a bite. It tasted good, so she went to Adam saying, "Look what I have fetched you! Try it.'"

"Adam took a bite, and when God heerd about the carryings-on, he got mad as all get out. 'Adam,' God said" —the righteous fervor on that stage driver's face was a sight to remember; thoroughly convinced that he was God lecturing Adam and Eve, Seymour continued—"Adam, you knowd better'n to eat that apple. You're old enough to know right from wrong. Now, don't be a-puttin' the blame on Eve. You didn't have to eat it."

The horses, taking advantage of Seymour's sermon, slowed to a walk, but he tolerated no interruption. Instead of tightening the reins, he reached for the whip in the socket at the right of the dashboard. "Now Eve," he continued, "don't you be a-snickerin' because Adam's goin' fer to ketch it."

Seymour gathered but did not tighten the slack reins in his left hand, and with zealous delight balanced the whip menacingly in his right. Devout triumph glistened in his eyes. "Yes, Eve"—Seymour was still God, dispensing justice to mankind—"you're guilty as Adam, and you know it. Both of you deserve a whippin', an' I'm a-goin' to give you what the Gentiles call a goddamned good one."

With righteous wrath, Seymour lashed the horses. My neck whiplashed as the stage jerked forward and sped through the sagebrush for the last seven miles to Jensen. The more I saw of this brave, new Out West the more I liked it.

The town of Jensen had just five buildings: the Kelly-Ashton Emporium; the New York Store, which was a two-room log cabin with the post office in one end; a blacksmith shop; a slab livery barn; and the Hotel de Atta. Cowboys, in idle moments, called it Atta Chatwin's Crystal Palace Dining Salon. "Aunt Atta" had married Postmaster Henry Chatwin, an elderly pioneer Indian trader with a good sense of humor and a sweeping black mustache too big for his face. A very kindly man, he arranged for some nearby ranchman to hire a horse for me at a dollar a day to ride over Blue Mountain to the fabled Pat's Hole.

"There's no road," Henry said, and I hoped my well-worn boots told him I was used to riding unfenced range. "Only a few cowboys have ever been there. The first house east of here is Bennie Dan'ls' ranch, just seven miles away. He's a cattleman who can tell you how to go from there. You've surely read *The Squaw Man* book? That story is pretty much true. The Indian girl lived at Bennie's ranch. The author, Ed Royle, spent a summer on his brother's ranch here."

I knew the book, and at the Walnut Street Theater in Philadelphia I had seen William Faversham play the leading role in the dramatized version. To see the ranch where the little Indian girl had been reared would be a treat for me. I followed what was called a road through badlands to reach it.

Mr. Daniels, a very intelligent man, drew, with his finger in the corral dust, a map of the country I must cross to find Pat's Hole.

"Follow up the crick here," he said, "and near the top of the mountain you'll come to a big log I've hewed into a cattle watering trough. When you get there, turn straight north up the steep rocky slope to the mountain's flat top. Then, keep going north for about two miles. Watch for a knob ahead with cedars on it. East of that knob you'll find a trail that zigzags down the steep mountainside into the upper part of Pat's Hole. It's only about twenty-five miles from here so you shouldn't get lost, but if you miss that cedar knob you can't get down."

I did not miss it, but on the rim I was not prepared for the dizzy chasm that, like the first glimpse of the Grand Canyon, stops an observer with breathless wonder. The dazzling confusion deep in the abyss—the alabaster-white outcroppings commingled with ocher-rimmed red strata—was more spectacular than any scenery I had ever beheld. The idea of finding the cabin of Dr. Decker's partner in that uninhabited chaos of color, and of running cattle down there, overwhelmed me. Here was an opportunity to see and be a part of the Old West before the last vestige of it vanished from the earth.

That summer I trailed my first herd of cattle into Pat's Hole, and for the next twenty years my range activities centered around this bizarre geological formation. Here I rode on summer roundups, explored cliff dwellings, raced horses with Indians, lived through one shooting scrape, a sheep-cattle war, and a devastating winter. I was now no longer a schoolboy, so these years were different. During them I worked hard to save the spectacular Pat's Hole country from exploitation. To interest the National Park Service in 1933 I outfitted a pack-horse expedition and, with an Indian to help wrangle the horses, guided Roger Toll, Superintendent of Yellowstone National Park, and Ben Thompson, of the National Parks Wild Life Division, through the unique canyon country. They recommended that the entire area of almost two hundred thousand acres be added to the already established Dinosaur National Monument in Utah. The new area was larger than the Jackson Hole National Monument and almost as large as the Grand Canyon Monument.

After this new monument was established it became a stopping place for transcontinental motorists on Interstate Highway 40. The spectacular canyons continued to display their color and breathtaking grandeur and I was justly proud of my part in preserving them, but they lacked something very important to me. The muleskinners, freighters, and cowboys who belonged in this sagebrush country had vanished, gone forever. Horsemen like Boston, Biscuits, High-Pockets, the Pink Angel, and Wagon-Tongue Jones could not be preserved on a national monument like deer and antelope, but the vast land did not look quite right without them. The official park entrance, the educated wardens pointing the way along automobile roads, the necessary signs telling tourists where to camp, where to get the best view, were foreign to the West I had known, loved, and hoped to preserve.

"Each man kills the thing he loves," Oscar Wilde has told us. Perhaps he was right, but it is more satisfying to remember the last request of Kipling's veteran soldier who, at the end of a hard life of danger and daring, said: "Write before I die, 'E liked it all.'"

Index